237

THE LUCID REFLECTOR

The Lucid Reflector

THE OBSERVER IN
HENRY JAMES' FICTION

by Ora Segal

New Haven and London, Yale University Press, 1969

Library of Congress catalog card number: 72–81431
Standard book number: 300–0–1143–1

Designed by John O. C. McCrillis,
Set in Baskerville type,
and printed in the United States of America by
The Carl Purington Rollins Printing-Office
of the Yale University Press, New Haven, Connecticut.
Distributed in Great Britain, Europe, Asia, and
Africa by Yale University Press Ltd., London; in
Canada by McGill-Queen's University Press, Montreal; and
in Mexico by Centro Interamericano de Libros
Académicos, Mexico City.

To Dorothea Krook, teacher and friend

CONTENTS

Preface   ix

A Note on Citations   xv

Chapter   1   *A Passionate Pilgrim*   1

Chapter   2   *Madame de Mauves*   15

Chapter   3   *The Portrait of a Lady*   33

Chapter   4   *Lady Barbarina*   56

Chapter   5   *The Aspern Papers*   74

Chapter   6   *The Liar*   93

Chapter   7   *Tales of the Literary Life*   107

Chapter   8   *The Sacred Fount*   144

Chapter   9   *The Golden Bowl*   170

Chapter 10   *The Beast in the Jungle*   211

Conclusion   233

Selected Bibliography   241

Index   259

PREFACE

What makes the Jamesian observer an interesting subject of analysis is the fact that he fulfills most of the authorial functions of the traditional omniscient author. It is well known that Henry James found the omniscient-author convention peculiarly uncongenial to his genius. In various places in his critical works he clearly and eloquently explains the grounds of his objection to the manner in which it was used by his English and French contemporaries. He objects to the Victorian practice of regularly interrupting the narrative by authorial addresses to the reader because it destroys the "illusion of life" which it is the novelist's first duty to establish. Thus, in "The Art of Fiction" (1884), he complains that "certain accomplished novelists have a habit of giving themselves away which must often bring tears to the eyes of people who take their fiction seriously."[1] Such a novelist is Anthony Trollope who, "in a digression, a parenthesis or an aside . . . concedes to the reader that he and this trustworthy friend are only 'making believe.' "

It should be noted that James does not refer to the convention as practiced by a writer like Sterne, who employs it with the utmost care and sophistication as a means of exhibiting his philosophical and literary ideas. He always has in mind its facile, uncritical use by a writer like Trollope. He finds the specifically Victorian authorial addresses to the reader objectionable not only for the reason that they destroy the "illusion of life" but also because they are employed in the sloppy, unreflective, indiscriminate manner which is to him a characteristic instance of that "comfortable, good-humoured feeling [prevailing in England] . . . that a novel is a novel, as a pudding is a pudding."[2]

1. "The Art of Fiction," *The Future of the Novel*, p. 6.
2. Ibid., p. 4

James also dislikes the Victorian heavy-handed didacticism —that is to say, the intrusive moral commentary of the omniscient narrator. He dislikes it in particular because it reflects what he describes as a tendency on the writer's part to load the dice against his peccable heroes. A striking instance of such moral tactlessness—or, as James prefers to call it, " 'moral' eagerness"—is found in Thackeray's desire in *Vanity Fair,* "to expose and desecrate poor Becky—to follow her up, catch her in the act, and bring her to shame."[3] Again, although James admires George Eliot's philosophical spirit, moral seriousness, and psychological penetration, he criticizes her discursive and insufficiently dramatic manner of presenting her psychological and moral analysis and her philosophical generalizations.[4]

James is equally critical of the French naturalists' impersonal, "scientific," and morally neutral method of omniscient narration. In this connection his critique of the literary theory expounded by Maupassant in his introduction to *Pierre et Jean* is instructive. Maupassant recommends the purely "epic" as opposed to the "analytic" manner of telling a story, claiming that the epic "avoids with care all complicated explanations, all dissertations upon motives, and confines itself to making persons and events pass before our eyes." He goes on to argue, on the grounds of realism, that "psychology should be hidden in a book, as it is hidden in reality under the facts of existence." James challenges Maupassant's concept of reality—a notion he finds too narrow— and maintains that "motives, reasons, relations, explanations, are a part of the very surface of the drama." If, therefore, psychology is "hidden," it is hidden only from the obtuse and the imperceptive. Though an admirer of Maupassant's concise, sharp, rapid stories, James adds the cutting remark that "a writer is fortunate when his theory and his limitations so exactly correspond."[5]

3. "The Lesson of Balzac," ibid., pp. 16–17.
4. "Middlemarch," ibid., pp. 80–89.
5. "Guy de Maupassant," ibid., pp. 203, 205.

That James had no wish to banish moral commentary, psychological analysis, and philosophical generalization from fiction but objected only to the intrusive, discursive, omniscient mode of their presentation in Victorian literature is sufficiently proved by the fact that his own observers are engaged in these very same analytical tasks. It is in this sense that James characterizes them in his Prefaces to the New York Edition of his works as "the author's deputies." The Jamesian observer appears in two principal guises: either as a central intelligence—as a first-person narrator or a dramatized center of consciousness—whose personal vision wholly controls the story; or in the subsidiary role of choric commentator, *raisonneur,* or confidant, intermittently present in the action.

The Jamesian observer is a most flexible and complex functional character. Unlike, for instance, Marlow, Conrad's famous *raconteur,* whose character traits and narrative tone never change, he appears in many guises and speaks in many voices. Indeed, James displays in his choice of observers the same inventiveness and experimental passion for trying out all possible combinations and permutations of his donnée as he does in his choice of dramatic situations. The observer may belong to any of the numerous Jamesian character types: young or old, male or female, innocent or sophisticated, provincial or cosmopolitan, American or European. Similarly, his attitude toward his objects of observation may range from the most detached amusement to the most intense emotional involvement and from the coolest irony to the deepest compassion. It is, in the last analysis, because James constantly varies the emotional, moral, and intellectual distance between the observer and the observed in accordance with the logic of the drama he projects that the device never hardens into a rigid, mechanical convention.

In view of the nearly ubiquitous presence of the observer in James' fiction, the important authorial functions he performs, and the variety of fictional types he embodies, it is to be hoped that an examination of his use of the observer as a technical device or, to use the Jamesian term, a "compositional resource" will yield some insight into the ways in which he contributes to the dramatization of James' great themes and to the dominant modes—tragic, comic, ironic, and satiric—in which these themes are articulated.

The observer's generic qualities—his reflective nature, sensitivity to impressions, analytical turn of mind, speculative propensities, and, above all, insatiable curiosity and capacity for appreciation—are qualities he has in common with many of James' principal protagonists or vessels of consciousness. James' conviction that "seeing" (a term covering all the above qualities) could be an authentic rather than merely a vicarious form of "being"—a form more intense and more valuable than any other—makes the observer a major Jamesian type. One of my objects, accordingly, was to explore the relationship between the observer's functional role and his fictional character. I have also attempted to trace two parallel lines of development: first, the growing importance of the observer whose role gradually changes from that of a mere subsidiary commentator to that of a central intelligence with a personal perspective that fully controls the story; second, the growing refinement of James' treatment of each different type observer he employs.

The method I have adopted is that of a detailed examination of the observer's role in a selected number of works, starting with *A Passionate Pilgrim* (1871)—the first work which James included in the definitive New York Edition of his works—to *The Beast in the Jungle* (1903). In each instance, while examining the observer's role, I have also tried to discuss all the important aspects of the drama he witnesses. I have been forced to abandon this method only in the chapter on *The Golden Bowl,* since the intractable complexity of the novel obliged me to postpone my discussion of the role of the two observers (the Assinghams) until I had first explained the nature of the central drama which they observe and interpret.

Each chapter may thus be viewed as an elucidatory study of an individual work and may be read independently of the others. In discussing the individual works, I tried to avoid any anticipatory generalizations; I let the results accumulate and then attempted to sum them up in the concluding chapter. I wish to emphasize, however, that any abstract general conclusions about the observer in James' fiction derive whatever value they may have from the detailed analysis of the individual works.

My choice of texts was determined by the importance of the observer's role, representativeness, literary merit, and the extent of previous analysis from similar points of view. I have accordingly concentrated mainly on the *nouvelles,* in which the observer performs a major function. Although James produced some of his greatest masterpieces in this form, the *nouvelles* have been sadly neglected by most critics in favor of his novels. The fact that there are only two comprehensive critical works on James' shorter fiction—Charles Hoffmann's *The Short Novels of Henry James* (New York, 1957) and Baldev Krishna Vaid's *Technique in the Tales of Henry James* (Cambridge, Mass., 1964)—provides an additional justification for my concentration on James' *nouvelles.*

Since there are no observers in most of James' full-length novels, I have not devoted special chapters to such major works as *The Spoils of Poynton, The Awkward Age, The Bostonians, The Tragic Muse, What Maisie Knew, The Wings of the Dove, The Sense of the Past,* and *The Ivory Tower,* though I have referred to them when relevant. Likewise, I have not devoted a separate chapter to any of James' apprentice works again because, apart from their minor literary value, the role the observer plays in them is negligible.

Although the governess in *The Turn of the Screw* and Maria Gostrey in *The Ambassadors* are eminent specimens of the Jamesian observer, I have not dealt with these works because they have already been discussed from points of view not very different from my own. Most of the critical studies of *The Turn of the Screw* focus on the question of the governess' narrative reliability, a subject involving a discussion of what she sees and understands in her role of observer.

Similarly, Sister Corona M. Sharp thoroughly examined Maria Gostrey, the central observer of *The Ambassadors,* in her *The Confidante in Henry James, Evolution and Moral Value of a Fictive Character* (1963); though her point of view differs somewhat from my own, I feel that she has done full justice to most of the issues I would have liked to raise.

James was, I believe, the kind of writer whose genius constantly matures. In addition, he was in the habit of using the same themes, situations, and techniques over and over again with ever-growing complexity, subtlety, and refinement. Since this is also true of his use of the observer in various roles, it seemed the most natural and promising procedure to examine chronologically the selected works in which the observer plays an important role.

For my discussion of *A Passionate Pilgrim* and *Madame de Mauves,* I have used Leon Edel's edition of the earliest versions. James extensively revised these two early works for the New York Edition, and since part of my purpose is to trace the development of his use of the observer, I preferred to use the original versions of these stories for purposes of analysis. I have, however, included a brief discussion of the changes which James' revisions introduced into the role of the early observer. Elsewhere I have used James' revised versions of the stories in the New York Edition, for I consider them improvements of the original versions that do not, unlike *A Passionate Pilgrim* and *Madame de Mauves,* introduce any significant changes into the role of the observer.

Throughout my study, I have used James' *Notebooks* to examine his initial conception of the observer in the stories discussed and to compare it with the finished product. These comparisons have generally proved very fruitful for an understanding of the role of the observer in the completed story.

O. S.

December 15, 1967

A NOTE ON CITATIONS

All quotations from Henry James' fiction, except *A Passionate Pilgrim, Madame de Mauves,* and *The Sacred Fount,* follow the text of the New York Edition (26 vols. New York, Scribner, 1907–17). Passages in *A Passionate Pilgrim* and *Madame de Mauves* are quoted from *The Complete Tales of Henry James,* ed. Leon Edel (12 vols. Philadelphia and London, Lippincott and Hart-Davis, 1961–64) and those in *The Sacred Fount* from the reprint edition (New York, Grove, 1953).

Footnotes at the first mention of each particular work indicate the volume or volumes, and page numbers where necessary, of the edition (New York or Edel) in which the text appears and also provide bibliographical information for quotations for James' nonfictional writings and all secondary studies.

In parenthetical citations within the text roman numerals indicate the chapter or section of the work being quoted and arabic numerals are used to indicate the exact volume where necessary (in italic type) and page number (in roman type) for the quotation. Hence the citation "(I; 288)" following the first quotation from *The Passionate Pilgrim* indicates that it is taken from section I of that tale and appears on page 228 of the Edel edition, and the citation "(V; *3,* 49)" following the first quotation from *The Portrait of a Lady* indicates that it is taken from chapter V of that novel and appears on page 49 of volume 3 in the New York Edition. Book numbers have also been included in citations of *The Golden Bowl;* hence the citation "(III, IV; *23,* 290)" following the first quotation from that novel indicates that it is taken from Book Third, chapter IV of that novel and appears on page 290 of volume 23 in the New York Edition.

CHAPTER 1

A PASSIONATE PILGRIM

A Passionate Pilgrim, to my mind one of the finest specimens of Jamesian early international fictions, is significantly the first story James included in his definitive edition in 1908. It exemplifies perfectly James' early use of the observer functioning as a witness-narrator, and at the same time, in spite of the traditional features of the technique, already foreshadows, as I shall try to prove, some of its most significant later characteristics.

The story centers upon Clement Searle's passionate pilgrimage to England, of which, in a characteristically American manner, he has always been deeply, almost obsessively enamored. Owing to a misspent youth, Clement Searle had never traveled abroad and seen the land of his dreams. At last, already in the decline of life, ill, wasted, and disillusioned, he discovers he has a rather tenuous claim to Lockley Park, an English estate, on which he of course immediately sets his heart. On the strength of this very dubious claim he impulsively leaves for England, only to discover on arrival that it has no legal basis. He visits Lockley Park and there he experiences his moment of glory—indeed, his great hour. Lockley Park remains in the hands of its lawful English owner, and the passionate pilgrim goes off to Oxford, dies, and is buried there in a little English churchyard, thereby fulfilling in death at least one of his favorite dreams. *A Passionate Pilgrim* thus depicts a sentimental journey in which James renders the romantic glamour that England inevitably assumes for the haunted American imagination famished for culture and tradition. It centers on the American mystique of England rather than on England itself, dramatizing an England of the spirit, just as *Four Meetings*, although a story in a completely different vein, dramatizes a Europe of the spirit. This inner-directed, subjective character of the pilgrimage is apparent in James' treatment of Searle's claim to Lockley Park. Its exact nature is never clarified; the precise legal state of affairs is to the end deliberately left obscure; and despite Searle's emotional intensity about the claim, he is never shown seriously attempting to do anything about it. Thus, although it is the immediate cause of his arrival in England, it is not the structural center of the story and never becomes its pivotal issue. James, in short, has internalized and spiritualized the conventional romance of "the American claimant," which had achieved in his time the status of a literary convention[1] and raised the pilgrim's state of dispossession to a symbolic plane.

Clement Searle, the single center of interest of *A Passionate Pilgrim*, is an early version of the late-Jamesian "poor sensitive gentleman"—Strether, Marcher, Spencer Brydon, Herbert Dodd, and Stransom.[2] His sensitivity, unlike theirs, is much more excitable, naïve, and often ridiculous; nevertheless, he is basically, like these later characters, a sadly disillusioned man in the decline of his life; and what this shows, interestingly, is that the international theme sounded in *A Passionate Pilgrim* blends with the existential theme of the "too late" experience which James was to explore on a much deeper level in *The Ambassadors*, *The Beast in the Jungle*, and *The Jolly Corner*.

Unlike Caroline Spencer in *Four Meetings*, Clement Searle does in the end arrive in England; yet *A Passionate Pilgrim*

1. On this subject see Ch. Wegelin, *The Image of Europe in Henry James* (Dallas, 1958), p. 37.

2. The complementary and contrapuntal relation of the two pilgrimages in *A Passionate Pilgrim* and in *The Jolly Corner* has not escaped the critics' notice. Witness S. Rosenzweig, "The Ghost in Henry James, A Study in Thematic Apperception," *Partisan Review*, II (Fall 1944), 435–55.

remains essentially a portrait of the American romantic and does not develop into a dramatized confrontation of the American and English sensibilities—a confrontation on which many of James' works in the vein of *emphasized* internationalism focus. As a consequence, that justly praised perfect balance which James achieves between the two conflicting sensibilities in, for instance, *An International Episode* and *Lady Barbarina* is not to be found in *A Passionate Pilgrim*. Here the American point of view predominates, and in this respect the story is closer to the novel *The American* than to the other shorter works of the same period.

As a consequence of this predominantly American note and, more important still, of the unmistakably "romantic" elements of its plot (a dispossessed heir visiting his estate for the first and last time before he dies), the question of the romanticism of this early story inevitably arises. Is it, one may ask, a nostalgic romance—or an ironic antiromance? This critical issue becomes more pointed if one bears in mind that in his Preface James frankly confesses to the autobiographical significance of *A Passionate Pilgrim*—to its having become "in the highest degree documentary of myself." The claim is reinforced by his vivid invocation of his own past uncurbed romanticism and unappeased passion for England:

> I had from as far back as I could remember carried in my side, buried and unextracted, the head of one of those well-directed shafts from the European quiver to which, of old, tender American flesh was more helplessly and bleedingly exposed, I think, than today: the nostalgic cup had been applied to my lips ever before I was conscious of it—I had been hurried off to London and to Paris immediately after my birth, and then and there, I was ever afterwards strangely to feel, that poison had entered my veins.

This confession appears to conflict with James' complementary claim that "the hovering disembodied critical spirit with a disengaged eye upon sneaking attempts to substitute

the American romantic for the American real," had been the
"Cerberus" of his "younger artistic conscience" and "the
keeper of the international 'books' "; and the two declara-
tions together nicely point the lines to be pursued in considering the romanticism of *A Passionate Pilgrim*—a question which engages James' own critical attention in his
Prefaces to *Roderick Hudson* and *The American,* as well as
to this story.[3]

Being narrated by an observer, the general tenor of the
story depends to a large extent on his personal perspective.
An analysis of the observer's role in *A Passionate Pilgrim*
might therefore shed light on the issue of its romanticism.
Although it is an early work, a characteristically rigorous consistency of point of view already prevails and complete authorial reticence is carefully maintained. This point is easily established by a glance at James' earliest short work, *The Story
of a Year.* Here the authorial narrator frequently addresses
the reader in a perfectly unself-conscious, almost Trollopian
manner (which James was later severely to criticize): he
"meddles with the characters," analyzing their shortcomings,
expatiating on their inner conflicts, and dilating on the
heroine's naïveté. In *A Passionate Pilgrim* there is no trace
of these lively Victorian addresses to the reader. Intrusive
omniscience is scrupulously excluded; instead, the definite,
and hence necessarily limited, personal perspective of an eye-
witnessing narrator rigorously controls the narrative. Having
as a consequence of this limitation of perspective no direct
access to the protagonist's inner life, the witness-narrator's
manner of narration necessarily differs from that of the authorial narrator, unhampered by the same limitation. Significantly, *A Passionate Pilgrim,*[4] like most of James' stories,
is not narrated retrospectively. If it had been, the witness-
narrator might have made use of at least some of the privileges of an authorial narrator, such as having acquired a full,

3. Preface to *The Reverberator,* New York, *13*, xx, xix, xviii.
4. Edel, 2, 227–306.

rounded-off view of Clement Searle's case. Instead, he records with a vivid sense of dramatic immediacy (a quality which James repeatedly commends in his critical writings) the progressive moment-to-moment unfolding of the case. However, if the later James exploits the observer's inherent epistemological limitation in order to register the flow of his impressions, conjectures, and analyses, in this early work he restricts his role to merely that of a witness who records the protagonist's adventures, which are for the most part dramatically exhibited.

Clement Searle's introduction into the scene, it will be remembered, is preceded by the narrator's detailed description of the Red Lion, the inn in which he is presently to meet him. The narrator's wealth of literary allusions—Dickens, Smollett, Boswell, and later Fanny Burney, Tennyson, and Jane Austen—his dwelling lovingly on all the minutiae of the Red Lion, his heavy emphasis on the "Englishness" of it all—"On the dark yellow walls, coated by the fumes of English coal, of English mutton, of Scotch whiskey, were a dozen melancholy prints, sallow-toned with age,—the Derby favourite of the year 1807, the Bank of England, Her Majesty the Queen" (I; 228)—immediately sound the recognizable note of the American in England. Thus what appears to be an objective, Balzacian concern with descriptive details in fact brands the narrator as himself an American passionate pilgrim—a pilgrim, however, whose passion is obviously pitched in a lower key than Clement Searle's and whose superiority is implicit in his greater cultivation and in his finer analytical powers, both indispensable for his narrative function. What this means is that despite his being undeniably a compositional resource, the witness-narrator, unlike the authorial narrator, inescapably belongs to the fictional universe of the story and cannot help being himself, however unobtrusively, a fictional character. Moreover, it is in virtue of his implied fictional characteristics that he becomes the Jamesian perfect mirror of Clement Searle's case; for his being himself an American pilgrim ensures a sufficient degree of intimate and sympathetic participation, and his implied superiority guarantees a sufficient degree of analytical discrimination and detachment.

The narrator's general reflections on the American pilgrim, prompted significantly by his own emotional state of being "ravished but unamazed," served as an indirect anticipatory comment on Clement Searle's particular case:

> The latest preparedness of the American mind for even the most delectable features of English life is a fact which I never fairly probed to its depths. The roots of it are so deeply buried in the virgin soil of our primary culture, that, without some great upheaval of experience, it would be hard to say exactly when and where and how it begins. It makes an American's enjoyment of England an emotion more fatal and sacred than his enjoyment, say, of Italy or Spain. (I; 227)

The presence of a second passionate pilgrim, as well as the impact of such general reflections, prevent Searle's case from being seen as merely a personal obsession, and indicate, without undue insistence, its typical nature—an emphasis common to all the international cases exhibited in James' early stories. If, however, the implied second case of passionate pilgrimage is sufficiently similar to the first to suggest the generic character of Searle's case, it is at the same time sufficiently different to bring out its extremity. Both pilgrims exhibit varying forms of "the latent preparedness of the American mind"; but whereas the narrator's dream of England has been cultivated by literature, poor Searle's vision is the pure product of his unappeased imagination—a completely self-generated dream. While the narrator is "ravished but unamazed," poor Clement Searle is both ravished *and* amazed. His expectations are much less specific, less definite, and certainly less literary than the narrator's; yet precisely for these reasons, his feelings for England, it is implied, are more intense, more incurably romantic—in short, more fatal.

This complementary and antithetical parallel between the
narrator and Clement Searle is most explicitly drawn by the
latter in the course of his confession. "You have the advantage over me," he says to the narrator, "in coming to all this
with an educated eye. You already know the old. I have
known it but by report. I have always fancied I should like
it. In a small way at home, you know, I have tried to stick to
the old. I must be a conservative by nature. People at home
—a few people—used to call me a snob" (I; 241). And again:
"I came into the world an aristocrat. I was born with a soul
for the picturesque. It condemns me, I confess, but in a
measure, too, it absolves me . . . Sitting here, in this old park,
in this old land, I feel—I feel that I hover on the misty
verge of what might have been! I should have been born here
and not there; here my vulgar idleness would have been—
don't laugh now!—would have been elegant leisure" (I; 245).

In his later phase James explicitly expresses his dislike for
"the *terrible* fluidity of self-revelation"[5] which characterizes
Gil Blas and *David Copperfield,* and scrupulously eschews
the subjective confessional in whatever form. His later observers almost invariably arrive at the necessary knowledge
of the protagonist's past (confession being ruled out) by a
complex process of speculative and conjectural activity, which
in many instances shifts the center of interest from the object
of detection to the process of detection itself. In *A Passionate
Pilgrim,* however, confession is still unhesitatingly used to
ensure smoothness and directness of narration, and the narrator plays the role of the traditional confidant rather than
that of a detective of the intelligence—a role consistent with
the prevailing dramatic objectivity of the story. James had
employed the device of the confession in many of his apprentice works—for instance, in *Guest's Confession, The
Sweetheart of M. Briseux, Eugene Pickering,* and others.
Compared with these, its artificiality in *A Passionate Pilgrim*
is reduced to a minimum and the seams of its expository
function hardly show. Searle's confession of his American

5. Preface to *The Ambassadors,* New York, *21,* xix.

malaise, for instance, which is as vague and unspecified as it is intense, is fully accounted for by his unexpected meeting with a sympathetic compatriot; and in a manner foreshadowing James' later technique in *The Ambassadors,* it serves simultaneously as exposition and self-characterization, exhibiting Searle's pathetic tendency to self-pity as well as his disarmingly naïve candor.

At this point in the story the narrator exceeds his unobtrusive role as an objective witness, embarking for once on a direct evaluative analysis of Clement Searle: "It was a simple mind enough, with no great culture, *I fancied,* but with a certain appealing native grace. I foresaw that I should find him a true American full of that perplexing interfusion of refinement and crudity which marks the American mind. His perceptions, *I divined,* were delicate; his opinions, *possibly,* gross" (I; 238–39; my italics). This extremely tentative manner of voicing his criticism, foreshadowing the epistemological and moral uncertainties of the late Jamesian observer, saves it from being merely patronizing.[6] Thus the "perplexing interfusion of refinement and crudity" which he particularly singles out succeeds in eliciting from the reader a corresponding interfusion of admiration and ridicule, sympathy and detachment, toward Searle's typically American case. (Searle's use of the adjective "picturesque" immediately brands him as an American romantic. Accordingly to Matthiessen, James was inclined to change the early adjective "picturesque" to "quaint," and whenever he did not change it, it was meant to emphasize the underlying romanticism of the character addicted to this expression.)[7] At the same time, it creates the required ironic distance between the narrator and Searle and therefore has the effect of

6. On the question of the narrator's reliability see W. C. Booth, *The Rhetoric of Fiction* (Chicago, 1961), pp. 339–64.

7. See F. O. Matthiessen's analysis of James' revisions of *The Portrait of a Lady* in *Henry James, The Major Phase* (New York, 1946), p. 155.

making Searle's own view of his case appear thoroughly melo-dramatic. His reiterated emphasis on his impending death, characterized by the narrator as "this intolerable flavor of mortality" (I; 247), his feverish melancholy tinged with hysteria, his wild rhetoric, all appear absurdly extravagant, and his sincerity, which has the unlucky trick of sounding affected, is clearly meant to be viewed as a pathetic example of the "simplicities and crudities" of the American mind.

Having set out upon their pilgrimage to Lockley Park, the narrator does not register his impressions of Searle's responses, but instead abounds in leisurely and detailed descriptions of an idyllic English countryside, which are periodically interrupted by his companion's excited exclamations. Again, as in the description of the Red Lion touched on earlier, these seemingly informative passages throb with subdued passion, and in this instance they provide an effective oblique commentary on Searle's more hysterical passion. On the one hand, being suffused with the love of the English countryside, they serve as a common objective correlative, thus rendering Searle's obsession basically understandable and indeed valuable; on the other hand, his exaltation, by being repeatedly played off against the narrator's quiet, cultivated comments, is exposed as absurdly exaggerated, sentimental, and melo-dramatic. Thus, for example: "Closely beneath us lay the dark, rich flats of hedgy Worcestershire and the copse-check-ered slopes of rolling Hereford, white with the blossom of apples. At widely opposite points of the large expanse two great cathedral towers rise sharply, taking the light, from the settled shadow of their circling towns,—the light, the ineffable English light! 'Out of England,' cried Searle, 'it's but a garish world!' " (I; 249–50).

In the course of this pilgrimage the gently ironic distance between the narrator and Searle, established by the former's critical comments and intensified by the latter's being viewed dramatically from the outside, is momentarily bridged as both points of view merge in a common appreciation—indeed, ado-ration—of the English countryside. This effect is achieved by

the narrator's repeated use of the pronouns "we" and "our"
in speaking of their shared responses: "with an equal attentive piety my friend and I glanced at these things" (I; 248);
"we allowed a couple of days to elapse in vague, undirected
strolls and sweet sentimental observance of the land . . . The
noble friendliness of the scenery, its subtle old-friendliness,
the magical familiarity of multitudinous details, appealed to
us at every step and at every glance. Deep in our souls a
natural affection answered" (I; 249). This sense of an identity
of feeling is, however, repeatedly canceled by Searle's exaggerated exclamations, which have the effect of breaking the
spell of the idyllic quiet narrative tone.

Upon their arrival at Lockley Park, as the emotional pitch
of the narrative steadily rises and the narrator's tone of
hushed ecstasy indicates that he too has lost his heart, the
ironic distance between the two pilgrims correspondingly diminishes. It is in particular Miss Searle's simplicity (later to be
exhibited again in Lord Warburton's sisters in *The Portrait
of a Lady* and in the elderly Miss Wenham in *Flickerbridge*)
expressing itself mainly in her complete obliviousness to the
romance of Lockley Park which marks her, for the narrator's
modern restless American imagination, as herself the incarnation of romance; and giving vent to his penchant for literary
allusions, he surrounds her simple, stolid figure with a wealth
of literary and historical associations. At this point we receive
our first hint of the reversal of the roles of the two pilgrims
which James gradually achieves, as a result of which a shift
in the reader's response to Searle's romanticism is effected.
The cultivated narrator's impressions now seem overwhelmingly, excessively literary, and it is now his effusions which
are set off by Searle's simpler remarks. If the narrator characterizes poor Miss Searle as "the Belle au Bois dormant,"
"a sequestered châtelaine of the feudal days," and "one of
Miss Austen's heroines," Clement Searle seems, in his moment
of glory, unerringly to hit upon the simplest expression:
"You're a woman of the past. You're nobly simple. It has
been a romance to see you" (II; 264). And still more simply:

"Let me dream, let me dream!" he said.

"What are you dreaming about?"

A moment passed before his answer came. "About a tall woman in a quaint black dress, with yellow hair, and a sweet, sweet smile, and a soft, low, delicious voice! I'm in love with her." (II; 266)

This change in the reader's response to Searle is helped by the fact that the reader is now invited to compare him with the English Searle "breathing the fumes of hereditary privilege and security" (II; 269). Set against the latter's English complacency (as yet unredeemed by the perfect breeding which James was later to attribute to his Englishmen), the extremity of Searle's agitated worship ceases to appear either ridiculous or sentimental: rather, more deeply appreciative of Lockley Park than its unimaginative owner, the American Searle seems to grow in stature and become in a true sense its real owner. Moreover, the narrator who at first regarded his compatriot's intensity about Lockley Park as exaggerated and slightly ridiculous is converted at this point in the story to a different view of it: "But a great frankness for the time makes its own law, and a great passion its own channel. There was, moreover, an immense sweetness in the manner of my friend's [Clement Searle's] speech. Free alike from either adulation or envy, the very soul of it was a divine apprehension, an imaginative mastery, free as the flight of Ariel, of the poetry of his companions' [the English Searle and his sister] situation and of the contrasted prosiness of their attitude" (II; 272–73).

The narrator communicates to the reader a sense of the mounting intensity of involvement which culminates in Searle's visitation by the old family ghost, and from that point onward the narrative tone undergoes a deeper change. The narrator, transcending his previous restricted role as an objective witness of events, now registers his more intensely personal impressions of Searle's "spectral presence," after having been visited by the ghost: "With his cadaverous, emaciated face, his tragic wrinkles, inten-

sified by the upward glow from the hearth, his drooping
black mustache, his transcendent gravity, and a certain high
fantastical air in the flickering alternation of his brow, he
looked like the vision-haunted knight of La Mancha, nursed
by the Duke and Duchess" (II; 288). Searle's spectral presence
is experienced by the narrator as sinister, grotesque, even
"tragic." Certain key phrases, such as "transcendent gravity"
or "fantastical air" suggest the grimness of a Hawthornesque
allegory. The narrator, who had been previously invoking
Smollett, Fanny Burney, Jane Austen, Tennyson, and other
English writers as food for his hungry American imagination,
reverts at this point to the poet of Salem (whom James had
praised for having among other things, "the feeling for the
latent romance of New England").[8] With a characteristic
Jamesian reversal of emphasis, the romance of England is
thus replaced by the romance of New England; and the reversal is completed by the narrator's further invocation of
the Knight of La Mancha—the perfect symbol for the Ro-
mantics of sublimity in ridiculousness, grandeur in derange-
ment.[9] This also effects the final transformation of the narrator's role as foil to the passionate pilgrim. His cultivation
and self-control, previously the signs of his superiority, now
seem dwarfed in the presence of his companion's "madness"
as he plays sober Horatio (though not Sancho) to Searle's
Don Quixote.

In a characteristically romantic manner Searle's peak moment of madness, in which he completely identifies himself

8. *The House of Fiction, Essays on the Novel,* ed. and introd. L. Edel
(London, 1957), p. 177.

9. It is interesting to note that James invokes Cervantes' knight only
in his early works, *Watch and Ward, Gabrielle de Bergerac,* and *Pro-
fessor Fargo.* Later on, his allusions are mostly to characters in Trollope,
Thackeray, Dickens, Balzac, and George Eliot. This fact is indicative of
James' abandonment of the Hawthorne-Poe tradition of the Gothic,
supernatural, allegorized moral fable in the interest of greater realism.
For a discussion of James' use of literary parallels see R. L. Gale, *The
Caught Image, Figurative Language in the Fiction of Henry James*
(Chapel Hill, 1964), pp. 102, 120.

with his English ancestor, coincides with his highest moment
of truth, in which he becomes aware of the romance of the
American imagination. He cries:

> Seriously, what does Oxford do for these people [the
> English]? Are they wiser, gentler, richer, deeper? . . . My
> soul reverts to the naked background of our own edu-
> cation, the dead white wall before which we played our
> parts . . . Naked come we into a naked world. There is a
> certain grandeur in the absence of a *mise en scène,* a cer-
> tain heroic strain in these young imaginations of the
> West, which find nothing made to their hands, which
> have to concoct their own mysteries, and raise high into
> our morning air, with a ringing hammer and nails, the
> castles in which they dwell. (II, 293–94)

What this signifies is that the ironic distance between the
two pilgrims has vanished in their common recognition of
the pathos and grandeur of the American romantic. The
final emphasis seems to fall not on the American as the disillusioned pilgrim (although this note is never entirely absent) but rather on the American as the romantic kind of
"wise fool." It is not therefore the romantic elements of the
plot (which could, quite conceivably, have served the opposite
purpose—that of enhancing the irony) but the final emphasis
on the value, rather than the absurdity, of the obsession, even
as disease or madness, which marks *A Passionate Pilgrim* as a
romantic rather than an ironic story of the American dream
of England.

This effect, I have indicated, is mainly determined by the
change in the observer's position vis-à-vis the protagonist.
Moreover, it is because the change from a mildly ironic detachment to a sad admiration is gradual rather than revolu-
tionary that the initial comic-ironic values of the fable are
not canceled but, rather, absorbed in its final note. It is,
partly at least, the observer's own passion which ensures a
neither too abrupt nor too aloof response on his part; and *A
Passionate Pilgrim* appears to be a genuinely romantic title,

lacking the ironic overtones of, for example, *The Madonna of the Future*.

It is worth mentioning that in revising *A Passionate Pilgrim* for the New York Edition, James introduced various touches of sophistication and knowledgeability in the narrator's description of the English scene which make it a good deal more ironic.[10] These changes give color to the claim that the protagonist is to be viewed in a wholly ironic light and the story interpreted as an antiromance. But although highly interesting as instances of the later James' growing predilection for a sophisticated narrator, the changes are nevertheless too slight to justify an unreservedly ironic interpretation of Searle's case. They undoubtedly add the witty, "amusing," late-Jamesian flavor to the early work, but being mere light touches, they are insufficient to invite a consistently ironic reading of *A Passionate Pilgrim*. Rather, by somewhat diminishing the narrator's own romanticism, they disrupt that delicate relationship between him and the protagonist which is essential to the exhibition of the latter's case. To express fully the specifically romantic values of the fable, it seems that precisely a less sophisticated, less amusingly witty narrator is required—indeed, just the kind of narrator James had in fact conceived of at the time of the actual composition of *A Passionate Pilgrim*.[11]

10. See Gegenheimer, "Early and Late Revisions in Henry James's *A Passionate Pilgrim*," *American Literature*, 23, 233–42.

11. For an account of James' revisions of *A Passionate Pilgrim* see F. A. Gegenheimer, "Early and Late Revisions in Henry James' *A Passionate Pilgrim*," *American Literature*, 23 (May 1951), 233–42.

CHAPTER 2

MADAME DE MAUVES

In *Madame de Mauves*[1] James uses the classical donnée of his international drama, that of "the European of position who marries the young American woman."[2] The heroine, daughter of a wealthy American widow, who has been brought up in a cloistered Parisian convent, exemplifies the American's fatal susceptibility to Europe, a susceptibility which in her case takes the form of an obsession with rank and with what she supposes to be the inherited virtues of the aristocracy:

> She dreamt of marrying a title,—not for the pleasure of hearing herself called Mme. La Vicomtesse (for which it seemed to her that she should never greatly care), but because she had a romantic belief that the best birth is the guaranty of an ideal delicacy of feeling. Romances are rarely shaped in such perfact good faith, and Euphemia's excuse was in the radical purity of her imagination. She was profoundly incorruptible, and she cherished this pernicious conceit as if it had been a dogma revealed by a white-winged angel. (II; 129)

This national romanticism, which James characterizes as "the great American disease," shapes the heroine's fate. She marries Baron de Mauves, an impoverished, cynical, superficial, morally corrupt French aristocrat and is exposed to the French "system," according to which the husband is free to have any number of love affairs, whereas the wife is expected

1. Edel, *3*, 123–209.
2. Preface to *The Reverberator*, p. x.

to accept his unfaithfulness with good grace and not to seem in any way either jealous or injured, lest it constitute an implicit criticism of her husband.

The story centers upon the international conflict between Madame de Mauves, the inexperienced, rigidly puritanical American bourgeoise, and the arrogant, rigidly traditional, aristocratic French family, whose code of conduct she quietly defies by adhering to her own American values. In his treatment of the international marriage in this story, James does not attempt any subtle portrayal of the European side. The Baron is an oversimplified, debased national type, almost a caricature of aristocratic corruption. Being superficial and unsubtle, he is devoid not only of the grace and perfect breeding which characterize the Englishmen of James' early fiction, but even of the aestheticism of Gilbert Osmond, the much more finely drawn villain of *The Portrait of a Lady*. In other words, the admirable balance which James strikes between the European and the American points of view in his comic-ironic short works of the same period *(An International Episode, The Point of View, A Bundle of Letters,* and *Lady Barbarina)* is not to be found in *Madame de Mauves*. This suggests that it is perhaps more rewarding to treat the story not as another drama of international contrasts but as a study of the Puritan conscience—a view of its central thematic issue which fully accounts for James' choosing as its reflector a young, inexperienced American who burns with "the sacred rage," instead of the witty, sophisticated, cosmopolitanized American who fulfills the same role in his comic-ironic international stories.[3]

As for the American wife—the story's center of interest—

3. This, it seems, was also James' own view of the matter, for he groups *Madame de Mauves* in the Preface to the New York Edition with *A Passionate Pilgrim,* a story which deals with the American romantic and does not develop into a confrontation of the American and European sensibilities. This is suggested also by the title—*Madame de Mauves*—which is significantly different from, for instance, *An International Episode.*

she by no means merely exemplifies a case of victimized innocence. Longmore, the tale's observer, fully and sensitively
records his impressions of her distinctive American traits: her
austerity, the absence in her of any of "the coquetry of unhappiness," and most important perhaps, her stoical reserve,
her exalted religion of conscience. These qualities Longmore,
her compatriot, of course inordinately admires. James, however, complicates the American woman's portrait by adding
to the story an ironic postscript in which it is reported that,
moved by his wife's steadfast virtue (in particular, her obstinate refusal to take Longmore as her lover in spite of his
own cynical encouragement), the Baron finally reforms. He
falls in love with the wife whom he has previously scorned,
only to discover that she refuses to forgive him, whereupon in
despair he blows his brains out. The Baron's sudden change
of heart is the kind of psychological miracle which is, as such,
totally unconvincing. Yet this melodramatic turn of the screw
admirably serves to bring out the more ominous implications
of Madame de Mauves' Puritan virtue.

The story marks the first important turning point in the
development of James' narrative technique. Instead of using
the observer as a first-person narrator, James presents him as
the story's single center of consciousness and dramatizes the
flow of his impressions, conjectures, and analyses of the case
he witnesses. Although the sequence of his reflections is
strictly determined by the logic of the case, the very fact that
the observer has become the story's center of consciousness,
and that the readers, instead of listening to his narrative, are
henceforth invited to watch his thought processes, makes him
a considerably more pronounced fictional character than the
earlier witness-narrator.

Since *Madame de Mauves* is James' earliest experiment in
this new technique, it is hardly surprising that he fails at
times to exploit all its possibilities, employing straightfor-
ward authorial narrative where he could use the new method
of dramatizing the observer's consciousness. Thus the ex-

pository material (the history of Madame de Mauves' convent life and her eventual marriage) is reported by the authorial narrator, and additional information is supplied by Mrs. Draper, a *ficelle* the later James would certainly have dispensed with. Moreover, James has recourse to the epistolary expedient for purposes of authorial commentary. Thus, for instance, Longmore sums up his view of Madame de Mauves' marital difficulties in a letter to Mrs. Draper (chap. IV), a summary which could easily have been recorded in the form of the observer's reflections.[4] This lack of a rigorous consistency of point of view remains, however, merely a technical flaw, for Longmore's personal vision fully controls the narrative of Madam de Mauves' international marriage, and the American note he strikes is, I will try to show, of the greatest significance.

Longmore contributes to Madame de Mauves' sad little tale the element of sympathetic appreciation, which James renders the more intense, indeed passionate, by making him fall in love with her. In this respect Longmore clearly functions, as, to use a Jamesian phrase, "the author's deputy":

> Again and again, on review, the shorter things in especial ... ranged themselves not as my own impersonal account of the affair in hand, but as my account of somebody's impression of it—the terms of this person's access to it and estimate of it contributing thus by some fine little law to intensification of interest. The somebody is often, among my shorter tales I recognise, but an unnamed, unintroduced and (save by right of intrinsic wit) unwarranted participant, the impersonal author's concrete deputy or delegate, a convenient substitute or apologist

4. A little later James is to employ the epistolary convention very successfully to present the international situation from a variety of conflicting angles of vision—French, German, English, and American (as in *A Bundle of Letters*)—or to achieve an ironic juxtaposition of the antithetical American and European points of view (as in *The Point of View*).

for the creative power otherwise so veiled and disembodied.[5]

The authorial narrator, however, is by no means completely effaced behind his fictional deputy, and he views Longmore's biased Americanism with a gentle and amused irony. Thus, for example, even before he learns the reason for Madame de Mauves' unhappiness, Longmore entertains not the slightest doubt that her French husband is its source: "Edified by his six months in Paris—'What else is possible,' he asked himself, 'for a sweet American girl who marries an unclean Frenchman'" (I; 127).

Madame de Mauves is the only instance in which an American burning with "the sacred rage"—a rage against anything European and a jealous belief in everything American—serves as the sensitive and intelligent observer through whose consciousness the narrative is filtered. The main reason is that the story deals with an American woman whose French husband completely fails to appreciate her, and consequently it is precisely a biased American who, by expressing his intense indignation and sense of outrage, extracts from the situation its maximum of sense.

A short passage will illustrate the tone and quality of Longmore's reflections.

> It was ten to one he [M. de Mauves] didn't know his wife was unhappy; he and his brilliant sister had doubtless agreed to consider their companion a Puritanical little person, of meagre aspirations and slender accomplishments, contented with looking at Paris from the terrace, and as an especial treat, having a countryman very much like herself to supply her with homely transatlantic gossip. M. de Mauves was tired of his companion: he relished a higher flavour in female society. She was too modest, too simple, too delicate; she had too few arts, too little coquetry, too much charity. M. de Mauves, some

5. Preface to *The Golden Bowl*, New York, 23, v.

day, lighting a cigar, had probably decided she was
stupid. (III; 152)

The Baron's point of view, which Longmore perceptively reproduces—"he and his brilliant sister had doubtless agreed to
consider their companion a Puritanical little person," and so
on—imperceptibly merges into Longmore's own point of
view—"she was too modest, too simple, too delicate; she had
too few arts, too little coquetry, too much charity"—so that
what began as a depreciatory European account of Madame
de Mauves' peculiarly American shortcomings ends up as an
American appreciative account of her virtues.

Despite Longmore's biased Americanism, James intimates
that—unlike Dr. Feeder in *Lady Barbarina,* Henrietta Stackpole in *The Portrait of a Lady,* and Waymarsh in *The Ambassadors,* all of whom burn with the sacred rage—Longmore
is not to be viewed as the protagonist's comic foil. Although
Madame de Mauves (like Jackson Lemon, Isabel Archer, and
Strether) is stricken with the American's fatal susceptibility to
Europe, her desire to marry a title is, in spite of its mitigating
"purity," romantic in the pejorative sense—unreal, immature, even crude; and what this means is that Longmore,
despite his unresponsiveness to Europe, is hardly her inferior.
Rather, Madame de Mauves' and Longmore's perspectives are
equally limited and, as such, exemplify two opposite but
complementary varieties of the American's "superstitious
evaluation" of Europe.

Longmore's impressions of M. de Mauves are clearly meant
to serve as an illuminating descriptive analysis of the social
type he represents; nevertheless, because they are registered
by an American of Longmore's sensibility rather than by a
more objective and detached observer, they are at the same
time self-characterizing. They dramatize the uneasiness, envy,
and indignation which the Baron's worldliness, frivolity, and
easy immorality inspire in the earnest, unworldly young
American:

He [the Baron] was by race and instinct a *grand seigneur*.
Longmore had often heard of this distinguished social
type, and was properly grateful for an opportunity to
examine it closely. It had certainly a picturesque boldness of outline, but it was fed from spiritual sources so
remote from those of which he felt the living gush in his
own soul, that he found himself gazing at it, in irreconcilable antipathy, across a dim historic mist. "I'm a
modern *bourgeois*," he said, "and not perhaps so good
a judge of how far a pretty woman's tongue may go at
supper without prejudice to her reputation. But I've not
met one of the sweetest of women without recognizing
her and discovering that a certain sort of character offers
better entertainment than Thérésa's songs, sung by a
dissipated duchess. Wit for wit, I think mine carries me
further. (III; 152)

Again, when the Baron discusses America with Longmore a
country he considers to be "a gigantic joke," we are told:

Longmore was not, by habit, an aggressive apologist for
our institutions; but the Baron's narrative confirmed his
worst impressions of French superficiality. He had understood nothing, he had felt nothing, he had learned
nothing; and our hero, glancing askance at his aristocratic profile, declared that if the chief merit of a long
pedigree was to leave one so vaingloriously stupid, he
thanked his stars that the Longmores had emerged from
obscurity in the present century, in the person of an
enterprising lumber merchant. (IV; 158)

While reflecting on M. de Mauves, Longmore, it appears,
contrasts him not only with his wife ("the Baron was a pagan
and his wife was a Christian, and between them, accordingly,
was a gulf" [III; 152]), but also with himself; and though
painfully aware of his own unworldliness, lack of sophistication, and humble bourgeois origin, he is at the same time

self-congratulatory on account of his superior American virtues, in particular his moral imagination, which he contrasts
with the Baron's "stupidity." (Lyon says to himself that the
Baron "was unable to draw a moral inference of the finer
strain, as a school-boy who has been playing truant for a week
to solve a problem in algebra III; 151–52.)

In other words, the observer, being a second illustrative case
of the American puritanical bourgeois, has in this story, in
addition to his role of the witness from whose point of view
the drama is projected, the task of acting as foil to the French
aristocrat, and this is one way in which James reinforces the
reader's sense of the generic character of the international
conflict in *Madame de Mauves*.

The spiritual and cultural gulf between Longmore and the
Baron is further exemplified in their conflicting literary
tastes. This is Longmore on the Baron: "It [the Baron's taste
in women] was the same sort of taste, Longmore moralized, as
the taste for Gérôme in painting, and for M. Gustave Flaubert
in literature" (III; 152). The Baron, on his side, tells Longmore:

> I doubt if your English authors . . . are very sound read-
> ing for young married women. I don't pretend to know
> much about them; but I remember that, not long ago
> after our marriage, Madame de Mauves undertook to
> read me one day a certain Wordsworth,—a poet highly
> esteemed, it appears, *chez vous*. It seemed to me that she
> took me by the nape of the neck and forced my head for
> half an hour over a basin of *soupe aux choux,* and that
> one ought to ventilate the drawing-room before any one
> called. But I suppose you know him,—*ce génie là*. I think
> my wife never forgave me, and that it was a real shock
> to her to find that she had married a man who had very
> much the same taste in literature as in cookery. (IV; 159)

Having in mind James' own literary views, it is clear that
he meant Longmore's and the Baron's tastes to appear equal-

ly limited; both, it transpires, profess contempt of foreign literatures, are totally insensitive to its merits, and are aware merely of its faults.[6] Thus, in his comment on Flaubert, Longmore voices James' own view of the French writers' deficiency in moral sensibility—a fault expressed, according to him, both in their choice of subject matter and in their addiction to the description of surfaces and sensations only. However, unlike James himself, who greatly admires Flaubert's impeccable style and his conscientious and indefatigable search for the *mot juste,* Longmore is characteristically unaware of the aesthetic perfection of his work. As for the Baron, his frivolous, philistine comparison of Wordsworth's poetry to a strong smelling, homely *soupe aux choux* may possibly express certain reservations James himself may have had with regard to Wordsworth's choice of the simplest characters, belonging to the lowest social strata; but again, the Baron, unlike James himself, completely fails to appreciate Wordsworth's moral seriousness and peculiar poetic virtue.

Because Longmore, unlike the earlier Jamesian witness-narrator, grows into a full-fledged fictional character, it is not surprising that he gets involved in the drama he witnesses and becomes a genuine dramatic agent of the greatest significance. M. de Mauves, wishing to undermine his wife's moral superiority and redress the moral balance between them, proposes to Longmore (whose love and admiration for his wife have not escaped him) that he become her lover. Thus Longmore's involvement in the plot precipitates the crisis and brings the international conflict between husband and wife to a head. The proposed arrangement is the ultimate proof of the Baron's cynicism and complete lack of scruple. (His sister, Madame Clarin, treats it as a "political" move to which all moral considerations are irrelevant.) Madame de Mauves, on her side, rejects Longmore's love, arguing that a liaison formed under the auspices of her hus-

6. For a useful and comprehensive discussion of James' literary views see R. Wellek, "Henry James's Literary Theory and Criticism," *American Literature, 30* (November 1958), 293–321.

band would amount to an acceptance of the French code and taint them both with the very corruption and "moral aridity" (III; 145) from which Longmore wishes to save her. In other words, the new situation in which the observer is involved serves as the final test of the American heroine's moral scrupulousness, dignity, and integrity, and furnishes the occasion for her ultimate triumph over her husband. (Madame de Mauves' rejection of her compatriot's offer to save her foreshadows, to some extent, Isabel Archer's similar rejection of Caspar Goodwood; but whereas in *The Portrait of a Lady* James dramatizes the heroine's consciousness, he prefers in *Madame de Mauves* to register the young man's point of view.)

Longmore's involvement in the drama he witnesses, however, is not merely instrumental to its development. He becomes deeply implicated, and in the second half of the story the reader's interest focuses on the inner struggle between his desire for "life" and "experience," on the one hand, and the requirements of his puritan conscience (that "inexpungable organ" which is "absolutely invincible" [V; 172]), on the other: between the "urgent egotism" of the young man's passion and "the principle of asceticism" which lurks in his nature (VII; 189, 184). This inner struggle is finally resolved in Longmore's affirmation of the American moral code. He rises in the end to Madame de Mauves' conception of the situation and decides "to do the handsome thing"—namely, to renounce her:

> But little by little her perfect meaning sank into his mind and soothed it with a sense of opportunity, which somehow stifled his sense of loss. (IX; 198)

> He was not to disappoint her, he was to justify a conception which it had beguiled her weariness to shape. Longmore's imagination swelled . . . he must do the handsome thing; he must decide that the handsome thing was to submit to the inevitable, to the supremely delicate, to

spare her all the pain, to stifle his passion, to ask no compensation, to deport without delay and try to believe that wisdom is its own reward. (IX; 199)

Longmore's involvement in the plot serves to crystallize rather than change the story's main thematic issue. By renouncing Madame de Mauves, Longmore too asserts the superiority of the Puritan conscience over French cynicism. In fact, the moral victory he scores over the Baron is in a way more effective than that of Madame de Mauves, for whereas she appears calm, determined, and inflexible, he arrives at his final decision to renounce only after a long and painful inner struggle. Indeed, it is made quite clear that Longmore's renunciation baffles the Baron, who cannot see its point any more than he can see his wife's.

Madame de Mauves is one of the first in a long line of Jamesian works in which the observer sets himself the task of rescuing the protagonist: Rolland Mallet tries to rescue Roderick Hudson; Pemberton tries to rescue his pupil; the governess in *The Turn of the Screw* tries to rescue Miles and Flora; and, perhaps the only case of a successful rescue, Mr. Longdon removes Nanda Brookenham from her mother's "set" in *The Awkward Age*. What accounts for the recurrence of the theme of the observer as the protagonist's savior is the double role of interpreter and fictional character which he plays in the Jamesian fiction. So long as the protagonist's plight is described by an authorial narrator who transcends the narrative framework, or even by an objective witness who functions merely as the author's deputy and whose fictional characteristics are effaced, the question as to why, being a witness of the protagonist's plight, he makes no attempt to rescue him is spurious and even illegitimate. As soon as the observer from whose point of view the drama is projected grows into a fictional character, however, and is drawn into the dramatic orbit, this same question becomes meaningful, and his urge to save the protagonist, along with his motives, become essential clues to his character. In *Madame de Mauves* Longmore's desire to rescue the heroine from the "moral aridity" of her marriage becomes, as we saw, a central moral issue of the greatest thematic significance. The rescue theme, however, takes on in this story an ironic twist, for Long-more's idea of saving the heroine by becoming her lover is shown to be morally wrong. It would be a false rescue, and he could be but a mock savior; and in the end he scores a moral victory precisely by giving up the project of saving his com-patriot.

The final twist the story takes—the Baron's sudden reform, his wife's unforgiveness, and his ensuing suicide—sheds, as has already been indicated, a highly ambiguous light on Madame de Mauves' salient American characteristic: her Puritan virtue. James records not merely the bare incident but its impact on Longmore:

> Longmore was strongly moved, and his first impulse after he had recovered his composure was to return immediate-ly to Europe. But several years have passed, and he still lingers at home. The truth is, that in the midst of all the ardent tenderness of his memory of Madame de Mauves, he has become conscious of a singular feeling, —a feeling for which awe would hardly be too strong a name" (IX; 209).

The term "awe," possessing the double connotation of both dread and reverence, appropriately conveys the effect of ambiguity. The irony is of course in the contrast between the uncharitableness and appalling coldness with which Madame de Mauves has treated her repentant husband and her com-patriot's belief in her Christian nature ("she was a Christian and her husband was a Pagan")—her "sweetness," "submis-siveness," "ingenuous reserve," "gentle stoicism," "ardent self-effacement," and what had in the past seemed to him "the wantonness of her patience." This ironic contrast takes on an added edge if one recognizes that far from being entire-ly new aspects of her character, Madame de Mauves' coldness and uncharitableness, which now inspire Longmore with obscure awe, are quite consistent with the moral inflexibility she had exhibited in her refusal to accept her husband's corrupt values, an inflexibility Longmore had inordinately admired. What this shows is that the biased American again proves to be the story's best reflector, for it is precisely his unreserved belief in his compatriot's moral sublimity (unimaginable in any of the Jamesian cosmopolitanized witty observers of the international scene) which reinforces the effect of James' ironic exposure of the double-edged character of her Puritan virtue.

Longmore emerges from this ordeal as a complementary case of the American disenchanted romantic. Madame de Mauves had entertained in her youth the romantic notion of the moral fineness of the European aristocrat—a notion of which she had been disabused by her marriage to the Baron. Longmore, on his side, it now transpires, was infected with the opposite brand of the national romanticism, that of a belief in the moral sublimity of the American woman, which the final incident deeply undermines.

Since Longmore, by now himself the butt of the Jamesian irony, ceases at this point of the story to function as its guiding intelligence, his final recoil from Madame de Mauves is not registered through his consciousness but instead reported by the objective authorial narrator—a technique creating the appropriate distancing effect. This dry, informative report reveals the cosmopolitanized, sophisticated author, who has not been effaced by his deputy.

The final ironic twist in *Madame de Mauves* is in many ways reminiscent of the Maupassantian "point."[7] There is, however, an essential difference between the way in which the two writers use this device. In a story by Maupassant, the final point throws a sudden, sharp retrospective light on the narrative, illuminating in a flash the central point of its

7. James was at that period very much under the influence of French writers. See W. C. D. Pacey, "James and his French Contemporaries," *American Literature, 13* (November 1941), 240–56.

theme. To take one famous example: the protagonist in *The Necklace* is a poor woman who had borrowed a necklace from a rich friend, enjoyed it but once in her life, and lost it at a ball. Henceforth she slaves quietly and uncomplainingly for many years in order to pay it back. In the closing passage the protagonist, ravaged and disfigured by her life of labor, meets her rich friend and learns that the necklace was artificial and therefore quite worthless. This information gives the story its twist by making the poor woman's life of hardship and sacrifice appear cruelly senseless—indeed, absurd.

The final ironic twist in James' *Madame de Mauves* serves, I suggest, a completely different purpose. Undeniably, it, too, has surprise value and throws a new light on the American wife's "virtue." Nevertheless, by hinting at some disturbing feature of the Puritan temperament, James did not change the reader's initial appreciation of the dignity, integrity, and moral rightness of Madame de Mauves' decision to reject Longmore's love. In other words, the final twist does not reverse the central point (or even moral) of the fable. Rather, it touches upon new aspects of the theme of the American woman which James was later to explore more thoroughly and tragically in *The Bostonians* in the character of Olive Chancellor, the neurotic Boston suffragette.

I have analyzed Longmore's functional value as an observer as well as his thematic value as a fictional character in his own right. It seems to me, however, that there is a certain unresolved contradiction between these two roles which, at this stage, James has not yet satisfactorily solved. As a young American who is totally insensitive—indeed, actually hostile—to the social traditions and conventions of the older civilization, Longmore is treated by the witty and critical authorial narrator with gentle irony, and his parochialism is mildly but persistently ridiculed. This effect is made possible by James' use of free indirect speech, a narrative technique which enables James to move from the observer's to the narrator's point of view and to introduce sly authorial reservations without thereby disrupting the inner rhythm of the

character's thoughts.[8] It is interesting to note in this connection that in this early work the authorial narrator, though
undeniably more sophisticated and cosmopolitanized than
the central observer, is yet himself an American. Thus he
clearly addresses himself in the following passage to the
reader as an American to a fellow-countryman: "Longmore
was not, by habit, an aggressive apologist for our institutions" (IV; 158). But if as a fictional character Longmore's
biased Americanism is ridiculed, as an observer he nevertheless appears to function as a perfect rather than as a distorted
mirror of the French family. That is to say, the scenic as
opposed to the reflective passages, in which M. de Mauves
and his sister are objectively presented, fully confirm Longmore's hostile view of them as odious, crude, and cynical.
And what this means is that there is nothing in the presentation of them which could justify James' implied critique of
Longmore's biased vision of Europe. A finer, more mature,
and much more complex work in which the later James has
solved this difficulty is *The Ambassadors*.

As in the case of *A Passionate Pilgrim*, an examination of

---

8. For an analysis of free indirect speech *(style indirect libre)* as a
stylistic device in Flaubert's fiction see M. Lips, *Le Style indirect libre*
(Paris, 1926); S. Ullman, *Style in the French Novel* (New York, 1963); and
V. Brombert, *The Novels of Flaubert, A Study of Themes and Techniques*
(Princeton, 1966). For an analysis of this narrative technique in James'
fiction see I. Watt, "The First Paragraph of *The Ambassadors:* An Explication," *Essays in Criticism*, 10 (1960), 250–74. For a summary of the
literature on the subject see Doritt Cohn, "Narrated Monologue: Definition of a Fictional Style," *Comparative Literature, 18* (1966), 97–112.

It is perhaps hardly surprising that both Flaubert and Henry James
favor this narrative technique. Both vehemently reject the traditional
omniscient-writer convention and prefer to project the drama through
the consciousness of one of their characters. At the same time, both feel
the need unobtrusively to amplify and comment on the characters and
the situation they present, and free indirect speech is the ideal narrative
technique for combining these two purposes. The authorial interpolations it makes possible serve as a delicate instrument of oblique criticism;
and it is, moreover, a perfect vehicle of irony—of which both novelists
are great masters.

James' revisions of *Madame de Mauves* for the New York
Edition sheds additional light on the relationship between
the observer's fictional character and his functional role as an
interpreter of the drama. For example, James changes "a
sweet American girl who marries an unclean Frenchman" (I;
127) into "a sweet American girl who marries an unholy for-
eigner";[9] "M. de Mauves had a stock of rigid notions" (III;
152) becomes "M. de Mauves had a stock of social principles";[10] "the Baron made those speeches with a remorse-
less placidity" (III; 151) becomes "M. de Mauves made these
speeches with a bright assurance."[11] The revisions are obviously a toning down of the original and have the effect of
making Longmore's view of the European seem less violent
and hostile. Again, James changes "Longmore had often
heard of this distinguished social type. . . . It had certainly a
picturesque boldness of outline" (III; 152) into "Longmore
had often heard of that historic type [which] had its elegance
of outline,"[12] a revision that weakens the grudging admiration of an unworldly young American for the social type M.
de Mauves represents, and makes his curiosity with regard to
it milder and more objective. James changes Longmore's view
of Madame de Mauves from "one of the sweetest women" (III;
152) into "one of the rarest women,"[13] and instead of "it
seemed one of fortune's most mocking strokes, that she
should be surrounded by persons whose only merit was that
they threw the charm of her character into radiant relief"
(III; 150), he says: "it seemed one of fortune's most mocking
strokes that she should be surrounded by persons whose only
merit was that they threw every side of her, as she turned in
her pain, into radiant relief."[14] By changing "sweetness"
into "rarity" and by emphasizing Madame de Mauves' "pain"

9. *Madame de Mauve,* New York, *13,* I, p. 220.
10. Ibid., p. 256.
11. Ibid., p. 254.
12. Ibid., pp. 255–56.
13. Ibid., p. 256.
14. Ibid., p. 253.

rather than "charm of character," James makes Longmore's
view of her more sober, more just, and less romantic, thus
reducing the ironic contrast between his view of her sweetness and gentleness and the final exposure of her coldness
and uncharitableness. Instead of "her husband thinks her too
rigid! What would a poet call it?" (V; 173) James makes
Longmore reflect: "her clever husband thinks her too prim.
What would a stupid poet call it?"[15] By changing "rigid"
into "prim" James weakens the harshness of the view Longmore takes of the French husband's inability to appreciate
his American wife, and by qualifying the poet as "stupid" he
adds a note of self-irony to Longmore's admiration for his
unappreciated compatriot. Again, while in the original version Longmore's state is that of "a muttering resentment that
he had not known her five years ago, and a brooding hostility
to those who had anticipated him" (III; 150), in the revised
version he is described as a friend who "nursed a brooding
regret for his not having known her five years earlier" and of
having "a particular objection to those who had smartly
anticipated him"[16]—a revision which makes Longmore sadly
rueful rather than resentful. Or again, "the lurking principle
of asceticism" (VII; 174) in Longmore's composition becomes
in the revised version "a lurking principle of sacrifice, sacrifice for sacrifice's sake."[17] By eliminating the term "asceticism," with its strong puritanical connotations, James again
mitigates Longmore's Americanism.

A study of James' revisions shows that apart from making
the style more flexible, concrete, and compact, he aims at
presenting the international marital drama of the De Mauves
in a subtler, less melodramatic light by somewhat mitigating
the impression of the odiousness of the French husband.
Since the drama is registered from Longmore's point of view
this change amounts, in effect, to making the manner in
which the drama is presented more sophisticated and dis-

15. Ibid., p. 283.
16. Ibid., p. 253.
17. Ibid., p. 299.

criminating than in the original version. But by making the
observer a finer interpreter of the case he registers, James
attenuates his distinctive fictional characteristics, those of a
young innocent American who serves as a second illustrative
case of American romanticism. It seems to me, therefore, that
despite the considerable stylistic gain of James' revisions,
there is a distinct loss in the resulting toning down of the observer's fictional character, which, as I have tried to show,
enriches the fable and serves to crystallize its central thematic
issue.[18]

18. The subject of James' revision is dealt with in the following
works: H. Harvitt, "The Revisions of Roderick Hudson," *PMLA, 39,*
(March 1924), 203–27; A. Gettman, "Henry James's Revision of *The
American,*" *American Literature, 16* (January 1945), 279–82; R. Mc-
Elderry, Jr., "Henry James's Revision of *Watch and Ward,*" *MLA, 72*
(November 1952), 457–61; Gegenheimer, *American Literature, 23,* 233–42;
S. J. Krause, "James's Revisions of the Style of *The Portrait of a Lady,*"
American Literature, 30 (March 1958), 67–88; I. Traschen, "Henry James
and the Art of Revision," *Philological Quarterly, 35* (1956), 39–47;
Matthiessen, *Henry James, The Major Phase,* pp. 152–86.

CHAPTER 3

THE PORTRAIT OF A LADY

The Portrait of a Lady,[1] whose subject is "the conception of a young girl affronting her destiny," grew out of James' "sense of a single character." In other words, the germ of his idea of the novel was not as usual a dramatic situation in terms of which the principal characters are conceived but rather a vision of "the unattached character, the image *en disponibilité.*" As James records in the Preface, only after he had a firm grasp of this image did he proceed, in a Turgenevian manner, to devise the action which leads the heroine to reveal her character, planning the whole cast of subsidiary characters as "a definite array of contributions to [her] history."[2]

In *Roderick Hudson,* the earlier novel whose subject was the rise and fall of a young American artist, James still chose to present the protagonist exclusively from the point of view of his friend and patron. This, in the long run, created an undesirable distancing effect, as a consequence of which the reader failed to become sufficiently involved in the young artist's predicament.[3] James' decision to present Isa-

---

1. New York, 3–4.

2. Preface 3, xii, viii. On Turgenev's influence on James, and in particular on the relation between James' *The Portrait of a Lady* (1881) and Turgenev's *On the Eve* (1859), see D. Lerner, "The Influence of Turgenev on Henry James," *Slavonic Review, 20* (1941), 28–54 (American Series I).

3. On control of distance see Booth, *The Rhetoric of Fiction,* pp. 243–64. Interestingly, James maintained in the Preface to *Roderick Hudson* that "the centre of interest throughout 'Roderick' is in Rolland Mallet's consciousness and the drama is the very drama of his con-

bel's drama from within shows that he must have recognized
that his method of registering the protagonist's case from an
observer's point of view, although very effective in his short
works, was unsuitable to a full-length novel in which one
needs to explore more deeply the protagonist's consciousness, in particular when its subject was preeminently develop-
mental. Indeed, having learned his lesson, James in all
his later novels consistently placed the center in the protagonist's consciousness—in *The Princess Casamassima, The
Tragic Muse, What Maisie Knew, The Ambassadors, The
Wings of the Dove,* and *The Golden Bowl.*[4]

Being preoccupied in the Preface to *The Portrait of a
Lady* with the "difficulties" and the "beauties" of his new
technique of "placing the centre of the subject in the heroine's consciousness,"[5] James, as critic, failed to do justice
to Ralph Touchett, the novel's central observer and its
second center of consciousness. Notwithstanding James' claim
that he employed but one center, an examination of the
novel shows that he supplemented the direct presentation
of Isabel's consciousness with a record of Ralph's feelings,
impressions, and analyses of her case.

Before being launched, Ralph is introduced in James'
early manner, by the authorial narrator who records his
past history and emphasizes his qualifications to serve as
the novel's guiding intelligence. He is, we learn, a Europeanized American, whose studies at both Harvard and
Oxford have placed in his hand "the key to modern criticism," by which James clearly means the ability to see with
equal clearness the merits and faults of both the American

---

sciousness," yet went on to discuss the problems involved in the dramatization of Roderick's development. In fact, unlike many later Jamesian
observers, Rolland Mallet remains basically a subsidiary character, who
fulfills the roles of interpreter and *raisonneur;* and his being the novel's
center of consciousness does not make him its center of interest.

4. The list does not include *The Awkward Age,* which is purely scenic,
and James' short novels, which may be considered as extended *nouvelles.*

5. Preface, p. xx.

and the European systems. In short, like the Freers in *Lady Barbarina*, it is Ralph's thorough acquaintance with the international scene which equips him to appreciate the international complexities of Isabel's tragic history. But since *The Portrait of a Lady* is a full-length novel, Ralph, its central observer, is a more fully imagined fictional character than the Freers, and his internationalism is correspondingly more fully explored than theirs. Not only is Ralph perfectly acquainted with both systems, he is actually a product of both; he has acquired European urbanity, sophistication, and refinement of manners, yet has never really lost those supreme American national traits—an independent mind and a lively imagination. In fact, it is clearly suggested that Ralph's Americanness goes deeper than his Englishness: "His outward conformity to the manners that surrounded him was none the less the mask of a mind that greatly enjoyed its independence, on which nothing long imposed itself, and which, naturally inclined to adventure and irony, indulged in a boundless liberty of appreciation" (V; *3*, 49).

As a sophisticated European, Ralph responds to Isabel's youthful enthusiasm and American romanticism with an ironic indulgence and an amused fascination; but it is as an American that he understands and admires her "presumptuous" desire for "the free exploration of life." Ralph's second qualification to serve as an observer of Isabel's drama is his invalid state, which forbids him "the rush of action" and confines him to "mere spectatorship at the game of life." As a consequence of his forced withdrawal from active life, he dedicates himself to "the joys of contemplation"[6]—the only activity he is allowed to indulge in, and into which all his passion, intelligence, and imagination seem to go. In

6. F. O. Matthiessen points out that in his revision of *The Portrait of a Lady* James was trying, among other things, to put greater emphasis on the chief attributes of the Jamesian sensibility, and that he therefore changed the rather colorless expression "delights of observation" to its more intense equivalent, "the joys of contemplation." See *Henry James, The Major Phase*, p. 159.

fact, as Isabel comes later to perceive, "the state of his health had seemed not a limitation, but a kind of intellectual advantage; it absolved him from all professional and official emotions and left him the luxury of being exclusively personal" (XXXIII; *4*, 59–60). Ralph is never bored in his role of spectator; he finds life extremely interesting and is naturally delighted to devote himself to the observation of an American cousin who embodies to perfection his "idea of an interesting woman" (II; *3*, 24). In other words, Ralph's functional traits—the keenness of his observations and the intensity of his interpretative activities—are fully accounted for in terms of his personal predicament.

The image of Ralph as the ugly and witty invalid is suggestively evoked in the opening chapter, in which James describes his first appearance on the scene:

> Tall, lean, loosely and feebly put together, he had an ugly, sickly, witty, charming face, furnished, but by no means decorated, with a straggling moustache and whisker. He looked clever and ill—a combination by no means felicitous; and he wore a brown velvet jacket. He carried his hands in his pockets, and there was something in the way he did it that showed the habit was inveterate. His gait had a shambling, wandering quality; he was not very firm on his legs. (I; *3*, 5–6)

The pathos of Ralph's sickly appearance is highlighted in two opposite and complementary ways: first, by being contrasted with Lord Warburton's splendid bloom (which, we are told, "would have provoked you to wish yourself almost blindly, in his place" [I; *3*, 5]), and second, by James' emphasis on the fact that the father as well as the son is an invalid— or, as Ralph humorously puts it, that both he and his father are "lame ducks" (I; *3*, 7).

Like Milly Theale in *The Wings of the Dove,* Ralph (James' "accessory invalid") is not addicted to self-pity; on the contrary, he is shown to be unfailingly cheerful and high-spirited—an invalid who is never "formally sick" (XXXIII;

4, 60). Ralph's good humor and self-irony are of course qualities of all the Jamesian vessels of consciousness, and here they save James' treatment of his case from the sentimentality with which the unattractive, sickly, and devoted cousin of the Victorian novel is commonly rendered.[7]

James, we recall, was in the habit of making the observer fall in love with the heroine for purely functional reasons: in order to deepen his sympathy and thereby give greater intensity to his narrative. However, having made the observer fall in love with the heroine, James could rarely resist the temptation of developing the potentialities of this new dramatic situation, adding to the observer's purely functional traits—curiosity, sensitivity, wit, and a lively sense of irony—the complicating elements of jealousy, resentment, vindictiveness, and exasperation. These feelings, where they occur, enrich his fictional character but may at the same time detract from his efficacy as a lucid reflector. In the case of Ralph, James does indeed make him instantly fall in love with Isabel, but no conflict between the exigencies of lucid reflection and those of convincing characterization arise. Because he is ill Ralph "loves without hope"; in fact, we are explicitly told in the introductory chapter that "the imagination of loving—as distinguished from that of being loved—had still a place in his [Ralph's] reduced sketch. He had only forbidden himself the riot of expression" (V; *3*, 54). In sum, since Ralph finds his spectatorship sufficiently absorbing and rewarding, his love for Isabel, though it intensi-

---

7. Oscar Cargill *(The Novels of Henry James* [New York, 1961], p. 90) draws an illuminating parallel between Ralph Touchett and another devoted invalid lover—the hunchback Philip Wakem in George Eliot's *The Mill on the Floss.* Whereas Cargill emphasizes Ralph's literary predecessors, E. Sandeen discovers an autobiographical parallel between Ralph's relationship with Isabel and James' relationship with his cousin Minny Temple, pointing out that at the time James might have regarded her with the eyes of a lover, he was himself an invalid, not qualified as a suitor *("The Wings of the Dove* and *The Portrait of a Lady:* A Study of Henry James' Later Phase," *PMLA, 69* [December 1954], 1060–75.)

fies the passionate interest he takes in her history, does not
obscure his vision by detracting from his disinterestedness.
If the Freers in *Lady Barbarina* are disinterested but detached, and Longmore in *Madame de Mauves* passionately
concerned but lacking in objectivity, Ralph combines Longmore's intense concern with the Freers' clear-sightedness.

The reader receives his first impression of the novel's
heroine through the impact she makes on Ralph's sensibilities, and it is only after his extremely sympathetic view of
her has been firmly established that James reverts to the
authorial narrator's record of her youth in Albany and to
his more critical analysis of her character. The authorial
analysis, which combines George Eliot's moral seriousness
with James' own distinctive ironic note, provides the reader
with a more comprehensive view of the young heroine, ap-
prising him not only of her charm and finer qualities but
also of her flaws: her extremely "theoretic" bent of mind,
her incorrigible American romanticism, her youthful self-
centeredness, and in particular, her "presumptuousness"—
the hubris of the American heroine. [8]

A few passages will illustrate the tone and quality of the
authorial analysis:

> Altogether, with her meagre knowledge, her inflated
> ideals, her confidence at once innocent and dogmatic,
> her temper at once exacting and indulgent, her mixture
> of curiosity and fastidiousness, of vivacity and indiffer-
> ence, her desire to look very well and to be if possible
> even better, her determination to see, to try, to know,
> her combination of the delicate, desultory, flame-like

8. Despite his preference for "rendering" over "stating," James still
uses in *The Portrait of a Lady* the staple Victorian expository technique
of block characterization. Clearly James has not yet mastered the art of
dramatizing the complex expository material of a full-length novel, so
perfectly exhibited in *The Ambassadors*. He uses the introductory authorial report again in *The Princess Casamassima* (in the story of Hyacinth's mother and of his adoption by the dressmaker) and in *The Wings
of the Dove* (in the story of Kate Croy's life with her father).

spirit and the eager and personal creature of conditions: she would be an easy victim of scientific criticism if she were not intended to awaken on the reader's part an impulse more tender and more purely expectant. (VI; *3*, 69)

Of course, among her theories, this young lady was not without a collection of views on the subject of marriage. The first on the list was a conviction of the vulgarity of thinking too much of it. From lapsing into eagerness on this point she earnestly prayed she might be delivered; she held that a woman ought to be able to live to herself, in the absence of exceptional flimsiness, and that it was perfectly possible to be happy without the society of a more or less coarse-minded person, of another sex. The girl's prayer was very sufficiently answered; something pure and proud that there was in her—something cold and dry an unappreciated suitor with a taste for analysis might have called it—had hitherto kept her from any great vanity of conjecture on the article of possible husbands. . . . Deep in her soul—it was the deepest thing there—lay a belief that if a certain light should dawn she could give herself completely. . . . It often seemed to her that she thought too much about herself; you could have made her colour, any day in the year, by calling her a rank egoist. She was always planning out her development, desiring her perfection, observing her progress. (VI; *3*, 71–72)

Although the authorial narrator's tone is somewhat more critical and less enthusiastic than that of the observer, he too is shown to be tenderly appreciative of the heroine's basically fine nature. His gentle irony (which plays about "poor Ralph" as well) never takes a satiric turn. In fact, in admitting to the reader that Isabel "would be an easy victim of scientific criticism if she were not intended to awaken on the reader's part an impulse more tender and more purely expectant," James dissociates his technique from the *impassibilité* advocated by Flaubert and the French naturalists, and indicates his intention of treating his heroine in a different spirit, a spirit of tender appreciation not unlike that in which Turgenev treats his heroines.[9] In short, by analyzing Isabel's case from two viewpoints essentially similar, though varying slightly in ironic distance, James arrives at the perfect balance of criticism and sympathy, irony and admiration, severity and gentleness with which he means the reader to respond to his heroine. Moreover, by dividing the interpretive function between an authorial narrator who impresses the reader as having a full, rounded view of Isabel's drama and an observer in whom the heroine gradually ceases to confide, and who is reduced to merely entertaining a suspicion of what her plight may be, James has combined the effect of dramatic irony—the sense that Isabel is acting out a preordained destiny—with the maximum suspense and dramatic immediacy.[10]

As Isabel begins her European career at Gardencourt, Ralph serves not only as the amused and delighted witness of her day-to-day activities but also as her initiator. He plays the role of cicerone to her—takes her round the old country house, shows her the galleries, anatomizes Lord Warburton for her benefit; and it is mainly through his lively, witty, ironic, amusing conversation that Isabel is first introduced

9. James describes Turgenev's heroines (Elena, Lisa, and Tatyana) in one of his critical essays as "radiant with maidenly charm" and as having "a touch of the faintly acrid perfume of the New England temperament, a hint of puritan angularity," a description which is perfectly applicable to Isabel Archer. See *French Poets and Novelists* (London, 1919), p. 216; quoted from Lerner, *Slavonic Review*, 35.

10. It is perhaps F. R. Leavis' failure to distinguish between the two complementary perspectives from which Isabel is seen, which accounts for his view that James fell in love with his own creation and that, because of this sentimental involvement with the heroine, he treated her with too great an indulgence and insufficient critical sharpness. (See his "Daniel Deronda; A Conversation" in *The Great Tradition* [New York: New

to the old world's sophistication. Actually, it is during this period of initiation that Ralph's European traits are most in evidence. He is thoroughly appreciative of Isabel, the fine, sensitive, ardent, imaginative specimen of the American Girl, whom he finds fascinating and adorable, but is irritated by Henrietta Stackpole, its cruder, more provincial representative, who serves as Isabel's comic foil. He is repelled by Henrietta's familiarity, loudness, bluntness, and lack of any "sense of privacy." What is more important, he is shown to be too Europeanized even to understand the workings of her incredibly simple mind, and jokingly confesses to Isabel that in Henrietta's case "to read between the lines was easier than to follow the text." Indeed, it is only after he has been in his turn initiated by Isabel into the simplicities of the American mind that Ralph comes in the end to enjoy the Henrietta type and even conceives a certain affection for the blunt, honest lady-journalist from Boston.

It is the unsubtle Henrietta who draws the reader's attention to the role Ralph is playing in her friend's Europeanization. She burns with the sacred rage and is extremely suspicious of Isabel's responsiveness to Europe ("Isabel's changing every day; she's drifting away—right out to sea. I've watched her and I can see it. She's not the bright American girl she was. She's taking different views, a different colour, and turning away from her old ideals" [XIII; 3, 170]). Within the framework of her simplified, black-and-white international scheme, Ralph naturally appears as the incarnation of European evil: she finds him lazy, indolent, and cynical, and accuses him, in her aggressive and comically exaggerated

York University Press, 1963; London, Chatto & Windus and Penguin Books, 1962]. Another reason for Leavis' criticism of James' attitude toward his heroine is that he sees her as an idealized version of George Eliot's Gwendolen Harleth, whereas she is much more like Dorothea Brooke. On this point see G. Levine, "Isabel, Gwendolen and Dorothea," *English Literary History*, 30 [September 1936], 244–57.)

manner, of having infected Isabel with European "corruption."

The hilariously comic conversations between Ralph and Henrietta in which they discuss Isabel (chap. VIII) serve an important analytical purpose. They direct our attention to the pivotal issue of Isabel's drama—namely, her exposure to Europe, its possibilities, and its dangers. Ralph, the representative of the European point of view, is alive mainly to the possibiilties for self-development which the European experience offers Isabel; whereas Henrietta, the representative of the American point of view, voices her fears of the effects European corruption might have on Isabel's moral nature. Besides having this analytical function, the discussions between Henrietta and Ralph constitute a comedy of international incompatibilities illustrative of the international conflict which rages among the various European and American spectators of Isabel's drama—Mr. Touchett, Mrs. Touchett, the Countess Gemini (Osmond's sister), Lord Warburton, and Caspar Goodwood.

During the period of Isabel's initiation, Ralph functions as the center through whose consciousness she is projected. His subsequent withdrawal from this post reflects Isabel's emergence from the sheltered existence of Gardencourt and marks the beginning of her European career. Her rejection of Lord Warburton's offer of marriage is already registered from her point of view, with Ralph no longer present as an eye-witness. James dramatizes Isabel's complex and conflicting reactions: her obscure fear of "the splendid security" Lord Warburton offers her, as well as her genuine desire to spare as much as possible a person she finds so immensely likeable; her conviction that she is doing the right thing in refusing him, along with her fear that her decision may perhaps prove her to be "a cold, priggish person." Isabel in this scene is presented with fine dramatic verisimilitude, as confused and uncertain about the full meaning of her act. James accordingly adds to the dramatic rejection-scene an analytical counterpart, in which Ralph, whose role is now restricted to that of a choric interpreter, attempts to diagnose Isabel's act and to provide a definition of its significance, supplementing her private, subjective analysis with his own, more objective evaluative commentary:

> "Tell me this," Ralph went on while she listened to him with quickened attention. "What had you in mind when you refused Lord Warburton?"
>
> "What had I in mind?"
>
> "What was the logic—the view of your situation—that dictated so remarkable an act?"
>
> "I didn't wish to marry him—if that's logic."
>
> "No, that's not logic—and I knew that before. It's really nothing, you know. What was it you *said* to yourself? You certainly said more than that."
>
> Isabel reflected a moment, then answered with a question of her own. "Why do you call it a remarkable act? That's what your mother thinks too."
>
> "Warburton's such a thorough good sort; as a man, I consider he has hardly a fault. And then he's what they call here no end of a swell. He has immense possessions, and his wife would be thought a superior being. He unites the intrinsic and the extrinsic advantages."
>
> Isabel watched her cousin as to see how far he would go. "I refused him because he was too perfect then. I'm not perfect myself, and he's too good for me. Besides, his perfection would irritate me."
>
> "That's ingenious rather than candid," said Ralph. "As a fact you think nothing in the world too perfect for you." (XV; *3*, 210)

At a glance from his companion, however, he became grave, and to prove it went on: "You want to see life—you'll be hanged if you don't, as the young men say."

"I don't think I want to see it as the young men want to see it. But I do want to look about me."

"You want to drain the cup of experience."

"No, I don't wish to touch the cup of experience. It's a poisoned drink! I only want to see for myself."

"You want to see, but not to feel," Ralph remarked.

"I don't think that if one's a sentient being one can make the distinction. I'm a good deal like Henrietta. The other day when I asker her if she wished to marry she said: 'Not till I've seen Europe!' I too don't wish to marry till I've seen Europe."

"You evidently expect a crowned head will be struck with you."

"No, that would be worse than marrying Lord Warburton. But it's getting very dark," Isabel continued, "and I must go home." She rose from her place, but Ralph only sat still and looked at her. As he remained there she stopped, and they exchanged a gaze that was full on either side, but especially on Ralph's, of utterances too vague for words.

"You've answered my question," he said at last. "You've told me what I wanted. I'm greatly obliged to you."

"It seems to me I've told you very little."

"You've told me the great thing: that the world interests you and that you want to throw yourself into it."

Her silvery eyes shone a moment in the dusk. "I never said that."

"I think you meant it. Don't repudiate it. It's so fine!"

"I don't know what you're trying to fasten upon me, for I'm not in the least an adventurous spirit. Women are not like men."

Ralph slowly rose from his seat and they walked together to the gate of the square. "No," he said; "women rarely boast of their courage. Men do so with a certain frequency."

"Men have it to boast of!"

"Women have it too. You've a great deal."

"Enough to go home in a cab to Pratt's Hotel, but not more." (XV; 3, 213–14)

Ralph interprets Isabel's rejection of Lord Warburton as the first grand example of her independence of mind and spirit of adventure—as an expression of her desire, which he inordinately respects and admires, "to see life" and "drain the cup of experience." As the novel's guiding intelligence he also emphasizes the extraordinary and exceptional nature of Isabel's decision:

> "What I mean is that I shall have the thrill of seeing what a young lady does who won't marry Lord War-burton."
>
> "That's what your mother counts upon too," said Isabel.
>
> "Ah, there will be plenty of spectators! We shall hang on the rest of your career. I shall not see all of it, but I shall probably see the most interesting years. Of course if you were to marry our friend you'd still have a career —a very decent, in fact a very brilliant one. But rela-tively speaking it would be a little prosaic. It would be definitely marked out in advance; it would be want-ing in the unexpected. You know I'm extremely fond of the unexpected, and now that you've kept the game in your hands I depend on your giving us some grand example of it." (XV; *3, 212*)

Ralph's analysis not only provides us with a clearer state-ment of Isabel's motives for rejecting Lord Warburton but also emphasizes its heroic character and its far-reaching sig-nificance as the first stage in a brilliant and highly prom-ising career.

What makes this analytical exchange between Ralph and Isabel so much more dramatic than its counterparts in, for instance, *The Ambassadors,* in which Miss Gostrey discusses with Strether the significance of his European experiences, is that, unlike the former, Isabel opposes her confidant rather than collaborates with him. Her unwillingness to cooperate, her evasiveness, irritability, and insistent self-depreciation, stem from a certain fear, a reluctance to assume the responsibilities which Ralph's great expectations impose on her. And these, in turn—the fear and the reluctance—spring from an ultimate modesty about her own capability for affronting her destiny and are an ironic comment on the charge of "presumption." (Can she be as presumptuous as all that, we are invited to ask, if she is so full of self-doubt and self-mistrust?)[11] Isabel, moreover, has all along been afraid lest her rejection of Lord Warburton might prove her to be "a victim of intellectual eagerness and vague ambitions." This fear, at first somewhat allayed by old Mr. Touchett's gallant pretense that her action was no more than an expression of ordinary feminine capriciousness, is presently aggravated by Ralph's insistence on its boldness and extraordinariness. Ralph, for whom watching Isabel act out her freedom constitutes *his* great personal adventure and fulfills the requirements of *his* imagination, constantly presses his cousin— indeed, beseeches her—to accept his interpretation of her action ("Don't repudiate it. It's so fine!") In sum, what gives the analytical discussion its dramatic intensity is the fact that, having his own personal stake in the matter, the confidant is not less deeply involved than the protagonist.

The second great scene in which Ralph figures which also combines analytical and dramatic values is the warning scene, in which Ralph attempts, rather hopelessly, to make Isabel see through Osmond and dissuade her from marrying him. Here again, Ralph's point of view supplements Isabel's own. Isabel delivers her defense in a tone of passionate agitation which she tries in vain to suppress. It expresses "the angry pain excited by his [Ralph's] words and the wounded pride of having to justify a choice of which she felt only the nobleness and purity":

11. In his Preface to *The Princess Casamassima* James characterizes Hyacinth Robinson, the novel's central vessel of consciousness, as "my little presumptuous adventurer" (New York, 5, xvii). The characterization as "presumptuous" of a hero who is so full of self-doubt and so tormented by uncertainty that he in the end commits suicide reinforces the view that James' earlier characterization of the heroine of *The Portrait of a Lady* as "presumptuous" is partly mock-ironic.

"I can't enter into your idea of Mr. Osmond; I can't do
it justice, because I see him in quite another way. He's
not important—no, he's not important; he's a man to
whom importance is supremely indifferent. If that's what
you mean when you call him 'small,' then he's as small
as you please. I call that large—it's the largest thing I
know. . . . There have been moments when I should like
to go and kneel by your father's grave: he did perhaps
a better thing than he knew when he put it into my
power to marry a poor man—a man who has borne his
poverty with such dignity, with such indifference. Mr.
Osmond has never scrambled nor struggled—he has
cared for no worldly prize. If that's to be narrow, if that's
to be selfish, then it's very well. I'm not frightened by
such words, I'm not even displeased; I'm only sorry that
you should make a mistake. . . . Your mother has never
forgiven me for not having come to a better understanding with Lord Warburton, and she's horrified at
my contenting myself with a person who has none of his
great advantages—no property, no title, no honours, no
houses, nor lands, nor position, nor reputation, nor
brilliant belongings of any sort. It's the total absence
of all these things that pleases me. Mr. Osmond's simply
a very lonely, a very cultivated and a very honest man."
(XXXIV; *4, 72–73*)

Although Isabel's ardent good faith in deciding to marry
Osmond is fully registered in such dramatic scenes, it is in
the end of the record of Ralph's impression of the impassioned rhetoric of her defense of Osmond which dispels any
remaining ambiguities on this score:

Ralph had listened with great attention, as if everything
she said merited deep consideration; but in truth he was
only half thinking of the things she said, he was for the
rest simply accommodating himself to the weight of his
total impression—the impression of her ardent good

faith. She was wrong, but she believed; she was deluded,
but she was dismally consistent. It was wonderfully
characteristic of her that, having invented a fine theory
about Gilbert Osmond, she loved him not for what he
really possessed, but for his very poverties dressed out as
honours. Ralph remembered what he had said to his
father about wishing to put it into her power to meet
the requirements of her imagination. He had done so,
and the girl had taken full advantage of the luxury.
Poor Ralph felt sick; he felt ashamed. Isabel had uttered
her last words with a low solemnity of conviction which
virtually terminated the discussion, and she closed it
formally by turning away and walking back to the house.
(XXXIV; *4*, 74–75)

Moreover, by contrasting Isabel's own certainty of the rightness of her choice with Ralph's painful awareness of her
delusion, James intensifies the irony of its tragic inevitability.

What makes the warning scene genuinely dramatic is again
the fact that protagonist and confidant are equally involved.
Ralph, who had persuaded his father to make Isabel an
heiress so that she should be free to realize her ideal of self-
development, considers himself to be in large measure responsible for her choice of a husband. Moreover, her decision
to marry Osmond—who (Ralph knows) is narrow, selfish, and
conventional a person who takes himself too seriously and
who, despite his exquisite taste, is nothing but a sterile
dilettante—shocks him and makes him feel "terribly 'sold.' "
To Isabel, on her side, Ralph's severe criticism of her future
husband and the doubt he casts on the wisdom of her decision
are naturally painful and offensive. Ralph exercises great tact
in his attempt to enlighten Isabel without unduly hurting her
feelings and without completely alienating her; Isabel, for
her part, tries to be scrupulously just to Ralph and makes a
great effort to stifle her deep agitation. Both, however, are
shown to be not entirely successful in their efforts; and this
conflict between two people who are forced, despite their

great affection, to hurt each other makes the warning scene one of the subtlest and most moving dramatic episodes in *The Portrait of a Lady*.

In the first part of the novel (the period of Isabel's initiation) Ralph, we recall, serves as the story's center of consciousness, and the witty, sophisticated, "amused" note he strikes dominates the narrative. In the second part (up to Isabel's marriage to Osmond) Ralph's role somewhat shrinks and he becomes a choric interpreter present only in the scenes of analysis. In the third part (up to Isabel's last visit to Gardencourt) Ralph's observational and interpretative activities becomes still more limited. Prompted by pride, a determination not "to publish her shame to the world," and a desire to spare her cousin, Isabel hides her unhappiness from Ralph, who, deprived of all the observer's privileges, turns into a silent, helpless, and resigned witness of his cousin's secret suffering.[12]

Significantly, the more Ralph's observational role shrinks, the greater his thematic significance grows, and the less he is physically present, the more does he come to occupy Isabel's thoughts. During her mediative vigil in which Isabel comes to a full awareness of the failure of her marriage (chap. XLII), she realizes that her cousin has been right in his criticism of Osmond and, more important, that she had deplorably failed to understand him. Her failure to perceive that Ralph's levity masked a deep seriousness appears now to have stemmed from the same source as her failure to see through Osmond's apparent seriousness. In both instances her susceptibility to fine appearances, coupled with her ignorance of European sophistication, made her mistake the surface for the substance.

---

12. Interestingly, this is Ralph's only role which James mentions in his detailed entry about *The Portrait of a Lady:* "Ralph's helpless observation of Isabel's deep misery; her determination to show him nothing, and his inability to help her. This to be a strong feature in the situation" (*The Notebooks of Henry James,* ed. F. O. Mathiessen and K. B. Murdock [New York, 1961], p. 17).

Having recognized her mistake, Isabel now devotes herself, with a characteristically passionate, almost religious intensity, to doing her wronged cousin full justice. He begins to stand in her mind for Osmond's polar opposite and becomes for her the touchstone by reference to which she now judges her husband. This polarity of the two men, counterpointed in Isabel's mind, is further elaborated in terms of light-darkness imagery. Osmond evokes in Isabel's mind a sense of darkness and suffocation: their house was "the house of darkness, the house of dumbness, the house of suffocation. Osmond's beautiful mind gave it neither light nor air" (XLII; *4*, 196). Their life together appears in retrospect to have been a process of gradual darkening: "Then the shadows had begun to gather; it was as if Osmond deliberately, almost malignantly, had put the lights out one by one" (XLII; *4*, 190), and Isabel comes to perceive that "Ralph's little visit was a lamp in the darkness" (XLII; *4*, 203). What makes this conventional image significant is the fact that Isabel used it earlier to convey her impression of Ralph's physical decline: "Blighted and battered, but still responsive and still ironic, his face was like a lighted lantern patched with paper and unsteadily held" (XXXIII; *4*, 59). The recurrence of the same image expresses the intimate interconnection in Ralph of physical decay and spiritual light.[13]

13. The lantern metaphor, which was introduced by James in his revision of the novel, may serve as an illustration of his method of revision. James frequently in his revisions replaces abstract by metaphorical expressions in order to achieve greater concreteness, compactness, and directness. He prefers, on the whole, to revitalize and expand the half-buried stock metaphors which are to be found in his original narrative rather than to introduce entirely new metaphorical expressions. The lantern metaphor is a case in point. As we saw, light continually figures in *The Portrait of a Lady* as a symbol of Ralph's intelligence, but in itself this mildly metaphorical element is not particularly impressive. By comparing Ralph's face to "a lighted lantern patched with paper and unsteadily held," James not only introduces an original metaphor which poignantly expresses the sad pathos of Ralph's precarious physical con-

James rarely treats disease as a purely physical phenomenon understood only on a literal level, and in *Daisy Miller, The Pupil, The Author of "Beltraffio," The Turn of the Screw,* and *The Wings of the Dove* the protagonist's affliction, which ends in his death, is always a symbolic expression of some kind of spiritual malaise. The same seems to be true of *The Portrait of a Lady.* Since Ralph lives solely for the purpose of seeing Isabel fulfill the requirements of her imagination and draws all his strength from the prospect of "watching the show," it is not surprising that the beginning of his decline should coincide with her engagement to Osmond. In other words, Ralph's affliction, initially introduced in order to account for his spectatorship, becomes, as the drama progressively unfolds, inseparable from the story of Isabel's downfall, which it both anticipates and echoes in a lower key. At first, Ralph's deterioration is sharply contrasted with Isabel's exuberance and vivacity; gradually, however, the converging lines of their tragedies intersect, and in the course of their last encounter in Gardencourt, Isabel at last comes to feel that her ache for herself and her ache for Ralph have become indistinguishable: "All her troubles, for the moment, became single and melted together into this present pain [of Ralph's impending death]" (LIV; *4,* 414). The darkest moment of her career—when she finally sees the ghost Ralph had once told her only those could see who had suffered greatly and gained the knowledge born of suffering—coincides with the moment of Ralph's death.

Many critics have held that the Ralph-Isabel relationship

---

dition, but at the same time invests the hackneyed light-intelligence comparison with a deeper meaning and greater point. James changed "His face wore its pleasant perpetual smile, which perhaps suggested wit rather than achieved it" into "Blighted and battered, but still responsive and still ironic, his face was like a lighted lantern patched with paper and unsteadily held." The example is taken from Krause, *American Literature, 30,* 83.

is similar in certain crucial respects to the Milly Theale-
Densher relationship in *The Wings of the Dove*. They have
argued that, like Milly Theale, Ralph assumes at the end a
Christlike role, that his death is sacrificial, and that his love
for Isabel (like Milly's for Densher) is the means of her salva-
tion.[14] The redemption motif is undoubtedly present in the
last scene and has, moreover, been prepared for by the religious terminology which Isabel uses whenever her thoughts
turn to Ralph. Nevertheless, it seems to me that to emphasize
this note to the exclusion of others is to obscure the full
thematic significance of Ralph's death.

It has already been indicated that Ralph's sickness is both
physical and spiritual, and that his decline, which sets in
when he learns that Isabel is going to marry Osmond, expresses a disappointment induced by his feeling that she has
forfeited her chance for a free life. If this is the case, it is
highly questionable that Ralph's death has the redemptive
implications it has been assigned. It is the logical culmination
of a long process of physical decline and, as such, the expression of Ralph's ultimate despair, his inability to face the
dreadfulness of Isabel's condition. In short, it constitutes
Ralph's final escape, and Isabel rightly comments on the
extraordinary ease with which he passes away: "If it was sad
to think of poor Touchett, it was not too sad, since death, for
him, had had no violence. He had been dying so long; he
was so ready; everything had been so expected and prepared"
(LV; *4, 420*). Ralph's lack of spiritual robustness brings into
high relief Isabel's stoic fortitude and greater powers of en-
durance, and intensifies the reader's sense that she is made of
sterner stuff. Indeed, we are explicitly told that despite her
envying Ralph his dying, "deep in her soul—deeper than any

14. See Q. Anderson, *The American Henry James* (New Brunswick,
N.J., 1957), p. 190; O. Cargill, "*The Portrait of a Lady*: A Critical
Reappraisal," *Modern Fiction Studies* (Spring 1957), pp. 11–32; and H.
Powers, "*The Portrait of a Lady*: The Eternal Mystery of Things,"
Nineteenth-Century Fiction (September 1959), pp. 150–55.

appetite for renunciation [of life]—was the sense that life would be her business for a long time to come" (LIII; *4, 392*).

James had undoubtedly intended Ralph's death-bed speech to express, most fully and most eloquently, the ultimate irony and pitifulness of Isabel's tragic fate. It is therefore not surprising that he incorporated into it the key phrases he used in the *Notebooks* entry about *The Portrait of a Lady*. Ralph speaks: " 'I always understood,' he continued, 'though it was so strange—so pitiful. You wanted to look at life for yourself —but you were not allowed; you were punished for your wish. You were ground in the very mill of the conventional! . . . I don't believe that such a generous mistake as yours can hurt you for more than a little' " (LIV; *4,* 415–17).[15] And this is the more analytical statement in the *Notebooks:* "The idea of the whole thing is that the poor girl, who has dreamt of freedom and nobleness, who has done, as she believes, a generous, natural, clear-sighted thing, finds herself in reality ground in the very mill of the conventional."[16] It is therefore of the utmost significance that Ralph, the novel's choric interpreter and Isabel's most genuine appreciator, should fail in the end to appreciate her decision to return to Osmond:

> Then he murmured simply: "You must stay here."
> "I should like to stay—as long as seems right."
> "As seems right—as seems right?" He repeated her words, "Yes, you think a great deal about that."
> "Of course one must. You're very tried," said Isabel.
>   (LIV; *4,* 416)

Ralph's last words express bafflement and a weary resignation. He had perfectly understood Isabel's desire "to see life

15. James had already employed the expression "a generous mistake" in *A Passionate Pilgrim,* in which the protagonist tells the narrator: "When I was thirty I married. It was a sad mistake, but a generous one" (I; 245). This is not the only instance of James' habit of turning an expression he had once casually used into a central key-phrase.

16. *Notebooks,* p. 15.

for herself," but obviously there is a certain austere, puritanical strain in his cousin's moral nature which Ralph (like many modern critics of Henry James), who is in all other respects unreservedly intelligent, is too Europeanized to sympathize with and to respond to. What Ralph himself offers Isabel—to stay at Gardencourt, which was the seat of her first happiness—is in fact but another kind of death, a romantic escape from the consequences of her choice; and his final bafflement of course intensifies the reader's sense of Isabel's isolation—the complete solitude in which she comes to perceive the "straight path." Had the novel ended with Ralph's death, James would have achieved an effect immediately moving but false and sentimental. But Ralph's death is not the last event in the novel. Isabel's life goes on; indeed, one of James' finest strokes is his making Isabel face her most harrowing ordeal—her "battle" with Caspar Goodwood—*after* Ralph's death.[17]

The fact that James dispenses precisely at this crucial moment with the observer's interpretative commentary and does not supplement it with that of the authorial narrator is, I suggest, neither an indication of his own reservation about the moral rightness of Isabel's decision nor an attempt to mystify the reader.[18] Rather, it is to be viewed as a strategy by means of which James emphasizes the growth of the heroine's tragic stature and her ultimate moral isolation. In his earlier short works, written in the comic-ironic key, James used to strike the authorial note in the closing as well as in the introductory passages, thus achieving a final ironic, distancing effect. In *The Portrait of a Lady,* which is

17. For an analysis of this scene see D. Krook, *The Ordeal of Consciousness in Henry James* (Cambridge, Eng., 1962), App. A, pp. 362–69.

18. James' revisions of *The Portrait of a Lady* show that he attempted to clarify the grounds of Isabel's decision to return to Osmond by making her "sacrificial" view of marriage more explicit. Thus "marriage meant that a woman should abide with her husband" is expanded in the revised version into: "marriage meant that a woman should cleave to the man with whom, uttering tremendous vows, she has stood at the altar." See Matthiessen, *Henry James, The Major Phase,* p. 162.

written in the tragic key, James has, I have shown, employed the opposite technique—that of gradual authorial withdrawal. The interesting point is that James experimented with this technique in an early novel like *The Portrait of a Lady,* in which he uses direct authorial commentary much more extensively and freely than in the more dramatic novels of his middle and late periods.

CHAPTER 4

LADY BARBARINA

Lady Barbarina,[1] like its companion piece *An International Episode,* is written in the vein of what James called *emphasized* internationalism. This means that the sense of Jackson Lemon's and Lady Barbarina's individualities never obscures that of their generic, national qualities, and that the reader is meant to respond to their marriage both as to a personal adventure and as to an experiment in Anglo-American relations. *Lady Barbarina* is an eminent instance of the sustained balance James sensitively strikes between the American and English points of view, represented in this work with equal imaginative insight and sympathetic irony. Perhaps the best proof of this scrupulous balance is the fact that no easy moral victory is scored, in the last analysis, on either side. James invariably depicted the American woman as morally finer than the European man. It seems that here, being disinclined to deviate from his myth of the American woman, James was forced, in order to strike a perfect international balance, to give up his classical donnée of "the European of 'position' [who] married the young American woman, or the young American woman [who] married the European of position,"[2] and experiment instead with the opposite, rarer donnée of the American doctor who marries a British noblewoman. In this story James displays with humorous acuteness a complex array of international contrasts and brings out with the lightest of touches and with a note of high amusement these crucial differences between American and English values

1. New York, *14,* pp. 3–142.
2. Preface to *Lady Barbarina,* p. x.

which account for the mutual attractions as well as the mutual misunderstandings between the American doctor and the British noblewoman.

Jackson Lemon and Lady Barbarina are depicted as the supreme exponents of all that is most characteristic, and in this sense "best," in the American and English traditions respectively. Indeed, the central irony of this international story is that their being the finest specimens of their kind explains, at one and the same time, the high hopes their marriage seems to evoke in all quarters, English and American, and its foredoomed failure or, rather, as James carefully qualifies it, "near failure."

Jackson Lemon, the son of a self-made man, an American millionaire in the medical profession, is unambiguously presented as "the heir of all the ages" (IV; 86); that is to say, he is immensely rich, highly intelligent, good humored, and strong-willed. Lady Barbarina, "the second daughter of the Cantervilles," now considerably impoverished, possesses for her part a title, personal grace, noble simplicity, perfect breeding, and the physical perfection of her type. Indeed, we are made to understand that what attracts Jackson Lemon is precisely Lady Barbarina's possession of these generic English qualities—her being, as he puts it to himself in his very American manner, "the fine flower of generations of privileged people and the centuries of rich country-life" (IV; 74). Jackson Lemon's admiration for Lady Barbarina's quintessential Englishness is of course seen as itself quintessentially American. Unlike Dr. Feeder, an earlier, less satirical version of Waymarsh in *The Ambassadors,* who is introduced as Jackson Lemon's foil, the heir of all the ages, having a greater capacity for the enjoyment of leisure than his "sturdy" medical friend, and being more imaginative, has the fatal susceptibility to Europe which is part of his supreme Americanness. The scales being evenly weighted, it is a characteristic irony of the Jamesian international situation that the very qualities which had made Jackson Lemon desire to transplant Lady Barbarina to American soil—namely, her being so

typically English—account for her absolute failure to adjust
to New York society. Not endowed with a "cleverness" which
her American suitor had contemptuously diagnosed while
he was in England as merely "a result of modern nerves"
(II; 40)—the lack of which he didn't at all seem to regret in
Lady Barbarina—she is doomed to be bored, intimidated,
and repelled by American society, in which she can discern
only the vulgarity, familiarity, and vociferousness epitomized in the terrible Mrs. Vanderdecken. This central ironic
intention is further emphasized by the contrast between Lady
Barbarina's pathetic rigidity and the farcical and highly
suspicious ease with which her younger sister, Lady Agatha
(a very flawed specimen of English nobility), is Americanized.
There is, by the way, an interesting parallel to be drawn
between the two foils—Dr. Feeder on the American side and
Lady Agatha on the English side. What characterizes Dr.
Feeder, the lesser American, is an excess of puritanical rigidity, a parochial narrowness of vision, whereas what characterizes Lady Agatha, the lesser Englishwoman, is precisely
the opposite taint, an excessively superficial, easygoing adapt-
ability.

Unlike the great majority of James' works, in which he
maintains "a beautiful consistency of point of view," *Lady
Barbarina* (like *A Bundle of Letters, The Point of View,* and
An International Episode, all written in the same period)
abounds in shifts of perspective. American and English
points of view alternate in quick succession, forming a sort
of a descending scale from the most deeply implicated participants (Jackson Lemon, Lady Barbarina, and the Cantervilles) to the peripheral spectators (Lady Beauchemin and
Lady Marmaduke on the English side and the Freers and Dr.
Feeder on the American side). These successive shifts of perspective, in which the American point of view is constantly
played off against the English, highlight the ironic comedy
of international incompatibilities and help maintain the
reader's balance of sympathy by keeping him from too intense
an identification with either point of view.

This symmetrical juxtaposition of points of view turns out to be as central to the exhibition of the international conflict as the dramatic plot in terms of which it has been conceived. The American impressions of Europe and the European impressions of America function not merely as penetrating, fresh insights into the workings of an alien society, highlighting its idiosyncrasies and shortcomings, but also as excellent self-characterizations. A case in point is Jackson Lemon's manner of viewing the question of the "settlement," which has the value of an American criticism of an English tradition but is also an exemplification of the fatal American "simplicity." Similarly, Lady Barbarina's vision of New York society is both an exposure of its more vulgar aspects, of which an English aristocrat is, in the nature of things, sharply conscious, and at the same time a most characteristic instance of the critic's own typically English limitations of vision.

Since, as has been indicated, James has chosen directly to dramatize the consciousness of the "bleeding participants," the role of the Freers qua observers shrinks considerably. Not functioning as the story's single centers of consciousness through whom the dramatic action is filtered, their vision does not fully control the narrative. In short, like Ralph Touchett in *The Portrait of a Lady* and, even more, the Assinghams in *The Golden Bowl* (whom the Freers foreshadow in many respects), theirs is the more traditional, subsidiary role of contributing to the case "a certain amount of criticism and interpretation of it."[3] They also contribute, as I will try to show, to the effect of an impartial balance struck between the English and American points of view and to the interplay of the individual and the typical, the personal and the national, which characterize this little international drama.

Before being launched, the Freers are introduced by the Jamesian authorial narrator, who emphasizes their qualifications to serve as intelligent commentators:

3. Preface to *The Golden Bowl*, p. v.

> They were native aliens, so to speak, and people at once
> so initiated and so detached could only be Americans
> . . . They had the American turn of mind, but that was
> very secret . . . they had the key to almost everything that
> needed to answer—because, in a word, they were able
> to compare . . . They were eminently a social pair; their
> interests were mainly personal. Their curiosity was so
> invidiously human that they were supposed too addicted
> to gossip, and they certainly kept up their acquaintance
> with the affairs of other people. They had friends in
> every country, in every town; and it was not their fault
> if people told them their secrets . . . People confided in
> her less than in him, but that mattered little, as she con-
> fided much in herself. (I; 4–5)

From this it is plain that the Freers are perfectly qualified
for their choric role. Impoverished, well-traveled American
expatriates, they are equally at home in both countries and
intimately familiar with both systems, which they view with
equal appreciation and sympathy. Significantly, their very
impartiality depends on their being Americans, for it is as
Americans that they possess the ability to compare (or to use
a more common Jamesian term, the ability to generalize),
which is, as James puts it, "the key to almost everything" on
the international scene. Apart from these purely intellectual
endowments, the Freers are also characterized by an "invidiously human" curiosity—that is, a genuine interest in the
private lives of their friends which, it is emphasized, they
make it their business to become intimately acquainted with.

It is through the Freers' conversations, in which Dr. Feeder
(the less initiated American, whose "social horizon," unlike
that of the Freers, does not include English nobility) joins in,
that the necessary information with regard to the central
characters in the drama is transmitted to the reader. (James'
abhorrence of "the mere seated mass of information" is
already in evidence.) These lively bits of conversation alternate with descriptive passages depicting the riders in Hyde

Park, the rich exuberance of which expresses the Freers' (and the author's) appreciation of "the great exhibition of English wealth and health, beauty, luxury and leisure" (I; 4). Thus, apart from its purely expository function, the introductory chapter furnishes us with a memorable scene in which Lady Barbarina appears most to her advantage—a scene that contrasts, sadly and ironically, with its later counterpart, in which the same Englishwoman is portrayed as helplessly languishing in her New York residence.

The characteristic tone and quality of the Freers' conversation may be discerned in the following passages:

> "The girls, I've no doubt, will be glad enough [of marrying Americans]; they have had very little chance as yet. But I don't want Jackson to begin" [says Mrs. Freer].
>
> "Do you know I rather think I do," said Dexter Freer. "It will be so very amusing."
>
> "For us perhaps, but not for him. He'll repent of it and be wretched. He's too good for that."
>
> "Wretched never! He has no capacity for wretchedness, and that's why he can afford to risk it."
>
> "He'll have to make great concessions," Mrs. Freer persisted.
>
> "He won't make one."
>
> "I should like to see."
>
> "You admit then that it will be amusing: all I contend for," her husband replied. "But, as you say, we're talking as if it were settled, whereas there's probably nothing in it after all. The best stories always turn out false. I shall be sorry in this case." (I; 8–9)

Again:

> "Of course they're his [Lord Canterville's] daughters," said Dexter Freer as these young ladies rode away with Lord Canterville; "and in that case one of them must be Jackson Lemon's sweetheart. Probably the bigger;

they said it was the eldest. She's evidently a fine creature."

"She'd hate it over there," Mrs. Freer returned for an
answer to this cluster of inductions.

"You know I don't admit that. But granting she
should, it would do her good to have to accommodate
herself."

"She wouldn't accommodate herself."

"She looks so confoundedly fortunate, perched up on
that saddle," he went on without heed of his wife's
speech. (I; 13–14)

The Freers' conversation, it seems, immediately touches upon
the pivotal issue of the (as yet merely nascent) drama—namely, upon the question of whether the international marriage
will, in fact, work. Mrs. Freer's profoundly skeptical pronouncement that she "doesn't believe in it at all" creates the
effect of intense dramatic irony, and the reader, aware of her
choric prophecies—that Lady Barbarina "would hate it over
there," that she would never "accommodate herself," and that
Jackson Lemon will have to make "great concessions"—
watches the budding of the latter's decision to propose to
Lady Barbarina, and his own inner conflicts on this score, as
the acting out of a preordained destiny. At the same time
suspense is kept alive by the alternation of Mrs. Freer's ominous predictions of future strains and disharmonies in the
protagonists' relationship with her husband's placid comments on their present happiness. Thus when Mrs. Freer
suggests that poor Lady Barbarina will "hate it over there,"
her husband rejoins, with characteristic inconsequence: "She
looks so confoundedly fortunate, perched upon that saddle."

The kind of discussion which takes place between the
Jamesian pair of choric observers is aptly characterized by
Austin Warren as "dialectical." It is, he says "a cerebral
process, pursued by two or more minds, in contrapuntal
movement of thesis, antithesis, synthesis. The topic is at-
tacked from without; the speakers circle around it. Like col-

laborating detectives they piece together their evidence, or like attorneys for the defence and prosecution they proceed alternatively, on rival systems. There are examinations and cross-examinations. There are mutual misunderstandings, false clues, shifts of position."[4] One cannot but take note of the finely-drawn differences between the two observers engaged in this dialectical activity, differences which ensure the dramatic vividness even of the purely analytic passages. Mrs. Freer's comments are, on the whole, sharp, lucid, and factual. She is perfectly impartial, and in refraining from displaying any animus and from passing any moral judgments on either of the protagonists, she emphasizes the social inevitability of the international relationship. By contrast, Mr. Freer, her collaborator in the dialectical activity, is less intense, less analytical, and less concerned than his wife. He pretends to be completely ignorant of Lady Barbarina's psychology—a pose which enables him to maintain a facile, optimistic view of the outcome of the marriage. Moreover, opposing his wife's belief in the inevitability of the development, he is not at all convinced that the mutual attraction of Jackson Lemon and Lady Barbarina will, in the final analysis, result in marriage. Apart, however, from having the merit of drawing his wife out (a device which James uses again with greater subtlety in *The Golden Bowl*), Mr. Freer's pose has additional thematic significances. His American simplicity is more assumed than real: he is not really as simple as he likes to pretend; but he delights in expressing confident ignorance of European values and an inability to perceive why on earth an English noblewoman should not be able to accommodate herself to a democratic society in which "everybody will be very nice to her."

There is another difference between Mr. and Mrs. Freer's attitudes toward the central conflict. Mrs. Freer is confident that things are bound to happen exactly as she predicts, but being sorry for the protagonists, she sincerely wishes they

4. A. Warren, *Rage for Order, Essays in Criticism* (Michigan, 1959), pp. 144, 145.

won't. Her husband, on his side, does not admit that things are bound to happen in the way his wife predicts they will, but maintains that it would be highly "amusing" if they did. In other words, the observers' discussion—"the contrapuntal movement of thesis and antithesis"—not only serves as a commentary on the central international conflict, but is also itself (almost in the manner of a Shakespearian subplot) a low-pitched comic exemplification of this very conflict, in which Mrs. Freer, being the more impartial of the two American observers, represents the English point of view and her husband the American point of view. This introductory social comedy is further developed when Dr. Feeder, whose American simplicity is genuine as Mr. Freer's is not, expresses his bafflement with regard to the English attitude toward a man who follows a profession, an attitude which is patiently explained to him by Mrs. Freer. An added edge is given to this comedy as Dr. Feeder's ignorance and even suspicion of the famous Cantervilles ("are they quite of the square?") is immediately succeeded by Lady Barbarina's equal ignorance of the well-known Freers and of Dr. Feeder, whose plebeian names are to her absolutely indistinguishable. Thus the analytical passages, themselves rich in comic interest, serve both to familiarize the reader with, and sensitize him to, all the shades of international contrasts later to be treated on a deeper, more personal level, and to underscore, without undue explicitness, the highly typical nature of the central international conflict.

However, having as choric observer (and unlike an authorial narrator) no direct access to the protagonists' inner lives, and being in this respect definitely less privileged than the reader, Mrs. Freer's otherwise authoritative and penetrating verdict is saved from appearing absolutely definitive and irrevocable. Consequently, the element of suspense is never completely eliminated at the expense of dramatic irony; on the contrary, it is in a sense intensified as the reader is kept wondering to what extent the final outcome of the drama will corroborate Mrs. Freer's verdict.

Her verdict, however, is neither a lucky guess nor an unerring intuition attributable to her in her capacity of author's deputy. In effect, not being in Lady Barbarina's social set, her understanding of the latter's attitude to American society is not based on any personal, esoteric knowledge of the English noblewoman, from which the reader is debarred. Rather, it is made amply clear that all Mrs. Freer has to go by is her familiarity with the national type—that is, her knowledge of the type-figure of the English noblewoman, of which Lady Barbarina turns out to be such a perfect example. This kind of choric commentary, which is based almost exclusively on a knowledge of national psychology, nicely points the fact that the particular case is meant to be viewed primarily as an illustration of the general international law.

In his Preface to *Lady Barbarina* James discusses the difference between the weight of the international factor in *Lady Barbarina* and in his late novels, *The Ambassadors, The Wings of the Dove,* and *The Golden Bowl,* maintaining that whereas the international factor is indispensable in *Lady Barbarina,* since without it the history of the British noblewoman would have no point, "the subject [in the late novels] could in each case have been perfectly expressed had *all* the persons concerned been only American or only English or only Roman or whatever."[5] While this may be an overstatement, it is surely undeniable that the protagonists in *The Golden Bowl,* for instance, possess complex individual traits which, although illuminated and deepened by the fact of their specific nationality, cannot be understood exclusively in its terms. This difference in the respective values of the international factor (due, partly at least, to the different requirements of a novel and a short work) is reflected in the different degrees of infallibility apportioned to the central observers in *Lady Barbarina* and *The Golden Bowl* respectively. The Assinghams in *The Golden Bowl* and the Freers in *Lady Barbarina* both engage in intense analytical activity, in an attempt to diagnose the protagonists' motives and

5. Preface to *Lady Barbarina,* pp. ix, vi.

anticipate the development of the drama. Yet although Mrs. Freer, qua fictional character, is neither more perceptive nor more sympathetic than Mrs. Assingham, and despite the fact that the latter is furnished with greater opportunities of directly observing the protagonists than the former, Mrs. Assingham often fails whereas Mrs. Freer never does. This difference is, I believe, to be attributed to their different functional roles rather than to a difference in their fictional characters. Whereas Mrs. Assingham's comic failures underscore the ever increasing motivational complexity of the protagonists, the unfailing correctness of Mrs. Freer's judgments serves to bring home to the reader the highly generic nature of the protagonists' motivations. This is not to say that their drama lacks its subtleties and complexities. Rather, it indicates that these subtleties and complexities operate primarily on the social, international level, and it is precisely complexities of this kind with which Mrs. Freer, by exercising her capacity to compare, can so beautifully cope.

I have tried to point out the various devices by means of which the observers' diagnostic activities intensify our sense of the representative nature of the case or, in James' own terms, of its *emphasized* internationalism. Seen in the light of the analytical passages (significantly, the first introductory chapter is preponderantly analytical), the central characters emerge as (unconscious) exemplifications of their respective nationalities and social classes, and this creates a distancing effect. It is instructive to observe, however, that James does not reinforce this effect either by narrating the dramatic action from an objective authorial point of view or by presenting it exclusively from the outside by the scenic technique. Rather, he dramatizes the consciousness of both Jackson Lemon and Lady Barbarina (although in Barbarina's case it is the author who gives expression to her inarticulate sense of her situation)—a treatment which engages the reader's sympathy. In other words, the analytical passages, which invite the reader to view the Jackson Lemon–Lady Barbarina case as an illustration of a general law and heighten its comic-ironic values, carefully alternate with dramatic passages, which invite the reader to view the same case as a personal entanglement and heighten its complementary near-tragic value.

It is, in the main, the inwardness of treatment in the dramatic passages which accounts for the conspicuous absence of any satirical effects in *Lady Barbarina*. Perfectly alive, however, to the amenability of his donnée to satirical treatment, James indicates its unrealized possibilities through the following conversation between Mrs. Freer and Dr. Feeder:

> "Oh if Thackeray could have done *this!*" And Mrs. Freer yearned over the lost hand.
>
> "You mean all this scene?" asked the young man.
>
> "No; the marriage of a British noblewoman and an American doctor. It would have been a subject for a master of satire." (I; 23)

Thus, while paying tribute to Thackeray's satiric genius, James at the same time dissociates himself from it, deliberately eschewing the satiric in favor of different values—namely, ironic humor alternating with a near-tragic seriousness. This dual effect shows James' well-known predilection for a complexity of effects ("It is for irony, for comedy, for tragedy," he says in his Preface to *What Maisie Knew*), all combined in one work and all contributing to what he termed the "intense illusion of life."

The interplay of the typical and the personal significances of the international drama is, however, even more complex than it seems. On the one hand, the typical constitutes a critique of the purely personal and sheds an illuminating ironic light on it. Thus, as has already been indicated, Jackson Lemon's refusal to accept the social implications of his marriage accounts, in some measure, for its ultimate failure. Lemon admits, of course, in the manner of a connoisseur, that in being attracted to Lady Barbarina he is attracted to the type rather than to the individual, yet he at the same time

obstinately insists on viewing the issue between himself and
the Cantervilles as purely personal, violently resenting their
different view on the matter. When Mrs. Freer, qua confidante, tells him that she doesn't see "where, in American
life, the daughter of a marquis would, [as she phrased it]
work in" (IV; 84), he is furious:

> Was he then so ignoble, so pledged to inferior things,
> that when he saw a girl who—putting aside the fact that
> she hadn't genius, which was rare, and which, though he
> prized rarity, he didn't want—seemed to him the most
> naturally and functionally founded and seated feminine
> subject he had known, he was to think himself too differ-
> ent, too incongruous, to mate with her? He would mate
> with whom he "damn pleased"; that was the upshot of
> Jackson Lemon's passion. (IV; 82)

The social nature of the obstacles is, evidently, a deep affront
to Jackson Lemon's strong, characteristically American in-
dividualism, and in this respect he resembles Isabel Archer,
whose American belief in the "romance of the self" leads her
to reject Lord Warburton and ultimately marry Gilbert
Osmond.[6] At this point, the interlocking of the analytical
and dramatic parts of the story becomes particularly promi-
nent, for Jackson Lemon is presented as violently resenting
the observers' insistence on the social, representative value of
his case. He winces under Lady Beauchemin's generalizations, as she tells him that she likes the idea of the marriage
as part of a "more general policy"; and he deeply resents his
marriage being characterized by Dr. Feeder as a "great precedent," as something "which has never been done before"
—a characterization which, he feels, turns his most personal
decision into "a curious and ambiguous phenomenon" (IV;
90). What deeply offends Jackson Lemon is not only the fact
that Mrs. Freer, his own compatriot, casts doubts on the
chances of success of his project, but also the fact that the

6. R. Chase, *The American Novel and Its Tradition* (New York, 1956),
p. 131.

others consistently refuse to view his case in purely individual terms. At this point (James' own different judgment notwithstanding) the international theme blends with the existential theme, as the interplay of agent and observer dramatizes the unbridgeable gulf between the way the self experiences its own situation and the way the other sees it.

The irony, however, is double-directed and seems to work both ways; that is to say, it is not only the personal which is criticized in the light of the typical; the typical, too, is criticized in its turn in the light of the personal. The presentation of Jackson Lemon's and Lady Barbarina's experiences in all their concrete particularity and personal intensity is an implicit critique of the facile generalizations, in particular those expressed by Lady Marmaduke and Lady Beauchemin (Lady Barbarina's sister), who hope that the marriage will initiate a new era in international relations and promote the ideal of "social fusion." The comic treatment of the ladies' great hope by no means implies that James wishes to debunk the ideal as such. (Indeed, in the Preface to *Lady Barbarina* James expresses this very ideal: "Behind all the small comedies and tragedies of the international, in a word, has exquisitely lurked for me the idea of some eventual sublime consensus of the educated.")[7] But by contrasting the abstract theory with the personal experience, it is made to sound hollow and flat. In fact, the amusement is increased as Jackson Lemon notes that Lady Beauchemin simply repeats (for her own purposes) the essentials of Lady Marmaduke's theory; and it reaches its peak when Lord Canterville, fumbling in his mind for a respectable pretext for marrying off his second daughter to the rich American doctor, innocently repeats in his turn the "great doctrine" he has had from his daughter Lady Beauchemin, who has had it from Lady Marmaduke:

> He threw out a remark to the effect that he thought it a capital thing the two countries should become more united, and there was nothing that would bring it about

7. Preface to *Lady Barbarina,* p. ix.

better than a few of the best people on both sides pairing off together. . . . They were all one race, after all; and why shouldn't they make one society—the best on both sides of course? Jackson Lemon smiled as he recognized Lady Marmaduke's great doctrine, and he was pleased to think Lady Beauchemin had some influence with her father. (III; 61)

This comic-ironic treatment of the generalizations is seen again in the closing passage, in which, after offering the reader a concentrated résumé of the outcome of the marriage as it is experienced by Jackson Lemon and Lady Barbarina, the authorial narrator, in the traditional manner of story-telling, gathering all the loose strands of the story, mock-seriously informs the reader about the effect the failure of the marriage had on the two ladies: "Lady Beauchemin and Lady Marmaduke are much disconcerted; the international projects has not, in their view, received an impetus" (VI; 141). Compared with the poignancy the failure has for the protagonists, the mention of the two ladies' disconcertment is deliberately anticlimactic and "amusing." Although the major issue of choosing the right reflector deeply engaged James' critical attention, the entries in his *Notebooks* (where he is seen in the workshop) show that he was in the habit of working out the specific details of the relation between the reflector and the central characters only in the course of the actual process of composition. It is therefore not surprising that despite the Freer's rather complex role in the finished tale, all James had to say about them in his *Notebooks* entry was the following: "He [the American] must have a pair of confidants there [in London], who bring him accidentally into relation with Lady B., and who watch his proceedings with amusement and dread."[8] That is to say, James simply indicates the general need for an observer who will be able to contribute to the drama the element of "appreciation." However, although (as the entry proves) James conceived of the

8. *Notebooks,* p. 51.

central situation independently of the observers, once he had introduced them, his dramatic inventiveness led him irresistibly to draw them into the dramatic orbit and turn their "interference" into a crucial event which finally clinches the crisis. Mrs. Freer, moving smoothly from her analytic role of interpreter to her dramatic role of confidante, urges Jackson Lemon to use the disagreement over the settlement as an excuse for breaking off a match which, she firmly believes, will never do. Ironically, it is precisely this advice coming from his own compatriot (and it is at this point that the Americanness of the observers becomes thematically significant) which finally determines Jackson Lemon to marry Lady Barbarina "on any terms." Thus, if traditionally the confidante's judicious advice is bound not to be heeded by the passionate protagonist, in this instance a further turn of the screw is effected—the confidante's advice precipitates the protagonist's decision to do the very opposite of what he is earnestly urged not to do, and what but for the confidante's advice he might perhaps never have decided to do.

It has been rightly pointed out that in many of James' works the growing involvement of the observer in the drama raises the critical issue of the double focus—namely, the uncertainty of the work's center of interest.[9] Since in *Lady Barbarina* the purely functional significance of the observer's interference in the drama seems beyond doubt, the controversy over the double focus is not likely to arise—a fact which makes it easier to analyze the characteristics of James' manner of drawing the observers into the dramatic action. First, it should be noted that the observer's secondary dramatic role grows out of their primary analytic role, for it is precisely in their primary capacity as sympathetic observers that they affect the course of events in the way they do. Second, the observers' interference serves to illuminate and deepen rather than change the point of the central theme as it was initially conceived independently of the observers;

9. See Booth, *The Rhetoric of Fiction,* pp. 339–46.

and its effects on Jackson Lemon are both psychologically accurate and dramatically effective. Thus Jackson Lemon's abrupt change of mind is a perfect expression of his most characteristic qualities as sketched in the *Notebooks* entry and fully dramatized in the finished tale. If at the start he opposes the Cantervilles because their demand for a settlement seems to him a reflection on his good faith and perfect equality with Lady Barbarina, his subsequent decision to give in to them springs from exactly the same motives. Presented as the kind of man whom opposition always puts on his mettle, Jackson Lemon is now as intent on proving the Freers wrong as he was previously intent on proving the Cantervilles wrong, the only significant difference being that his own countrymen's doubts affect him more deeply than those of the Cantervilles.

The wryly sophisticated authorial note which pervades *Lady Barbarina* shows that at this stage in his literary career James was not yet so uncompromisingly intent on eliminating the author's voice from the fictional work.[10] The authorial narrator in *Lady Barbarina,* although in basic agreement with the central observers (whose point of view is more objective and cosmopolitan than Longmore's in *Madame de Mauves),* is unmistakably distinguishable from them, and if they contribute to the tale the elements of sympathy and interest, he contributes the note of sophisticated irony.[11] The authorial voice is most clearly heard at the beginning and at the end of the little fable. It is the authorial narrator who introduces the Freers, and although they are meant to be the vehicles of his impartial judgment, they are not spared a touch of humorous censure as the ambiguous nature of their

10. On the question of whether James ever achieved complete authorial withdrawal (as P. Lubbock and Blackmur have claimed), see J. E. Tillford, Jr., "James the Old Intruder," *Modern Fiction Studies* (Summer 1956), pp. 157–64.

11. On the subject of the distance between the author and the narrator see W. C. Booth, "Point of View and Distance in Fiction: An Essay in Classification," *Essays in Criticism* (January 1961), pp. 60–79.

qualifications is slyly intimated. Thus, for instance, the
Freers' curiosity is characterized as "invidiously human"—
an adjective meant, of course, to express the keenness and
intensity of their interest, yet at the same time hinting at certain more ominous possibilities. Another amused note is
struck when the fact that Mrs. Freer's horizon included even
Cincinnati (Dr. Feeder's town) is produced as the clinching
proof of her social omniscience. It is, in fact, in virtue of this
distinctive authorial note that *Lady Barbarina* is exempt
from the characteristically Jamesian ambiguities present in
those works in which the authorial point of view cannot so
clearly be distinguished from that of the story's guiding intelligence.

In the closing passage the authorial narrator reports on
the final outcome of the international marriage and on its
repercussions in various quarters, moving from the central
characters' point of view to that of the more peripheral spectators' (Lady Marmaduke's and Lady Beauchemin's on the
one side and Sidney Feeder's on the other), and achieving
in this way the effect of a growing ironic distance. The report
—a narrative technique which in itself creates a distancing
effect—touches also on Jackson Lemon's relation to the central observers, definitely dissociating them from the authorial
narrator, and transforming them in the process of ironic
distancing, from commentators on the international scene
into mere elements of it: "He's [Jackson Lemon] exceedingly
restless, and is constantly crossing to the Continent; but he
returns with a certain abruptness, for he hates meeting the
Dexter Freers, who seem to pervade the more comfortable
parts of Europe. He dodges them in every town" (VI; 142).
It is by dispensing in the concluding passage with the deeply
interested choric commentators, and by adopting the point
of view of a fully omniscient and completely aloof authorial
narrator who provides the reader with a dryly informative,
pointedly non-committal report on the outcome of the great
international experiment that James strikes the final ironic
note of *Lady Barbarina*.

CHAPTER 5

THE ASPERN PAPERS

The first-person narrators of James' middle period *The Aspern Papers, The Turn of the Screw, The Figure in the Carpet,* and *The Lesson of the Master)*[1] differ greatly from those of his early period in being agent-narrators as well as witness-narrators.[2] Thus the narrator in *The Figure in the Carpet* records not only his impressions of the enigmatic Hugh Vereker, the subtlest, most maddeningly allusive of authors, but also his (and other critics') attempts to discover the central meaning of his work. Similarly, the narrator in *The Aspern Papers,*[3] who attempts to secure an American poet's love letters which his aged former mistress is jealously guarding, not only registers his impressions of the poet's old mistress, but also recounts his attempts to get hold of the precious documents.

The Jamesian narrator was initially conceived of in functional terms, as the story's right reflector, and his dramatic role was, as has already been indicated, an outcome of his primary observational and interpretative role. A perusal of the *Notebooks* entries about *The Aspern Papers* shows that,

1. James wrote these structurally compressed works, which he classifies as *nouvelles,* during the same period in which he produced his most expansive, panoramic novels, *The Bostonians, The Princess Casamassima,* and *The Tragic Muse,* where he portrays, in addition to the central vessels of sensibility, an almost Dickensian gallery of types from various social strata, and elaborates (in *The Tragic Muse,* for instance) a double plot comparable to the best double-plots in George Eliot's novels.

2. On this distinction see N. Friedman, "Point of view in Fiction: The Development of a Critical Concept," *PMLA, 70* (December 1955), 1160–84.

3. New York, *12,* pp. 3–143.

unlike his predecessors, the narrator in this story was initially conceived of as the story's dramatic agent or protagonist, whose adventures (his quest for the illustrious papers) form its center of interest: "Then the plot of the Shelley fanatic [who becomes in the finished tale a Byron fanatic]—his watchings and waitings—the way he *couvers* the treasure. . . . The interest would be in some price that the man has to pay —that the old woman—or the survivor—sets upon the papers. His hesitations—his struggle—for he really would give almost anything."[4] As a first-person narrator whose personal perspective controls the narrative, he fulfills also, in recording his impressions and analyses of the poet's mistress and her niece, a secondary observational and interpretative role.

Although James turned again in the stories of his middle period from dramatization of consciousness to first-person narrative, an analysis of his narrative technique shows that his marked preference for "showing" over "telling" remains unabated. Thus James does not exploit in *The Aspern Papers* the narrative distance between the two temporal planes— that of the experiencing and that of the narrating or reminiscing self.[5] Although written in the form of a personal reminiscence, the narrator in *The Aspern Papers* hardly ever reminisces; instead, he imaginatively projects himself into the past, reproducing with a vivid sense of dramatic immediacy the adventures of the experiencing self. Moreover, the narrating self, who has (somewhat like the omniscient author) a full, rounded-off view of the story he tells, rarely comments from his narrative vantage point on the experiencing self. In sum, James makes narrative as similar as possible to dramatization of consciousness, imposing upon it the very restrictions and advantages of this more dramatic

4. *Notebooks,* p. 72.

5. The distinction between "erlebendes Ich" (experiencing self) and "erzählendes Ich" (narrative self) was first suggested by L. Spitzer in his essay "Zum Stil Marcel Prousts" included in *Stilstudien,* 2 (München, 1928), 389.

method of presentation.[6] There is, however, one important respect in which the first-person narrative necessarily differs from dramatization of consciousness. In dramatizing an observer's consciousness James uses free indirect speech, a technique which enables him to slip in directive authorial comments that provide an unobtrusive running commentary. Since this procedure is, of course, ruled out in a first-person narrative, the dangers of misinterpretation and unintentional ambiguity become considerably greater.

Some critics (Charles G. Hoffmann, Wilson, and Wayne C. Booth) have described the narrator in *The Aspern Papers* as an insensitive and unscrupulous "publishing scoundrel," an unredeemed journalistic villain embodying that mania for publicity which James considered to be one of the most striking signs of his times.[7] In fact, as I shall try to show, his true affinities lie not with George Flack, the vulgar enterprising reporter in *The Reverberator,* with Mathias Pardon, the odious, shameless newspaperman in *The Bostonians,* or with the insufferable Mr. Morrow, in charge of the "Smatter and Chatter" department of *The Tatler* in *The Death of the Lion,* but rather with the narrator in *The Sacred Fount,* who is not a mere scandalmonger, and whose prying, however reprehensible, is prompted by his intense imaginative curiosity.

The introductory narrative shows the literary detective to be deeply and genuinely appreciative of Aspern's heroic character and poetic genius. "One doesn't defend one's God," he tells Mrs. Prest, his confidante, who pretends to make light of the poet's genius; "one's God is in himself a defence" (I; 5). The quasi-religious expressions which he uses in speaking

6. James' autobiographies, *A Small Boy and Others* (1913), *Notes of a Son and Brother* (1914), and *The Middle Years* (1917) are his only works written in the retrospective mode.

7. C. G. Hoffmann, *The Short Novels of Henry James* (New York, 1957), p. 45; E. Wilson, "The Ambiguity of Henry James," *The Triple Thinkers* (New York, Oxford University Press, 1963), p. 98; W. C. Booth, *The Rhetoric of Fiction* (Chicago, 1961), pp. 355, 358.

of Aspern, although mainly ironic in intention, are also partly serious. "The world, as I say, had recognised Jeffrey Aspern, but Cumnor [a fellow worshiper] and I had recognised him most. The multitude to-day flocked to his temple, but of that temple he and I regarded ourselves as the appointed ministers" (I; 6). The narrator's extravagant adoration of the poet is, however, combined with a fine critical sense; and there is no doubt that in his perceptive reflections on the case of the American poet, his narrative voice is indistinguishable from James' own:

> When Americans went abroad in 1820 there was something romantic, almost heroic in it, as compared with the perpetual ferryings of the present hour, the hour at which photography and other conveniences have annihilated surprise . . . It was a much more important fact, if one was looking at his genius critically, that he had lived in the days before the general transfusion . . . His own country after all had had most of his life, and his muse, as they said at that time, was essentially American. That was originally what I had prized him for: that at a period when our native land was nude and crude and provincial, when the famous "atmosphere" it is supposed to lack was not even missed, when literature was lonely there and art and form almost impossible, he had found means to live and write like one of the first; to be free and general and not at all afraid; to feel, understand and express everything. (IV; 49–50) [8]

8. James reminisces in his Preface about his "amusing" experiment of transposing the Byronic poet to "the banks of the Hudson": "I am afraid I must add, since I allow myself so much to fantasticate, that the impulse had more than once taken me to project the Byronic age and the afternoon light across the great sea, to see in short whether association would carry so far and what the young century might pass for on that side of the modern world where it was not only itself so irremediably youngest, but was bound up with youth in everything else. There was a refinement of curiosity in this imputation of a golden strangeness to American social facts—though I cannot pretend, I fear, that there was any great wisdom" (Preface to *The Aspern Papers,* pp. x-xi).

The literary analyses with which the introductory narrative is sprinkled indicate that the narrator's motives in his quest for the poet's love letters are not those of the mere sensation-hunting newspaperman. Rather, one's impression is that the narrator's interest in Aspern's biography is intimately connected with his interest in his lyric poems—which are, he believes, comparable in beauty and mystery to Shakespeare's sonnets. In fact, one may almost imagine him as a nineteenth-century Leon Edel, forever hunting after new biographical material which might illuminate the writer's character and fiction.

The narrator affirms his certainty that nothing ignoble and unworthy of the poet was likely to be discovered in his love letters. Indeed, when he discusses the rather delicate subject of Aspern's many amorous adventures, his tone—a shade too protesting and apologetic—hints at the opposite possibility—namely, that far from desiring to expose Aspern, the narrator tends to judge his moral lapses too leniently.

> Each of these cases [i.e. love affairs] Cumnor and I had been able to investigate, and we had never failed to acquit him conscientiously of any grossness. I judged him perhaps more indulgently than my friend; certainly, at any rate, it appeared to me that no man could have walked straighter in the given circumstances. These had been almost always difficult and dangerous. Half the women of his time, to speak liberally, had flung themselves at his head, and while the fury raged—the more that it was very catching—accidents, some of them grave, had not failed to occur. (I; 7)

Undeniably, the narrator does give Aspern away in the very attempt to protect him; but this, I suggest, is not a deliberate rhetorical stratagem on the part of a self-conscious narrator, but rather a wholly unconscious betrayal, the irony of which is directed at the narrator himself.

What further confirms the reader's impression that the

literary critic's adoration for Aspern is both deep and sincere, and that he is not merely after the spoils, is that at the very moment in which he becomes aware that he will never get the papers, he is still capable of relishing the mere contact with Aspern's Juliana: "Let me say that even at first this [the realization that Juliana is not going to give up the letters] didn't make me too miserable, for the whole situation had the charm of its oddity. I foresaw that I should have a summer after *my own literary heart,* and the sense of playing with my opportunity was much greater after all than any sense of being played with" (IV; 42; my italics).

It is possible, of course, in the absence of explicit authorial comment and, in particular, in a first-person narrative, to view the narrator's admiration for Aspern as an insincere pose and to insist that the high-minded view he takes of his mission is an ingenious bit of rationalization, the kind that an impure conscience easily produces. Such a failure to appreciate the impassioned fervor which informs the critic's account of Aspern can be explained only by the fashion, current in recent criticism, of preferring an ironic to a straight reading of James' narratives.

Although on the plot level *The Aspern Papers* is the story of the narrator's quest and ultimate frustration, one of its major themes is the recreation of the past. This is a theme James treated in other stories, and with the most elaborate ingenuity in his posthumously published work *The Sense of the Past,* in which Ralph Pendrel, a late-Jamesian passionate pilgrim, is granted his wish and is temporarily transplanted into a past century. As he states in his Preface, James' intention in this story was to recreate "the palpable *visitable* past" not yet protected by the "dignity" of history, "in which the precious element of closeness, telling so of connexions but tasting so of differences, remains appreciable."[9] His choice of the Byronic age and of Juliana, the Byronic poet's mistress and only surviving contemporary (whose name evokes in the

9. Preface to *The Aspern Papers,* p. x.

reader the memory of the beautiful and seductive Donna Julia of the first Canto of Byron's *Don Juan*), combines to perfection those elements of familiarity and strangeness which James considered to be essential to the evocation of the visitable past. In spite of the fact that qua dramatic agent who is after the spoils he is Juliana's ruthless opponent, the narrator turns out to be a perfect medium for the successful evocation of the Byronic age and of the Byronic poet's mistress. His adoration of Aspern enables him imaginatively to project himself into the Byronic age and vividly to conjure up the image of Juliana's younger self. At the same time, although in love with the past, he is perfectly aware of the most salient characteristics of contemporary life, which he characterizes as "the age of newspapermen and telegrams and photographs and interviewers" (I; 8), and of which he is himself an eminent instance. In other words, possessing the sense of the present as well as the sense of the past, the narrator is capable of communicating to the reader not only his romantic vision of Juliana's younger self but also his feeling for the incongruity and extraordinary strangeness (the recurring adjectives "strange" and "queer" strongly color the narrative) of her survival into the present "age of publicity." In fact, it is his possession of these two senses which enable the narrator to communicate to the reader the full ironic horror of Juliana's present state of decrepitude and to evoke so powerfully the death-in-life motif she embodies: "She was too strange, too literally resurgent. Then came a check from the perception that we weren't really face to face, inasmuch as she had over her eyes a horrible green shade which served for her almost as a mask . . . At the same time it created a presumption of some ghastly death's-head lurking behind it. *The divine Juliana as a grinning skull—* the vision hung there until it passed" (II; 23–24; my italics).

This motif is sounded again in the climactic scene, in which the narrator, caught red-handed by the dying Juliana, at last gets a glimpse of the grinning skull behind the mask:

Juliana stood there in her night-dress, by the doorway of her room, watching me; her hands were raised, she had lifted the everlasting curtain that covered half her face, and for the first, the last, the only time I beheld her extraordinary eyes. They glared at me; they were like the sudden drench, for a caught burglar, of a flood of gas-light; they made me horribly ashamed. (VIII; 118)

The sharp contrast between Juliana of the past and Juliana of the present is forcefully brought home to the reader not only through the narrator's acute sense of the old lady's extreme physical decrepitude but also through his accumulating impressions of her cynicism, greed, and hardheadedness. The recognition of these unexpected qualities introduces a nice "deflatory" note of the harshly antiromantic into his vision of the subject of Aspern's most exquisite lyrics.

It is, however, made perfectly clear that the narrator's theories with regard to Juliana are unsupported by any facts. He admits that all he and Cumnor had to go upon were some of Aspern's verses, in which they had detected certain clues to the nature of his relationship with Juliana. We are told that after infinite conjectures they had managed to establish, "solidly enough," the date of these verses (IV; 47); but this, we are soon made to see, is their only "solid" hypothesis. Both critics, it transpires, instead of carefully and "scientifically" reconstructing the past, give free rein to their speculative imaginations and invent, each according to his own fancy, richly elaborate biographies of the poet's mistress. Thus we are told that whereas Cumnor held the theory that Juliana had been a governess in some family which the poet used to visit, the narrator preferred to picture her as the daughter of an expatriate American painter or sculptor, in whose studio she must have met Aspern—a theory he proceeds to amplify with many exquisitely imagined details, whose very specificity emphasizes their fancifulness (IV; 47).

The narrative clearly betrays the narrator's speculative ex-

cesses. Like the narrator in *The Sacred Fount,* he too suc-
cumbs to the fatal weakness of all the Jamesian "supersubtle
fry"—namely, the disposition to read too much into the situation they are confronted with; and this points to the continuity between the thematic preoccupation of these two
stories. In fact, all the elements of the epistemological theme
which James was later to develop in *The Sacred Fount* are
already present in *The Aspern Papers.* Because, however,
James' interest in *The Aspern Papers* lay elsewhere, his treatment of the narrator's speculative excess is quite different.
In *The Sacred Fount,* which dramatizes the observer's epistemological predicament and deals with the dangers of his
solipsistic, overingenious imaginative activity, the question
of the truth value of his theory naturally becomes a major
thematic issue. The case is different in *The Aspern Papers,*
in which James' main purpose is vividly to capture the
romance of the past.[10]

It is precisely by virtue of his speculative extravagance (of
which the reader is made fully conscious) that the narrator so
beautifully evokes the romantic charm of the Byronic age.
Unlike the narrator in *The Sacred Fount,* who is constantly
preoccupied in proving both to himself and to others the
truth of his theory, the narrator in *The Aspern Papers* frequently abandons his quasi-scientific talk of "theories,"
"hypotheses," and "confirmations," and quite openly characterizes his proceedings as "the hatching of a little romance."
In other words, the narrator is himself conscious of his role
as romancer and knows perfectly well that in concocting his
delightful theories he is merely "fantasticating" the past (to
appropriate the term which James applies to his own prac-

10. He admits in the Preface that he saw the story "at the very first
blush as romantic" (ibid., p. vii). Romance means for James a work
which deals with "experience disengaged, disembodies, disencumbered,
exempt from the conditions that we usually attack to it," and he playfully pictures the romancer as "one who 'for the fun of it' insidiously
cuts the cable" which ties the balloon of experience to the earth (Preface
to *The American,* New York, 2, 339–46).

tice in *The Aspern Papers).* In the last analysis, the reader of *The Aspern Papers* is invited to surrender deliciously to the vision of the past which the narrator evokes, without bothering to appraise (as he is compelled to do in *The Sacred Fount)* the pros and cons of the narrator's theory.

While the narrator serves as a perfect mirror of Juliana, he functions as a distorting mirror of her niece. He consistently misinterprets the nature of her unbelievable simplicity and totally fails throughout their developing relationships to realize that he is cruelly using her. Significantly, *The Aspern Papers* is the first work in which James fully exploits, for comic-ironic purposes, the epistemological limitations inherent in the observer's position, turning him from a guiding intelligence into a misguided and self-deceived victim of his literary obsession.

The observer in *The Aspern Papers* is a first-person narrator. Since the primary function of narration is to tell a story, its basic convention is a confidence in the narrator's reliability and good faith. In fact, the reader who is *told* what the observer sees is in a sense invited to accept the former's views as true. The case is quite different when the observer is a dramatized consciousness. The reader is *shown* rather than told what the observer sees, and what this means is that the reader is not in any way committed to accepting the observer's view as true. Rather, he is invited to decide for himself whether or not the observer is reliable. Narration being by its nature a more persuasive and less objective narrative mode than dramatization of consciousness, the fact that the observer in *The Aspern Papers* functions as a first-person narrator and not as a dramatized consciousness intensifies the ironies of his self-deception.

The dramatic irony is not achieved through the narrator's retrospective commentary on his past blindness. Instead, James makes him unconsciously betray himself in and through his narrative in such a way that all the necessary information about the true state of Miss Tina's feelings is disclosed. The narrative devices which James employs to achieve this effect are worth lingering on. First, since the narrator does not fight Miss Tina but tries to win her over to his side, it is not surprising that he should draw his metaphorical expressions from the field of love rather than from the fields of war and diplomacy. He sends the "tremulous spinster" flowers, he talks of "winning his suit," and he appeals to her "to believe in him"; and although used nonchalantly, these metaphorical flourishes evoke in the reader's mind the idea of courtship, thus preparing the ground for the final ironic revelation of the truth. Second, the narrator not only uses love metaphors but is himself repeatedly struck by the thought that his gallant chivalry looks suspiciously like an attempt to win Miss Tina's heart, and that in begging the middle-aged spinster to believe in him, in an Italian garden on a midsummer night, he lays himself open to the charge of having "made love to her" (V; 62). Believing, however, that "one couldn't allow too much for Miss Tina's simplicity," he repeatedly dismisses this grotesque idea (whose drollness he relishes) as preposterous and impossible. Thus, coming one night to the garden in the hope of meeting Miss Tina, he reflects:

> It [the breath of the garden] was delicious—just such an air as must have trembled with Romeo's vows when he stood among the thick flowers and raised his arms to his mistress's balcony. I looked at the windows of the palace to see if by chance the example of Verona—Verona being not far off—had been followed; but everything was dim, as usual, and everything was still. Juliana might on the summer nights of her youth have murmured down from open windows at Jeffrey Aspern, but Miss Tina was not a poet's mistress any more than I was a poet. This however didn't prevent my gratification from being great as I became aware on reaching the end of the garden that my younger padrona was seated in one of the bowers. (V; 52–53)

Affected by the setting, the narrator gives rein to his literary imagination: he evokes the famous couples belonging to the tradition of romantic love—Romeo and *Juliet,* Aspern (the Byronic Romeo) and *Juliana,* enjoying the feeling of walking in the kind of Italian garden in which these great lovers of the far and of the near past might have met. Possessing a keen sense of the ridiculous, he cannot help seeing his own meeting with the plain, homely Miss Tina, the polar opposite of the glorious Juliana, as a comic travesty of a lovers' meeting. The constant evocation of these elements of parody in the relationship prepare the reader for the grotesque and moving proposal scene, in which, with a characteristic Jamesian reversal of emphasis, the very idea the subtle narrator had definitively dismissed is confirmed. The narrator, we recall, had told Mrs. Prest, his confidante, that "there was no baseness he wouldn't commit for Jeffrey Aspern's sake," that, if necessary, he would even "make love to the niece" (I; 14). The principal irony of his case is that this pronouncement, intended as a mere piece of bravado, a kind of rhetorical extravagance (and not, as some critics have maintained, a Yago-like cynical revelation of his diabolical intentions), turns out in the end to have been right. The narrator comes to realize during the proposal scene that he *had* enacted in his intercourse with Miss Tina the role of a lover, and that in trifling with the poor woman's feeling he *had* in fact committed the greatest baseness.

A comparison of the finished story, in which the narrator's relationship with Miss Tina is the central moral issue, with the preliminary *Notebooks* sketch, in which the "niece" is conceived of as a mere appendage to Juliana, sheds light on a characteristic feature of James' process of composition ("the triumph of intentions never entertained.") Miss Tina begins her career as a mildly ridiculous but useful *ficelle,* through whom the narrator is to try to establish contact with Juliana. Struck, however, by the promising possibilities of the posited relationship between the narrator and the *ficelle,* James, never hesitating to stray from the straight and narrow path of his initial subject, proceeds to develop it in a way which adds to the ironic comedy of the literary critic's unsuccessful quest a dimension of poignant pathos.

The Aspern Papers is a literary detective thriller (a Jamesian genre) which develops, up to a point, along the lines of conventional detective stories. Since the story is told from the point of view of the detective himself, the reader who shares his viewpoint evaluates his proceedings in strategic rather than in moral categories. The literary detective's narrative accordingly abounds in strategic metaphors generously drawn from the fields of diplomacy, war, and card games. He talks to Mrs. Prest, his confidante, of "laying siege," of "a plan of campaign," and of using all his "ingratiating diplomatic arts"; he chooses a "nom de guerre," hopes that his chance lies in being, unlike Cumnor, "a fresh hand," and suspects that Miss Tina's "sudden conversion to sociability" might be "a design to make him show his hand." The literary detective, like all the Jamesian supersubtle fry, is moreover a veritable intellectual *alazon,* whose narrative bristles with his bragging about his strategic ingenuity.[11] And his story, which follows the comic pattern of the deceiver deceived, ends in his ultimate frustration when he finds himself unable to pay the price the diabolical Juliana had set upon the papers —namely, to marry her "ancient" niece.

James, however, who always strove to achieve a complexity of effects—comic, ironic, satiric, tragic, pathetic, all combined in one work[12]—rarely followed a purely comic pattern, and *The Aspern Papers* perfectly illustrates this. Instead of turning the proposal scene into the apotheosis of the comic action, he chooses to exploit its pathetic rather than comic possibilities; in other words, instead of emphasizing the ridiculousness of Miss Tina's grotesque proposal, James fully and sen-

11. On the *alazon* in comedy see N. Frye, *Anatomy of Criticism, Four Essays* (Princeton, 1957), pp. 163–86.

12. W. C. Booth discusses the problem of the incompatibility of various effects, and criticizes James for not realizing that in always striving to achieve a complexity of effects, some of them inevitably cancel each other (*The Rhetoric of Fiction,* p. 47).

sitively renders the poor spinster's embarrassment, shame, anguish, and humiliation, as experienced by the narrator himself. Thus, when at last the significance of Miss Tina's words dawns on him, the narrator reflects:

> That was the price—that was the price! And did she think I wanted it, poor deluded infatuated extravagant lady? My gondolier, behind me, must have seen my ears red as I wondered . . . whether her delusion, her infatuation had been my own reckless work. Did she think I had made love to her even to get the papers? I *hadn't,* I *hadn't;* I repeated that over to myself for an hour, for two hours, till I was wearied if not convinced. . . . It took it out of me to think I had been so much at fault, that I had unwittingly but none the less deplorably trifled. But I *hadn't* given her cause—distinctly I *hadn't.* I had said to Mrs. Prest that I would make love to her; but it had been a joke without consequences and I had never said it to my victim. I had been as kind as possible because I really liked her; but since when had that become a crime where a woman of such an age and such an appearance was concerned? . . . It only comes back to me that there were moments when I pacified my conscience and others when I lashed it into pain. I didn't laugh all day—that I do recollect; *the case, however it might have struck others, seemed to me so little amusing.* I should have been better employed perhaps in taking the comic side of it. At any rate, whether I had given cause or not, there was no doubt whatever that I couldn't pay the price. (IX; 136–37; my italics)

The passage shows that the narrator's first reaction to the preposterous proposal is not that of exasperation but that of incredulity, pity, shame, guilt, and an agony of embarrassment—the embarrassment being for the spectacle of a poor woman's self-abasement he has been obliged to witness, the guilt and shame for the part he himself has or may have had in precipitating it. Nor are these the feelings, recollected in tranquillity, of the narrating self, but the reproduced *immediate* reactions of the experiencing self: this is clear from the frenzied narrative tone, in particular the excited repetition of the phrase "I hadn't" and the succession of rhetorical questions which swiftly pile upon each other. In this transformation of the comic *cognitio,* in which the infuriated *alazon* finally discovers that he has been made a fool of, into a genuine moment of truth of a Jamesian vessel of consciousness, the story most significantly deviates from the conventional comic pattern of the deceiver deceived.

James' emphasis on the narrator's feelings of guilt and shame enriches the bare *Notebooks* idea of a price ("the interest would be in some price the man has to pay—that the old woman—or the survivor sets upon the papers"),[13] with a moral depth and subtlety not originally conceived of. For the reader no longer understands by the price merely Juliana's condition—that the narrator must marry her niece if he is to get hold of the papers. It comes to signify also the price which he has actually, visibly paid—the humiliation of having plunged the innocent Miss Tina into such a painfully embarrassing situation.[14]

The interplay of the comic and the near-tragic in the final chapter is one of the most brilliant achievements of the story. The narrator's violent fluctuations of feeling are rendered with exquisite verisimilitude. After the first shock he feels that it is impossible to pay the price for "a bundle of tattered papers" and loses himself in wonder of the importance he had attached to what he now characterizes as "Juliana's crumpled scraps" (IX; 137, 138). But the next morning —and this is both psychologically right and dramatically effective—the obsession reasserts itself with positive ferocity,

13. *Notebooks,* p. 72.

14. One is reminded of Dostoyevsky's *Crime and Punishment,* in which Raskolnikov, who has decided to kill an old woman who, according to his Napoleonic theory, deserves to die, kills her innocent sister as well. (For this point I am indebted to Professor Lea Goldberg, of the Hebrew University of Jerusalem.)

and his imagination reinvests the tattered papers and crumpled scraps of yesterday with the highest value:

> As soon as I came into the room I saw that she [Miss Tina] had done so [i.e. understood the narrator's recoil of the day before], but I also saw something which had not been in my forecast. Poor Miss Tina's sense of her failure had produced a rare alteration in her, but I had been too full of stratagems and spoils to think of that. Now I took it in; I can scarcely tell how it startled me. She stood in the middle of the room with a face of mildness bent upon me, and her look of forgiveness, of absolution, made her angelic. It beautified her; she was younger; she was not a ridiculous old woman. This trick of her expression, this magic of her spirit, transfigured her, and while I still noted it I heard a whisper somewhere in the depths of my conscience: "Why not, after all—why not?" It seemed to me I *could* pay the price. (IX; 141–42)

Miss Tina's "transfiguration" comes to the narrator as a surprise after all his "stratagems and spoils." What the passage invites us to feel is that the transfiguration is not the projection of the narrator's renewed desire to possess Aspern's papers, but rather the product of a genuinely appreciative response to the moral beauty of the poor woman's forgiveness—function of the same imagination which was capable of detecting in the decrepit Juliana of the present the glorious Juliana of the past.

But the next climactic passage casts a backward light of the Jamesian ambiguity on this supposition. The narrator is still obsessed with the papers, and his obsession proves stronger than either his shame or his pity. He presses Miss Tina, and in three short sentences hears the devastating truth:

> "What shall you do—where shall you go?" I asked.
>
> "Oh, I don't know. I've done the great thing. I've destroyed the papers."

> "Destroyed them?" I wailed.
>
> "Yes; what was I to keep them for? I burnt them last night, one by one, in the kitchen."
>
> "One by one?" I coldly echoed it.
>
> "It took a long time—there were so many." The room seemed to go round me as she said this and a real darkness for a moment descended on my eyes. When it passed Miss Tina was there still, but the transfiguration was over and she had changed back to a plain dingy elderly person. (IX; 142–43)

If Miss Tina's momentary transfiguration was possibly the product of the narrator's moral imagination, its sudden extinction is certainly the result of his realization that the poor woman is no longer in possession of the precious documents; and in that case the question arises whether the belief that she did possess the precious documents did not powerfully cooperate with the moral imagination to produce the miraculous transformation.

The closing passage runs as follows:

> I have never forgotten it [the last look Miss Tina gave the narrator] and *I sometimes still suffer from it,* though it was not resentful. No, there was no resentment, nothing hard or vindictive in poor Miss Tina; for when, later, I sent her, as the price of the portrait of Jeffrey Aspern, a larger sum of money than I had hoped to gather for her, writing to her that I had sold the picture, she kept it with thanks; she never sent it back. I wrote her that I had sold the picture, but I admitted to Mrs. Prest at the time—I met this other friend in London that autumn—that it hangs above my writing-table. *When I look at it I can scarcely bear my loss—I mean of the precious papers.* (IX; 143; my italics)

The final effect is that of an open ending.[15] No emotional

15. R. M. Adams characterizes works of art in which the reader is intentionally left baffled about the crucial question they raise, that is works "which are not ultimately unified thematically, ideologically, emo-

resolution is effected. Like his successors, the narrators in *The Figure in the Carpet* and in *The Sacred Fount,* the narrator in *The Aspern Papers* has not been dispossessed; his imagination is still unappeased and his conscience still unpacified. When Aspern's portrait was first offered to him by Juliana, he had felt Aspern's mockery ("He seemed to smile at me with mild mockery; he might have been amused at my case. I had got into a pickle for him—as if he needed it!" [IX; 131]). Now the same portrait hangs over his writing table, a perpetual reminder that he has never really got out of the pickle, and the final effect is that of the narrator transfixed, as it were, as an everlasting butt of the Jamesian irony.

As has already been indicated, instead of recollecting, the narrator in *The Aspern Papers* faithfully and vividly reenacts his past adventures, with the result that the reader is hardly ever aware of the temporal gap between the distinct temporal planes of experience and narration. Indeed, only in the two crucial scenes, that of the narrator's last nightmarish meeting with the dying Juliana and that of Miss Tina's proposal, does he speak (very briefly) from the temporal plane of narration:

> *I never shall forget* her strange little bent white tottering figure, with its lifted head, her attitude, her expression; *neither shall I forget* the tone in which as I turned, looking at her, she hissed out passionately, furiously:
>
> "Ah you publishing scoundrel!" (VIII; 118; my italics)
>
> "Ah Miss Tina—ah Miss Tina," I stammered for all reply. I didn't know what to do, *as I say,* but at a venture I made a wild vague movement in consequence of which I found myself at the door. *I remember* standing there and saying: "It wouldn't do, it wouldn't do!"— saying it pensively, awkwardly, grotesquely, while I looked away to the opposite end of the sala as at some-

---

tionally, imagistically, and on the narrative level" as having an "open form" *(Strains of Discord: Studies in Literary Openness* [Ithaca, New York, Cornell University Press, 1958, p. 207]). Following in his footsteps I here use the term "open ended" in a somewhat more restricted sense.

thing very interesting. *The next thing I remember* is that
I was downstairs and out of the house. (IX; 135, my
italics)

The purpose of these small intrusions of the narrating self is
not to create a sense of the pastness of these scenes but rather
to emphasize some of their present qualities. In the first passage it serves to reinforce the dramatic intensity of the encounter, emphasizing its unforgettable nature; and in the
second passage it brings out more forcefully the experiencing
self's extreme confusion during the painfully embarrassing
moment of Miss Tina's proposal.

In the closing passage the hitherto unemphasized temporal
gap between the experiencing and the narrating self is gradually bridged, till the moment of experience actually coincides
with the moment of narration, and narrative becomes "instantaneous."[16] Significantly, the switch from the past to the
present tense in the closing passage occurs in the two crucial
sentences in which we are told that the narrator is still
haunted by Miss Tina's "look" of reproach and that he is
still tormented by the loss of "the precious papers" (they are
again "precious papers" and not the "tattered papers" and
"crumpled scraps" they had become during the narrator's
momentary revulsion). This use of the present tense, which
characterizes instantaneous narration, reinforces the effect
of an open ending and the reader's sense that the narrator's
double torment is continuing to the present moment.

16. I appropriate here the expression Ian Watt has coined in *The
Rise of the Novel* to characterize the diary technique, in which narration
immediately follows experience. See I. Watt, *The Rise of the Novel:
Studies in Defoe, Richardson and Fielding* (Berkeley: University of California Press, 1957; London, Chatto & Windus and Penguin Books, 1963),
p. 199.

CHAPTER 6

THE LIAR

The Liar[1]—like *The Aspern Papers,* written a year earlier—
is another of James' subtle and witty psychological studies of
a self-deceived observer, written in a comic-ironic key. In this
story James returns to his favorite narrative method—dramatization of consciousness. Under the influence of first-
person narrative, however, James now uses a minimum of
authorial comment and altogether dispenses with the expository chapter in which the authorial narrator introduces
the observer and discusses his qualifications to serve as the
center through whose consciousness the story is projected.

Oliver Lyon, a successful young portrait painter, arrives at
Sir David Ashmore's house party and there meets Everina
Brant, a woman he had known as a student at Münich and
who had rejected his offer of marriage. Lyon learns that she
is now married to Colonel Capadose and is shocked, disgusted, and deeply irritated when he discovers that the
woman he still greatly admires appears to be in love with
a husband who is a pathological liar—a kind of English
Münschausen, whose lying is, as the host aptly puts it, "a
natural peculiarity—as you might limp or stutter or be
left-handed" (II; 344).

James, we recall, frequently made the observer fall in love
with the heroine in order to intensify his sympathetic appreciation of her plight and thus extract from it its maximum
of sense. But in *The Liar* matters are somewhat more complicated. Whereas all the earlier Jamesian observers who fall
in love with the heroine meet her for the first time at the

1. New York, *12*, pp. 313–88.

beginning of the story, Lyon, we learn, had known Mrs. Capadose in the past. His past involvement with the heroine affects Lyon's observational and interpretative role in two complementary ways. On the one hand, he possesses a deeper, finer, more intimate understanding of the heroine's nature than other observers do. On the other hand, being a rejected suitor, his impressions of Mrs. Capadose are strongly colored by feelings of frustration and resentment—a fact which casts an initial doubt on his reliability as the center through whose consciousness Mrs. Capadose's case is projected.

While there is no mention of the observer in James' *Notebooks* entry to *The Liar*,[2] this does not mean that Lyon functions in the finished tale as merely a medium through which the relationship between Mrs. Capadose and her husband is registered. Rather, having posited his past attachment to the heroine, James proceeds to develop the potentialities of this new relationship. By turning the relationship between the observer and the heroine into the story's other and perhaps main center of interest, James complicates and enriches its initial conception. *The Liar* is, in this respect, a characteristic transitional work. On the one hand, the observer does not only contribute, as he does in *Madame de Mauves, The Portrait of a Lady* and *Lady Barbarina,* to the story's original theme, but initiates a new thematic interest.[3] On the other hand, unlike the narrator in *The Sacred Fount,* he has not yet become the story's sole center of interest. Thus *The Liar* may be seen as one of James' "hybrid" works (to appropriate J. F. Blackall's term).[4]

James in the finished tale changed his original intention to portray in Colonel Capadose a person who lies consciously,

2. *Notebooks,* pp. 61–62.

3. According to W. C. Booth all the Jamesian stories which developed in this manner exemplify an "incomplete fusion" of the two subjects (*The Rhetoric of Fiction,* p. 341).

4. J. F. Blackall, *Jamesian Ambiguity and "The Sacred Fount"* (Ithaca, N.Y., 1965), p. 150.

"mainly out of vanity, the desire to be interesting, and a peculiar irresistible impulse,"[5] and has instead inflicted upon the jovial husband an innocent and harmless impulse to exaggerate and romance. The slightness of the husband's foible and the light-heartedness with which it is treated by everyone else immediately creates an uncertainty as to the validity of the grimly tragic view Lyon takes of it—a view touched on by the authorial narrator with pointed humorous irony: "If our friend hadn't been in love with her [Mrs. Capadose] he would surely have taken the Colonel's delinquencies less to heart. As the case stood they fairly turned to the tragical for him, even while he was sharply aware of how merely 'his funny way' they were to others—and of how funny his, Oliver Lyon's, own way of regarding them would have seemed to every one" (II; 349–50).

This uncertainty is further reinforced by Lyon's own vacillating attitude toward the Colonel's "delinquency." Irritated and humiliated by Mrs. Capadose's air of perfect happiness, he cannot help regarding this delinquency as disgustingly vulgar—"the most contemptible, least heroic of vices" (II; 349); at the same time, in his desire, characteristic of a Jamesian vessel of consciousness, to do full justice to the man Mrs. Capadose has preferred to himself, he tries to take the most sympathetic view of it:

> "He's the liar platonic," he said to himself; "he's disinterested, as Sir David said, he doesn't operate with a hope of gain or with a desire to injure. It's art for art— he's prompted by some love of beauty. He has an inner vision of what might have been, of what ought to be, and he helps on the good cause by the simple substitution of a shade. He lays on colour, as it were, and what less do I do myself?" (II; 350)

In earlier works the observer's chief function was sensitively to record the heroine's predicament, and the gradual

5. *Notebooks,* p. 61.

process of its discovery served merely as a dramatic expository device. In *The Liar* the question whether the heroine is made unhappy by her husband's foible becomes a central issue, and the fact that the answer is given only at the end of the story clearly shows that the process of the observer's discovery of Mrs. Capadose's predicament constitutes the story's principal action. In other words, *The Liar* which—like *The Aspern Papers, The Figure in the Carpet,* and *The Sacred Fount*—defines itself as the story of the observer's search, perfectly exemplifies James' growing tendency to turn purely functional techniques into central thematic issues. Although the search for the truth concerning Mrs. Capadose's feelings for her husband constitutes the principal action of *The Liar,* it is not, like the other Jamesian quest-stories of the same period, a purely intellectual detective story. Lyon's obsessive curiosity, far from being of a purely intellectual nature, proceeds from frustration and resentment, and as a consequence the reader's interest focuses more on its moral and psychological significances than on its epistemological implications. It is not surprising, therefore, that the conception of the quest as "a game of skill" *(The Figure in the Carpet)* or "a high sport" *(The Sacred Fount)* is entirely absent in *The Liar.* The conclusive proof of the matter is that Lyon is not satisfied with the discovery of the truth which has so long eluded him. On the contrary, as we shall see, he presses on, impelled by an ulterior interest—that of inducing Mrs. Capadose to confess her shame and humiliation.

Lyon remembers Mrs. Capadose as a fine specimen of the type of the simple, proud, and fastidious Englishwoman, not stupid but essentially unsophisticated and unimaginative: "She was simple and good; inexpressive but not inhuman, not stupid . . . She had no imagination and only the simpler feelings, but several of these had grown up to full size" (I; 330). Indeed, we are told that, struck by Mrs. Capadose's simplicity, Lyon had once sketched her as Werther's simple but adorable Charlotte, cutting bread and butter while the children cluster around her (I; 324)—a detail indicating his view of his own plight as analagous to that of Werther, the agonized witness of Charlotte's love for his rival, the simple, unimaginative, but honest, upright, and kind-hearted Albert. Lyon feels sure that because of this combination of qualities in her, nothing could be more repugnant to Mrs. Capadose than the Colonel's peculiar vice. Being essentially simple, she can only be struck by the indignity of the lies, and being too much of a lady and too little of the artist, she is, he believes, constitutionally incapable of considering her husband's lies as "art for art."

Lyon secretly hopes that the woman he adores has preserved her integrity and has not been contaminated by her husband, and his vision of her integrity is composed of three complementary elements. Intellectually, her integrity should mean an awareness of the indignity of her husband's foible; emotionally, it ought to induce in her a deep sense of shame about it; and practically, it should involve an aloofness from any form of complicity in it. Vividly recalling, however, the loving attention Mrs. Capadose bestowed on her husband, and faced with her humorous but essentially serious confession that her husband "hadn't a fault" and that "he is everything that's good and true and kind. He's a soldier and a gentleman and a dear!" (II; 348), Lyon grows increasingly anxious lest Mrs. Capadose has failed to preserve her pristine candor, and finds solace in imagining her secret anguish with the most poignant vividness:

> That was her pride: she wished not to be even suspected of not facing the music. Lyon had none the less an importunate vision of a veiled figure coming the next day in the dusk to certain places to repair the Colonel's ravages, as the relatives of kleptomaniacs punctually call at the shops that have suffered from their depredations.
>
> "I must apologise; of course it wasn't true; I hope no harm is done: it's only his incorrigible—" oh to hear that woman's voice in that deep abasement! Lyon had

no harsh design, no conscious wish to practise on her
sensibility or her loyalty; but he did say to himself that
he should have liked to bring her round, liked to see her
show him that a vision of the dignity of not being married to a mountbank sometimes haunted her dreams.
He even imagined the hour when, with a burning face,
she might ask *him* not to take the question up. Then he
should be almost consoled—he would be magnanimous.
(II; 353)

In this passage James brings out, with a fine sense of
comic irony, the extraordinary mixture of acuteness and
bad faith, sensitivity and cruelty, genuine compassion and
vindictiveness, which characterizes the workings of the mind
of the self-deceived observer. But although Lyon's moral
indignation is prompted by self-interested motives, this in
itself is not enough to establish the perversity of his view of
the debasing effect the Colonel's delinquency might have
on his wife. Lyon's reflections may in the end prove to be
a form of self-indulgent wishful thinking—in which case
he would be merely a comic dupe, the victim of James'
scathing ridicule. He may, however, quite as plausibly be
the only person in this drawing-room society endowed with
the kind of fastidious discrimination (sharpened, of course, by
his resentment) which enables him to divine and fully sympathize with Mrs. Capadose's predicament—that of a woman
capable of experiencing intense agony because her husband
has failed at some point to satisfy her high conception of dignity and refinement.

We are told that, like the narrator in *The Sacred Fount,*
"Lyon was at once too discreet and too fond of his own intimate inductions to ask other people how they answered his
conundrum—too afraid also of exposing the woman he
once had loved" (II; 347). Ironically, however, his method
of arriving at the truth turns out to be even more indelicate
and insidious than that of discussing Mrs. Capadose's case
with other people. Lyon desires to force Mrs. Capadose to

confess her dissatisfaction with her lot as a wife, a confession which would amount to an admission on her part that she entertained at least some regret for having preferred the Colonel to himself. In this Lyon too evidently exhibits a strain of ungenerous egotism mixed with his love. It is his bad faith that makes him believe that in asking Mrs. Capadose for "some *visible* contrition," he asks very little ("He didn't ask much after all; not that she should love him to-day or that she should allow him to tell her that he loved her, but only that she should give him some sign she didn't feel her choice as *all* gain" [II; 354]), whereas the ironic truth is, of course, that he asks a great deal too much. An open avowal would have created an intimate bond between them, and bearing in mind the significance attributed to a community of knowledge in the Jamesian universe, one realizes that the establishment of such a bond of mutual understanding between Lyon and Mrs. Capadose would have amounted, on her side, to a betrayal of her husband. More-over, a compliance with Lyon's demand would have been deeply humiliating to a woman characterized by the very man who makes this demand as "the proudest, most re-served of women," possessing "a sort of nobleness of the Roman type" (I; 321, 323). Since Lyon's hope that Mrs. Capadose has not been contaminated by her husband has largely depended on his knowledge of her proud nature, there is intense irony in the fact that he should now demand of her an act which such a woman could not, by her nature, bring herself to perform.

Like the obsessed narrators in *The Aspern Papers, The Figure in the Carpet,* and *The Turn of the Screw,* Lyon must know the truth, and instead of letting go, he presses on and on. He asks as a special favor that the Colonel should sit for his portrait, pretending that he finds his interesting face a subject preeminently suited to his art. The truth, how-ever, is that he desires to bring out in the portrait the Colonel's essential vulgarity, and by thus exposing him, find an outlet for his accumulated anger:

The desire grew in him to paint the Colonel also—an operation from which he had promised himself a rich private satisfaction. He would draw him out, he would set him up in that totality about which he had talked with Sir David, and none but the initiated would know. They, however, would rank the picture high, and it would be indeed six rows deep—*a masterpiece of fine characterisation, of legitimate treachery.* (II; 355; my italics)

The passage admirably dramatizes Lyon's twisted logic. Although he is aware that his plan constitutes a "treachery," he yet considers it to be a "legitimate"—that is to say, a morally justifiable treachery.

In the following highly ambiguous conversation Lyon persuades Mrs. Capadose to let him paint her husband:

"Well, if you won't take it [the picture] why not let him [the Colonel] sit just for my own pleasure and profit? Let it be a favour, a service I ask of him. All the generosity and charity will so be on your side. It will do me a lot of good to paint him and the picture will remain in my hands."

"How will it do you a lot of good?" Mrs. Capadose asked.

"Why he's such a rare model—such an interesting subject. He has such an expressive face. It will teach me no end of things."

"Expressive of what?" said Mrs. Capadose.

"Why of the inner man."

"And you want to paint his inner man?"

"Of course I do. That's what a great portrait gives you, and with a splendid comment on it thrown in for the money. I shall make the Colonel's a great one. It will put me up high. So you see my request is eminently interested."

"How can you be higher than you are?"

"Oh I'm an insatiable climber. So don't stand in my way," said Lyon. (III; 359–60)

Then she gently lets him know that she trusts him not to betray her husband: " 'Well, everything in him is very noble,' Mrs. Capadose gravely contended. 'Ah trust me to bring everything out!' Lyon returned, feeling a little ashamed of himself" (III; 360). The ambiguity of this important colloquy deepens our sense of Lyon's disingenuousness, for the indirectness of Mrs. Capadose's appeal enables him to abuse her faith without his needing to have recourse to a literal lie.

James, it will be remembered, was always intensely preoccupied with the dialectics of artistic excellence versus moral evil (three of his most famous stories—*The Aspern Papers, The Sacred Fount,* and *The Author of "Beltraffio"* —turn upon this theme), and in *The Liar* the theme is restated in an interesting way. The fact that Lyon's inspiration feeds upon vindictiveness and exasperation does not, it turns out, detract from the artistic perfection of the portrait he paints of the Colonel. If the Colonel is "the liar Platonic," Lyon's portrait is the fullest expression of the "Idea of Lying."[6] It appears, in other words, that the painter's per-

---

6. Interestingly, James had already been preoccupied with the theme of portrait painting as a form of exposure in *The Story of a Masterpiece,* one of his earliest apprentice works. In this story a gifted young portrait-painter paints an excellent portrait of a young girl who had once disappointed him and who is now going to marry his friend. The portrait expresses not only the girl's youthful charm and beauty but also a certain coldness and fatuousness with which the painter had been struck. Upon seeing this portrait the girl's fiancé becomes deeply perturbed, and in a fit of impotent rage, not unlike that of the Colonel in *The Liar,* destroys the portrait, but later overcomes his scruples and marries the girl.

I should like to mention in this connection Matthiessen's claim that it was Hawthorne who taught James the use of a portrait as a means of bringing out character: "In *The House of the Seven Gables* Holgrave's daguerreotype pries beneath Judge Pyncheon's smooth appearance and shows his real kinship to his hard and grasping ancestor." See his "James and the Plastic Arts," *The Kenyon Review,* 5 (Winter 1943), 535.

sonal frustration has only sharpened his insight into the
Colonel's peculiar temperament; and the fact that the portrait came into being as a result of unscrupulous manipula-
tion is not at all detrimental to its essential justness of vision.

Although Lyon had painted the Colonel's portrait merely
for his "private satisfaction," it serves in the end to precipitate
the crisis and resolve the story's central ambiguity. One fateful day, when Lyon is supposed to be out of town but in
fact returns in time to witness the scene unobserved, the
Colonel brings his wife to the studio to have a look at the
portrait. Her quick discernment of the point of the portrait
and her agonized outburst in front of this cruel exposure
of her husband finally gives Lyon the knowledge he craves
—that Mrs. Capadose is, as he had guessed, deeply ashamed
of her husband's vulgar "peculiarity." Angered by his wife's
outburst (the meaning of which, it is made quite clear, completely eludes him), the Colonel destroys the calumniating
portrait. Lyon barely regrets its destruction, and this is not
surprising, since in painting it he had not been impelled
by a properly artistic motive.

> The strangest part of all was—as will doubtless appear
> —that Oliver lifted neither voice nor hand to his
> picture. The point is that he didn't feel as if he were
> losing it or didn't care if he were, so much more was
> he conscious of gaining a certitude. His old friend *was*
> ashamed of her husband, and he had made her so, and

R. J. Keene and E. Rosenberry have detected an even closer analogy
between James' *The Liar* and Hawthorne's *The Prophetic Pictures*. In
Hawthorne's tales the artist reproduces in the portrait of Walter Ludlow
his latent madness, thus committing the unpardonable sin of violating
the human heart. As in *The Liar*, the artist is at last confounded by the
sitter's wife, who though quick to discern the truthfulness of the portrait,
yet remains devoted to her husband. See R. J. Keene, "Hawthorne's *The
Prophetic Pictures* and James' *The Liar*," *MLN*, 65 (April 1950), 257–58;
and E. Rosenberry, "James' Use of Hawthorne in The Liar," *MLN*, 76
(March 1961), 234–38.

he had scored a great success, even at the sacrifice of
his precious labour. (III; 376)

Lyon's unforgivable sin, however, is that he is not willing to
content himself with a proof which has been given unin-
tentionally and unknowingly. The destruction of the portrait by the Colonel provides him with the ideal opportunity to extract from Mrs. Capadose the long-desired face-
to-face avowal of her shame, and in resolving to extract it
he forfeits his chance to prove his delicacy. The story's crown-
ing irony is that this last attempt on Lyon's part to exert
more pressure turns his "success" into a pyrrhic victory.
When subsequently he challenges the Capadoses about the
portrait, the Colonel flatly denies his act of vandalism, and
his wife sides with him, pretending to believe that the portrait must have been destroyed by some drunken model who
wandered into the studio after the Colonel had left. Lyon's
last exasperated attempts to strip the "inscrutable mask"
off Mrs. Capadose fail completely: "Her hypocrisy revolted
him. And yet by way of plucking off the last veil of her
shame he broke out to her again, shortly afterwards: 'And
you *did* like it [the portrait], really?' To which she returned,
looking him straight in his face, without a blush, a pallor,
an evasion: 'Oh *cher grand maître*, I loved it!' " (III; 386).
As Mrs. Capadose, under Lyon's pressure, suggests that had
she and her husband returned, they might have saved the
picture, Lyon cannot resist a last desperate thrust:

> "Yes; you'd have saved the picture."
> For a moment she said nothing; then she smiled. "For
> you, *cher maître,* I'm very sorry. But you must remember
> I possess the original!" (III; 387–88)

Thus, without removing her mask, Mrs. Capadose gently
but firmly conveys to Lyon her pity for him as well as her
love for her husband. The skill with which she communicates
what she wished him to know without transgressing the rules
of her game, and her mock-ironic reiteration of the title

"cher maître," which emphasizes her decision to meet her opponent only on the most impersonal ground, marks her as a master of the Jamesian irony. Mrs. Capadose's final triumph is precisely her refusal to tear off her mask. Unlike the immature boy in *The Turn of the Screw,* who breaks down under the pressure of the governess, the fact that Lyon is reduced to challenging her only indirectly and ambiguously, without daring to violate the rules she has established for both of them, forms a formidable part of her subtle victory over him.

Lyon, we remember, had entertained two mutually exclusive theories concerning Mrs. Capadose's probable state of mind. Either she had been unconscious of her husband's indignity, and her love had therefore never abated, or if she had guessed the truth, her lucidity must have killed her love. This was Lyon's theory. What we are made to see, however, is that his imagination had failed to take account of the finest and most touching *third* possibility. A secret unwillingness to fathom the depths of Mrs. Capadose's loyalty to another man had narrowed his speculative range, and he had accordingly failed to imagine a case in which a highly scrupulous woman, whose lucidity had been powerless to quench her love, might consent to depart from her ideal of decency in order to shield the man she loves.[7] This

7. In *The Tree of Knowledge,* a late short-story, James exhibits the same relationship between a refined woman married to a tainted husband, whom she loves in spite of his taint, and an observer who is in love with her. The observer in *The Liar* tries, we saw, to force the wife to admit her secret shame, whereas the observer in *The Tree of Knowledge* tries to prevent her at all costs from realizing the truth about her husband. Interestingly, despite this difference in moral sensitivity, which makes the two observers appear as polar opposites, James attributes to both the same "bad faith," the same inability to envisage the possibility that the woman they hopelessly adore loves her husband in spite of her perfect lucidity about him. Thus the observer in *The Tree of Knowledge* comes, in his moment of truth, to realize that his attempts to spare the wife the bitter knowledge about her husband's taint stemmed, in the last analysis, from his unconscious need to spare himself by attributing her extraordinary loyalty to her husband to her ignorance about him.

last failure of the imagination in the observer establishes, of course, an intimate link between his moral and intellectual weaknesses. His failure of perception is finally to be attributed to the spirit of vindictiveness and resentment which has impelled him to press on, and the new insight, which operates as a painful enrichment of his imaginative range, has a bitter-sweet savor. The observer's "interference" in the plot (his painting of the Colonel's portrait) is not only instrumental to the resolution of the ambiguity and the discovery of Mrs. Capadose's life-long devotion to her husband. It is also itself a highly significant dramatic situation, which serves as the final test of both Mrs. Capadose and Lyon. It furnishes the occasion for the finest expression of Mrs. Capadose's devotion to her husband and at the same time most forcefully brings out Lyon's uncharitableness. In other words, it equally illuminates the story's two cases—that of Mrs. Capadose's relationship to her husband (the initial *Notebooks* donnée) and that of Lyon's relationship to Mrs. Capadose.

Like so many of James' stories, *The Liar* combines pathos and irony, for whereas the heroine's case is sad and touching, the observer's case is clearly the stuff of an ironic comedy. These two distinct notes are struck with equal force in the closing passage in which James dramatizes Lyon's final appreciative response to the phenomenon of loyalty—his moment of truth: "He [Lyon] would never go back—he couldn't. Nor should he ever sound her abyss. He believed in her absolute straightness where she and her affairs alone might be concerned, but she was still in love with the man of her choice, and since she couldn't redeem him she would adopt and protect him. So he had trained her" (III; 388). Since James employs, in this instance, the method of dramatization of consciousness, his record of Lyon's moment of truth has none of the retrospective flavor of an episode recollected in tranquillity. James depicts the living moment of Lyon's recognition, and it is a recognition marred by his irrepressible resentment, to which he gives vent in the last

sarcastic remark, "so he had trained her"—a remark which
is jarringly out of resonance with the rest of the passage
and which Lyon compulsively repeats for the second time.
(He had already used it earlier. When Mrs. Capadose tells
him: "Oh, *cher grand maître,* I loved it [the picture]!" he
reflects: "Truly her husband had trained her well" [III; 386]).
In reflecting upon Mrs. Capadose, Lyon functions as the
interpreter who contributes to the case which he witnesses
the element of appreciation. His last self-revelatory comment,
however, immediately switches our attention from the contemplation of the beauty of the heroine's devotion to her
husband to the observer's unresolved comic-ironic predicament. As in *The Aspern Papers,* the closing passage dramatizes the reaction of a man who has not yet fully assimilated
what might be called his lesson in devotion, and creates the
same effect of an open ending: Lyon's emotional conflict has
clearly not yet been resolved, and his "special torment" (a
phrase James uses in *The Sacred Fount*) is not yet over.

CHAPTER 7

TALES OF THE LITERARY LIFE

During his middle period James wrote a number of short masterpieces—*The Coxon Fund, The Next Time, The Death of the Lion, Greville Fane, The Great Good Place, The Middle Years, The Lesson of the Master, The Author of "Beltraffio,"* and *The Figure in the Carpet*—in which he dramatizes the embarrassments and predicaments, difficulties and joys, of the artist's life. In these tales he treats such themes as the nature and conditions of artistic integrity—the difficulties of true craftsmanship, the dedicated artist's desire for perfection, and the sacrifices he has to make in order to attain it; the dangers of artistic deterioration and the waning of the artist's creative powers; the effect on the artist of "the odd numbness of the general sensibility" and the shallowness and obtuseness of his critics, as well as his craving for the right kind of appreciation; the pressures exercised on him by domestic and social life; and the disappointments attendant upon his failure to achieve fame and financial success.

Although these tales are characterized by a common thematic preoccupation, they are written in a variety of modes ranging from the mordant social satire of *The Death of the Lion* to the weird melodrama of *The Author of "Beltraffio,"* from the elegiac lyricism of *The Middle Years* to the farcical comedy of *Greville Fane,* from the sad humor of *The Next Time* to the intense irony of *The Figure in the Carpet.*

James excelled as a critic in the art of the literary portrait, of which his essay on Hawthorne is perhaps the finest example. (*Partial Portraits* is the title of one of his collections of critical essays.) He conceived of the task of the literary critic as not merely that of analyzing and judging the single passage or the single work, but rather as that of evoking, analyzing, and evaluating the full, complete, rounded literary personality. Accordingly, his tales of the literary life are essentially literary portraits. James' imaginary authors— Hugh Vereker, Neil Paraday, Ray Limbert, Frank Saltram, Dencombe, Mark Ambient, and Henry St. George—are treated in the fictional mode in a spirit similar to that in which Turgenieff, Maupassant, Balzac, Dickens, Flaubert, and George Eliot are treated in the critical mode; and the literary merits and faults of the masterpieces of his imaginary novelists, which he pretends the reader is familiar with (Mark Ambient's *Beltraffio,* Dencombe's *The Middle Years,* Ray Limbert's *The Major Key, The Hidden Heart,* and *Derogation,* Henry St. George's *Shadowmere,* and Paul Overt's *Ginistrella)* are discussed in precisely the same critical idiom that James uses in his nonfictional literary studies —a technique which, one may add, affords delightful intellectual amusement.[1]

These tales, insofar as they are also concise anecdotes illustrative of some literary idea, are the most "intellectual" of James' works. Many of them take on the quality of a parable, and the point (or even moral) they so tellingly and wittily make is in many ways reminiscent of the Maupassantian point. At the same time, their tone is never didactic or dryly discursive, and their principal characters, far from being allegorized symbols (as in Hawthorne's parable—*The Artist of the Beautiful,* for instance) or primarily vehicles for the expression of the author's ideas (as in a Shavian "problem play"), are fully realized and intensely living men. In short, these intellectual stories possess the concreteness, dramatic vividness, and psychological realism which characterize other Jamesian works, and combine in a most felicitous

1. On the different types of reader ("mock-reader") every fictional work assumes, see W. Gibson, "Authors, Speakers, Readers and Mock Readers," *College English, 11* (February 1950), 265–69.

manner idea and story, wit and sensibility, intellectual content and human interest.

Although the most intellectual of James' works, these stories are at the same time his most personal—indeed, most autobiographical—and may be viewed as dramatizations of his own problems and his own situation. Far from being, as James claimed in his Preface to *The Lesson of the Master*, "portraits without models" for whom he was unable to give "chapter and verse,"[2] they are, in many crucial respects, self-portraits. Significantly—unlike other Jamesian artist-heroes, who are either sculptors or painters—all the principal characters in these tales are masters of the art of fiction and, specifically, novelists of rare distinction. (In this connection it is interesting to note that Mark Ambient, the artist-hero in *The Author of "Beltraffio,"* is conceived of in the *Notebooks* entry as "poet or novelist or both,"[3] but is presented in the finished tale as a novelist only.) Moreover, the experience which these novelists undergo and the critical problems which occupy them are remarkably like James' own. Paul Overt in *The Lesson of the Master* accepts the doctrine, which James himself practiced, of the necessity of renouncing "all human and material appendages" in order to achieve perfection; and Hugh Vereker, the enigmatic author in *The Figure in the Carpet,* suffers the distinctly Jamesian fate of being forever misunderstood by his critics—a fate to which, like James himself, he ultimately reconciles himself. All these autobiographical elements are, however, incorporated into fully objectivized tales, which are remarkably free of the self-indulgence and self-pity that frequently vitiate the fictional autobiography. As usual, James achieves this objectivity by projecting the "troubled artistic consciousness"[4] from the point of view of an interested observer.

These observers possess, besides the generic characteristics of the Jamesian observer, certain additional common fea-

2. Preface to *The Lesson of the Master*, New York, *15*, p. xi.
3. *Notebooks*, pp. 56–57.
4. Preface to *The Lesson of the Master*, p. viii.

tures. They are the only Jamesian observers who are professional men of letters: strict connoisseurs rather than amateurs—critics, reviewers, or aspiring young writers who wish
to model their work upon that of the Master. Consequently,
they appropriately combine literary passion with critical discrimination: they are sensitive to and appreciative of the
finer shades of the Master's work, which they hold in high
esteem, but are at the same time its sharpest critics, quick
to detect any false note which might be indicative of artistic
decline. In short, their intimate familiarity with the artistic
temperament, their profound interest in the aesthetic questions with which the artist struggles, and their intellectual
sympathy with his predicaments account for the authority,
critical acumen, and authenticity of their narrative and
make them the most intelligent interpreters of the perils of
the artist's vocation.

In order to extract the maximum of sense from the literary
case he registers, the narrator of the literary tale must be,
in his own way, no less supersubtle than the artist-hero. Thus,
in contradistinction to the works in which the authorial narrator's voice is quite distinct from that of the observer, in
these literary tales the observer's voice is indistinguishable
from James' own. James appears to be fully aware of this,
and in the *Notebooks* entry to *The Next Time* he is explicit
about it. He says: "The narrator [of Ray Limbert's case] must
be fully and richly, must be ironically *conscient*. . . . I become
the narrator, either impersonally, or in my unnamed, unspecified personality"[5]—a statement of the identity of author
and observer conspicuously different from, for instance, his
description of the observer in the Preface to *The Golden
Bowl*, as "the impersonal author's concrete deputy and dele-
gate."[6]

Since the observers of the literary tales are professional
men of letters who possess extraordinary gifts of expression,

5. *Notebooks,* p. 201.
6. Preface to *The Golden Bowl,* p. v.

they are fully conscious of their narrative role, in which they frankly delight, and at times directly address the reader, disclosing to him their principles of narrative, selection, and emphasis.[7]

It is the presence of the deeply sympathetic and spiritually involved critic-observer whose narrative serves to crystallize the major art theme which sharply distinguishes these tales of the literary life from James' more objectively dramatized full-length novels about the artist's life—*Roderick Hudson* and *The Tragic Muse*. In *Roderick Hudson* the process of the young sculptor's moral and artistic disintegration is seen through the eyes of Rolland Mallet, his friend and patron, who in spite of being a Jamesian vessel of sensibility, does not possess the kind of sympathetic understanding and critical insight into the artist's temper which characterize the observers in James' shorter tales. He is a New England Puritan, impeccably moral and somewhat priggish and provincial, and although he is quick to perceive Roderick's talent and enthusiastically takes it upon himself to help him develop his gifts, he is incapable of understanding his protégé's "romantic" personality—his egotism, impulsiveness, self-indulgence, and grandiloquence. Since his temper is moral rather than artistic, he cherishes the rather naïve belief in "the essential salubrity of genius" and views with disapproval Roderick's "large capacity for ruin." In effect, he serves not only as a center through whose consciousness Roderick's case is projected and *raisonneur* but also as Roderick's foil, a role which conflicts, to some extent at least,

7. See *The Death of the Lion*, New York, *15*, II, 103; and *The Figure in the Carpet*, New York, *15*, VIII, 262–63. These observers belong to the family of "self-conscious narrators" in the sense in which this expression is used by W. C. Booth in "The Self-Conscious Narrator in Comic Fiction before *Tristram Shandy*," *PMLA*, 67 (1952), 163–85; and H. Fluchère in *Laurence Sterne, de l'homme à l'oeuvre. Biographie critique et essai d'interprétation de Tristram Shandy* (Paris, 1961). These writers use this expression to designate narrators who are conscious of their narrative role and whose practice it is to intervene in the story in order to discuss their method and art.

with his interpretative activity. In *The Tragic Muse* James exhibits the implications of the artist's struggle between the rival claims of art and life by the device of the double plot—that is, by presenting both a "political" and a "theatrical" case—and dispenses altogether with the interpretative observer. (Gabriel Nash is too whimsical a character and his presence is too sporadic to qualify as such an observer.)[8]

James had always been intrigued by the potentialities of the artist-hero as a fictional character, and it is worth noting that many of his characters are, in fact, practicing artists, usually painters. This is true not only of the heroes of such apprentice works as *The Story of a Masterpiece, A Landscape Painting,* and *The Sweetheart of Mr. Briseux* but also of the heroes of the more mature and sophisticated *The Madonna of the Future, Mrs. Temperley,* and *The Liar.* It should, however, be emphasized that with the exception of *The Madonna of the Future* James never deals in these early works with the artist and with art as "a human complication and a social stumbling-block,"[9] but rather with the artist as a young man in love. In other words, the central theme of these works is not art but personal relationships, and the fact that the young man in love happens to be an artist merely contributes, in all these instances, an additional intensity to the domestic or international drama he is involved in. The reason for James' long hesitation to treat the art theme is fully stated in his Preface to *The Tragic Muse,* in which he discusses the immense difficulty of "doing something about art[10]—namely, of depicting the artist qua artist

8. James delighted in presenting two symmetrical cases, both of which dramatize, in interestingly different ways, the same idea for purposes of emphasis, intensification, irony, and generalization. Apart from *The Tragic Muse,* James uses the double-case technique only in his shorter works, such as *Fordham Castle, Broken Wings,* and *The Abasement of the Northmores,* in which he had little scope for a more linear development of his subject. There are minor symmetries in other novels—such as, for instance, the remarriage of both parents in *What Maisie Knew.*

9. Preface to *The Tragic Muse,* New York, 7, p. v.

10. Ibid.

rather than qua man, and in making his artistic preoccupations and predicaments dramatically "interesting." I shall try to show that in the last analysis it is in the small canvas of the structurally compressed *nouvelle* rather than in the larger canvas of the panoramic novel characteristic of his middle period that James at last discovered the perfect medium for the treatment of the art theme and consequently the solution of its inherent difficulties. (A discussion of the merits and felicities of this "beautiful and blessed" form is to be found, appropriately, in the Preface to *The Lesson of the Master.)*

I have already indicated that it was James' practice to develop the possibilities latent in the relationship between the observer, initially introduced for narrative and interpretative purposes, and the principal character, whose case the observer was intended to render. In *Madame de Mauves, The Portrait of a Lady,* and *The Liar* James, we saw, explored the relationship between the observer and the principal feminine character with whom he is in love; in the tales of the literary life it is the relationship between the man of genius and his admiring observer (who is also a member of his craft) which James dramatizes. This relationship follows a similar pattern throughout the tales. It is presented in each instance as a relationship between an elderly Master in the decline of life and a young, promising, hopeful disciple, at once timid and impertinent, modest and vain. The elderly Master is, invariably, an amiable, charitable, though somewhat aloof person, mellowed by experience, whereas the young observer though sharp-witted, is innocent, inexperienced, and vulnerable; he is also generally less self-possessed than the Master, who has the disarming naturalness and simplicity of a great man. The Master is generally a bourgeois family-man, while the young observer is a bit of a Bohemian, single and as yet unattached.

My main object in this chapter is to trace the development of this relationship in *The Author of "Beltraffio"* and *The Lesson of the Master,* which treat, though with differences in emphasis, the conflict between the artist's domestic life and the quest for artistic perfection. I want to indicate the increasing depth and significance of writer-observer relationship in these two stories and, in particular, to show that the elements which possess an almost purely functional value in *The Author of "Beltraffio"* are transformed in *The Lesson of the Master* into the fable's central thematic issue.

In *The Author of "Beltraffio"*[11] James deals with the philistine's deep-seated fear and hatred of art and with their impact on the sensitive writer wholly dedicated to his art. James projects this theme in a marital drama, in which the case of Mark Ambient, an exquisitely fine writer, whose wife is an aristocratic upper-class Englishwoman possessed of a deep, insurmountable aversion to his work, which she has never read, and the aesthetic value of which she is constitutionally incapable of comprehending.

The wife, moreover, is shown to be mortally afraid that her husband's "horrors" (as she calls his novels) will have a corrupting influence on their boy, the frail, delicate, sensitive and, precocious Dolcino: she feels, as her husband puts it, that one "shouldn't cultivate and enjoy it [beauty] without extraordinary precautions and reserves" (II; 46). The conflict between the artist husband, possessed with the love of beauty and the passion for form, and his narrow, rigidly moralistic wife, who doesn't approve of her husband's "ideas," centers on the child whom both adore and upon whom both continually exercise a relentless moral pressure. In the end the wife's morbid fear that the child will be contaminated by his father's immoral books and her desire to "redeem" him from such a monstrous contamination drives her to sacrifice him. She deliberately fails to summon medical help when Dolcino falls ill, and he dies.

The theme of moral pressure mercilessly exercised on a helpless child by a self-appointed redeemer, which is of subsidiary importance in *The Author of "Beltraffio,"* is more

11. New York, *16*, III, 46.

fully and more subtly dramatized in *The Turn of the Screw,* written some years later. In both stories a young, extremely beautiful, and intelligent child dies at the hands of a morbidly possessive woman who wishes to redeem him from what seems to her an evil and corrupting influence. There are, of course, important differences between the two cases. First, the child in *The Author of "Beltraffio"* is a perfectly innocent victim of the struggle which rages between his parents, whereas Miles, the child in *The Turn of the Screw* (if, ignoring for the moment the Jamesian ambiguity, we accept as true the governess' account of the matter), is actually possessed by some evil, corrupting influence. Second, the inarticulate English wife differs greatly from the psychologically complex governess, who is a genuine Jamesian vessel of consciousness. Third, the wife in *The Author of "Beltraffio"* deliberately decides to let Dolcino die, while the governess in *The Turn of the Screw* wishes only to make Miles confess, and his death, which is the result of the pressure she exercises on him, comes to her not only as a terrible shock but also as a complete surprise. Finally, *The Author of "Beltraffio"* is free of the moral and epistemological ambiguity which is at the very center of *The Turn of the Screw,* and the reader is left in no doubt as to how he is to judge the wife's terrible action.

Although *The Author of "Beltraffio"* belongs to the tales of literary life, it also treats, like most of the works of James' middle period, the English theme. Appropriately, the wife who hates her husband's art is the quintessential English noblewoman, a genuine "Barbarian" (to use Arnold's epithet), combining physical grace with a deep distrust and incomprehension of the things of the mind. She is, we are told, "a wonderfully cultivated human plant" (III; 49).[12] She is slim, fair, and pretty, with "a vague air of race" (I; 11).

12. Lady Barbarina, another Jamesian specimen of the English aristocracy, is also described in terms of plant imagery, as "the finest flower of generations of privileged people and of centuries of rich country life" (IV; 74).

Indeed, she appears to the American observer-narrator as having come out of a Gainsborough, a Reynolds, or a Lawrence—painters with a keen eye for the English national character.[13] She has perfect breeding, personal grace, and impeccable social manners, but hardly any conversation and no sense of humor. As the observer-narrator notes, she has a "monosyllabic correctness" and possesses "the enviable English quality of being able to be mute without unrest." In spite of her great reserve, she seems to burn, like Julia Dallow, in *The Tragic Muse,* "with a cold thin flame" (III; 48).

Although James is clearly on the artist's side, he presents the husband's and the wife's positions with an impartiality comparable to that which he shows in *The Tragic Muse.* He never makes the philistine wife the target of his satire; and his account of the marital conflict which culminates in Dolcino's death is unbiased and without a trace of special pleading. Indeed, in order to make the scales evenly weighted and achieve a perfect balance between the two incompatible viewpoints, James adds certain details designed primarily to extend our sympathy to the wife by making her position appear somewhat less monstrous and more understandable.

First, James associates Mark Ambient with the aesthetic movement of the nineties, and we learn that *Beltraffio,* his celebrated masterpiece, which produced quite a scandal at the time of its publication, was then considered as "the most complete presentation that had yet been made of the gospel of art," that "it was a kind of aesthetic war-cry," and that "nothing had been done in that line from the point of art for art"—the "fond formula" for the period (I; 3–4). As for Mrs. Ambient, nothing (we are made to see) could be more repugnant to a woman of her type than the air of scandal which clung about her husband's work; being incapable of

13. For James' attitude toward Gainsborough, Sir Joshua Reynolds, and Lawrence, whom he considered to be "deeply English painters," see *The Painter's Eyes, Notes and Essays in the Pictorial Arts by Henry James,* sel. and ed., with an Intro., by J. L. Swenney (London, 1956), pp. 69–71, 126–27, 193–94.

distinguishing between *Beltraffio* and other, inferior works, her husband's seemingly decadent novels were bound to seem to her particularly horrifying and immoral.

The introduction of Miss Ambient, the writer's sister, into the drama is James' second way of making Mrs. Ambient somewhat more sympathetic. Miss Ambient is presented as a fatuous, affected, attitudinizing spinster who incarnates in her person all the false values of the aesthetic movement and functions as a grotesque travesty, a preposterous caricature, of her great brother. Since Mrs. Ambient's total incomprehension of art makes her incapable of discriminating between the genuine aestheticism of her husband and the spuriousness of his sister's, the latter's presence clearly serves to intensify Mrs. Ambient's profound dislike of her husband's work and to deepen her mortification. Indeed, the perceptive observer informs the reader that unfortunately Mrs. Ambient was not the only one who failed to distinguish between the original and the imitation: "her [Miss Ambient's] affections rubbed off on her brother's renown, and as there were plenty of people who darkly disapproved of him they could easily point to his sister as a person formed by his influence. It was quite possible to regard her as a warning, and she had almost compromised him with the world at large" (II; 25). Miss Ambient, it should be observed, is one of James' few subsidiary characters whose primary function is not that of a *ficelle* (the information she imparts to the narrator could easily be gleaned some other way). Rather, her false artiness makes her the perfect foil to her sister-in-law and thus enhances the latter's value. Appropriately, the narrator, who conceives of Mrs. Ambient—the perfect specimen of her type—as a Gainsborough, a Reynolds, or a Lawrence, conceives of her sister-in-law—the second-rate imitation—as a Rossetti.

Perhaps the most memorable, most amusing illustration of the two women's contrasting natures is the account of their behavior during a literary conversation which the writer—a prodigious and charming talker—conducts with the observer. Mrs. Ambient, who cannot appreciate the interesting, inspiring, humorous, and amusing things her husband is saying, and who clearly dislikes "art-talk" during dinner, is detached and inscrutable, meeting neither her husband's nor his guest's eye, and attends with brusque efficiency to the dinner. Her sister-in-law, on the other hand, is intensely, perversely attentive:

> Her "die-away" pupils continued to attach themselves to my countenance, and it was only her air of belonging to another century that kept them from being importunate . . . It was as if she knew in a general way that he must be talking very well, but she herself was so at home among such allusions that she had no need to pick them up and was at liberty to see what would become of the exposure of a candid young American to a high aesthetic temperature. (II; 27)

James' success in making Mrs. Ambient more sympathetic to the reader is to be seen again in his treatment of the two parents engaged in the struggle over their boy. It is the wife who is the more tragic character, for it is she who, consumed with the passion of philistinism, is driven to commit the horrible deed by which her son, to whom she is deeply attached, is allowed to die rather than be contaminated by his own father.

The narrating observer in *The Author of "Beltraffio"* is a young American of literary tastes and critical pretensions on his first visit to England. An ardent admirer of Mark Ambient's novels (which he carries about in his trunk), he calls on the writer to pay his homage. He is one of James' "exquisite provincials," a passionate pilgrim deeply conscious of the cultural bareness of his own country and delighted with everything European, in particular English and Italian. In effect, his love of both England and Italy is intimately bound up with his appreciation of Mark Ambient's work, for the latter is known to be saturated with the spirit of Italy and Italian art, in particular that of the cinquecento, and the scenes of of his early novels are, we learn, laid in Rome and Florence.[14]

The Author of "Beltraffio" is one of James' very few works in which he exploits to great effect the narrative distance between the two temporal planes—that of the experiencing and that of the narrating or reminiscing self. The young observer (i.e. the experiencing self) is eager, rash, lacking in self-restraint, pitiless, overinsistent, meddlesome, and impertinent. He is an aesthete who wholeheartedly, almost religiously, espouses all the slogans and mannerisms of the aesthetic movement, and his boundless uncritical admiration for the English national character is matched only by his ignorance of it. The older observer (the narrating self), through whose running commentary this somewhat ironical portrait of his younger self emerges, is much more self-critical, mellower, kinder, and more humane. He is also subtler, more ironical, and critically more blasé, but although he is no longer an enthusiastic partisan of the aesthetic movement, he is still as great an admirer of Mark Ambient's work as he was in his youth.

The tale's structure is governed by the principle of contrast. It consists of a series of alternating encounters between the observer and the husband and the observer and the wife respectively, each encounter offsetting and highlighting the other with a progressively growing intensity. The best illustration of this contrapuntal structure is the ironic juxtaposition of the scene in which the wife explains to the observer her view, according to which their young son should not be allowed to dip into his father's books because they are a grave danger to his moral well-being, with the scene in

14. The appreciation of the cinquecento in a story by James is always a sign of cultivation and of an aesthetic temperament. Both the diarist and the young man in *The Diary of a Man of Fifty* like the early Florentines best of all, and so does the painter-hero in *Mrs. Temperley*. On the other hand, Sir Claude, the stepfather in *What Maisie Knew*, regards, as an Englishman of his type would, a taste for the Primitives as a "silly superstition." On this point see V. Hopkins, "Visual Art Devices and Parallels in the Fiction of Henry James," *PMLA*, 76 (December 1961), 567.

which the husband, in his turn, explains to the narrator his view (which serves as an indirect comment on his wife's), according to which young people in general and his son in particular shouldn't read good novels because, not being sufficiently mature, it would be "too bad for the poor dear old novel" (III; 45). The indirectness of the marital dialogue has the effect also of forcibly bringing out the estrangement between husband and wife and impressing upon the reader the impossibility of a direct, face-to-face confrontation between them on the art question.

To the enthusiastic "juvenile pilgrim from overseas" who idealizes everything English the realization of Mrs. Ambient's hatred of art comes, of course, as a great shock. The presentation of the wife's attitude toward her husband's work from the point of view of a young, inexperienced American rather than from that of a blasé cosmopolitan greatly heightens the dramatic vividness of the marital situation and most fully expresses its horror. The observer arrives at the truth by degrees. In fact, far from perceiving at once that the Ambients are sadly mismated, the American observer, who is naturally much struck by Mrs. Ambient's Gainsborough-like beauty and grace, feels at first that she is indeed the proper wife for the English genius, and it is only when he notices her strange behavior toward her son that he begins to entertain some doubts on the matter: "I have seen poets married to women of whom it was difficult to conceive that they should gratify the poetic fancy—women with dull faces and glutinous minds, who were none the less, however, excellent wives. But there was no obvious disparity in Mark Ambient's union" (I; 11). The initial false impression of a harmonious relationship between the great novelist and his wife reinforces the irony of the latter's unhappy marital situation. What gives this ironic effect an added edge is the fact that Mrs. Ambient as well as her son have Italian names—Beatrice and Dolcino. For if Italy stands for beauty and the artistic life, Mrs. Ambient, far from being the incarnation of the spirit of Italy, perversely and bitterly detests everything that country stands for. Thus, without any discussion of the couple's past, these details conjure up the image of Mark Ambient as a young man who falls in love with a woman possessing the perfect breeding, grace, and beauty of the Englishwoman, and whose Italian name touches his poetic fancy and fires his imagination.

The process of the American observer's initiation into Mark Ambient's case follows a pattern similar to that of his initiation into his wife's. At first he is surprised to find out that the celebrated master of the art-for-art school looks "at once an English gentleman and a man of genius," but being an admirer of the English he finds this, on second thought, "a happy combination" (I; 7). Only by degrees does the observer come to realize that far from being happy, this combination reflects a sad compromise on the English writer's part, whose marriage to a philistine wife in itself places him in the falsest of positions. The first indication of this fact is brought home to the observer when he sees the author of *Beltraffio*, that book which expresses the most profane view of life, "in communion with the Church of England" (I; 12) —that is to say, entertaining the district's vicaress, with whom he discusses the unobjectionable subject of chrysanthemums.

This sad incongruity between the writer's artistic convictions and his personal life (a subject to be more fully treated in *The Lesson of the Master*), of which the observer gradually becomes aware, is already foreshadowed in his first impression of the exquisite novelist: "Mark Ambient was grave and gay at one and the same moment. There were other strange oppositions and contradictions in his slightly faded and fatigued countenance. He affected me somehow as at once fresh and stale, at once anxious and indifferent" (I; 7).[15]

The international complication which the presence of the

15. This curious combination in the English of freshness and staleness is experienced also by the Prince in *The Golden Bowl*, who confesses to being puzzled "as to the elements of staleness in all the freshness and of freshness in all the staleness." See *The Golden Bowl*, New York, III, IX, 23, p. 354.

American observer introduces into *The Author of "Beltraffio"* thus enriches and deepens our understanding of the
artist's marital drama.[16] But in addition to the observer's
narrative and interpretative roles, to which his Americanness
gives special poignancy, he also plays the part of a fictional
character and in this capacity serves various dramatic purposes. First, it is made abundantly clear that Mrs. Ambient
has no great taste for the enthusiastic admirer of her husband's art and finds his conversation profoundly irritating—
in particular, since he is in the habit of loudly professing his
aesthetic creed in the idiom of the aesthetic movement of the
period. He is presented as wedded to the view that it is Life
which imitates Art. He views Mark Ambient's country house
in Sussex as a masterpiece of one of the Pre-Raphaelites, confessing that "that was the way many things struck me at the
time, in England—as reproductions of something that existed
primarily in art or literature. It was not the picture, the poem,
the fictive page, that seemed to me a copy; these things were
the originals, and the life of happy and distinguished people
was fashioned in their image" (I; 8).

Ignorant at first of Mrs. Ambient's attitude toward art, the
observer does not hesitate to express these aesthetic ideas in
her presence. Thus, wishing to praise her house, he tells her
that "it is like one of his [Mark Ambient's] pictures"—a most
unfortunate remark, to which she coldly replies that she
doesn't in the least consider that she is living in one of her
husband's books, adding that she shouldn't care for that in
the least. But the colder and more reserved Mrs. Ambient
grows on the painful subject of her husband's art, the more
does the exasperated, obstinate observer indulge in extravagant praise of it. When he relentlessly presses on, appealing
to Mrs. Ambient to acknowledge at least the beauty of her

16. *The Author of "Beltraffio"* serves, therefore, to disprove Jefferson's
contention that since for James the sense of national type was the basis
of successful portrayal of the individual, his literary men for whom he
fails to give "chapter and verse" are failures. See D. W. Jefferson, *Henry
James and the Modern Reader* (London, 1964), p. 121.

husband's "tone," she is at last forced to tell him point-blank that she doesn't read her husband's works, and to his incredulous question: "Don't you admire his genius? Don't you admire *Beltraffio?*" she gives the classical vague and noncommittal answer of the English philistine: "Oh of course he's very clever!" (I; 20). Thus, apart from the purely expository function of drawing Mrs. Ambient out, these conversations are a delightful international comedy of errors, which serves as a comic exemplification of the unbridgeable gulf between the aesthetic and the philistine viewpoints which is the central subject of the story.

As in many of his other works, James cannot resist the temptation of involving the observer in the plot and of making him the person who finally brings things to a head. One evening Mark Ambient gives the observer, as a mark of friendship and confidence, the early pages of his forthcoming book. Meeting Mrs. Ambient, the observer suggests "by a kind of fatality, a perversity that had already made [him] address her overmuch on that question of her husband's powers" (II; 35), that she read them. Surprisingly, she accepts his suggestions, and it is her reading of these pages (which she must have found even more horrible than she thought) that determines her to let her boy die rather than expose him to the contaminating influence of his father's work.

It should be emphasized that this interference on the observer's part, which precipitates the crisis, is never with James a mere mechanical device. The observer does not function as a deus ex machina, and his action is always shown to be in perfect keeping with his fictional character. In this instance, it is mainly the desire to "convert" Mrs. Ambient to her husband's religion, to force her to see and admit the beauty of his works, which prompts the observer to offer her the sheets. At the same time, however, this action also exhibits in the narrator an absence of charity, a strain of cruelty, perhaps even of sadism—a note which strongly recalls Lyon in *The Liar*.

In the concluding passage it is the wry, amused tone of the reminiscing narrator which predominates: "I ought to mention that the death of her child in some degree converted her. When the new book came out (it was long delayed) she read it over as a whole, and her husband told me that during the supreme weeks before her death—she failed rapidly after losing her son, sank into a consumption and faded away at Mentone—she even dipped into the black *Beltraffio*" (IV; 73). This sober, informative tone of the résumé, in which the reminiscing narrator sums up the events following the tragic dénouement, creates a distancing effect. The main emphasis is on the painfully ironic fact that the death of the child at last "converted" Mrs. Ambient, so that before she died she "even dipped into the black *Beltraffio*"—a remark which sounds the only ironic note directed against her. As for the Ambients' great sorrow, it is deliberately understated. The husband's sorrow is not explicitly touched on but merely hinted at in the parenthetical remark ("it [his book] was long delayed"), and the wife's despair is similarly mentioned in a merely parenthetical fashion: "—she failed rapidly after losing her son, sank into a consumption and faded away at Mentone—."

In *The Author of "Beltraffio"* the observer's subsidiary role as a dramatic agent who gets involved in the plot serves, we saw, to deepen and intensify the artist's drama as it was originally conceived in the *Notebooks*. By contrast, the observer in *The Lesson of the Master*[17] grows in stature and becomes a central character equal in thematic value to the writer whose case he sets out to record in his capacity of the story's single center of consciousness. In other words, a reversal of emphasis takes place, and the observer's role as the medium through which the writer's case is projected becomes subsidiary to his dramatic role. Similarly, the Master-disciple relationship between the writer and his observer, the primary function of which, in *The Author of "Beltraffio,"* is to enable

17. New York, *15, pp.* 3–93.

the observer better to understand and appreciate the writer's case, becomes in *The Lesson of the Master* the tale's central dramatic relationship, in terms of which its art theme is exemplified.

In *The Lesson of the Master* James sounds the theme of the conflict between the artist's vocation and the fulfillment of his humanity, of the price he has to pay and the sacrifices he must make in order to achieve perfection—which is, James claims, the artist's "only business." In order to fulfill his only duty—that of "having drawn from his intellectual instrument the finest music that nature had hidden in it, of having played it as it should be played"—the artist must renounce all "human and material appendages" which are bound, by their nature, to hamper, falsify, and limit his creative powers; he must entirely and wholeheartedly give up the full human life, the "responsibilities and duties and burdens and sorrows and joys" of domestic and social life, and live the unworldly life of a "disfranchised monk," single-mindedly pursuing his artistic aim (V; 69, 73, 72, 77).

It is married life with all that it involves which stands in *The Lesson of the Master* for the "full rich masculine human general life" (V; 72) the artist must give up if he is to achieve real greatness. In the *Notebooks* entry to his tale James sees as an interesting subject "the situation of an elder artist or writer who has been ruined (in his own sight) by his marriage and its forcing him to produce promiscuously and cheaply—his position in regard to a younger *confrère* whom he sees on the brink of the same disaster and whom he endeavours to save, to rescue, by some act of bold interference—breaking off the marriage, annihilating the wife, making trouble between the parties."[18] It is this younger *confrère* of the *Notebooks* whom the elder artist wishes to save from a fate similar to his own who becomes in the finished tale the center through whose consciousness the elder artist's case is filtered. Significantly, this is one of the few cases in which the character

18. *Notebooks,* p. 78.

who has in the finished tale both interpretative and dramatic functions is conceived of in the *Notebooks* in terms of his dramatic rather than, as usual, of his interpretative role.

Paul Overt, whose promising first book, *Ginistrella,* has already caught the eye of criticism, considers himself immensely in the debt of Henry St. George, the Master whose fiction, in particular *Shadowmere,* he inordinately admires. At the same time, he cannot but perceive inequalities and superficialities, a certain "comparative absence of quality" in the Master's late work, a perception which fills him with tender pity for "the great misguided novelist."

If in many cases the characteristics which enrich the observer's dramatic character at the same time detract from his efficiency as a lucid reflector, in the case of Paul Overt there is no such conflict between his two roles. Rather, the same traits of character which qualify him to serve as a perfect mirror of Henry St. George's case admirably equip him, at the same time, for his dramatic role. *Qua* center through whose consciousness St. George's case is presented, his painful awareness of the Master's artistic decline—of which, it is suggested, very few critically perceptive people are aware— makes him lucid about his case. His love and pity for the Master make Paul Overt sympathetically appreciative of his dilemma; and the fact that he himself is a writer who possesses a first-hand knowledge of the torments and difficulties of "keeping it up" serves to intensify the passionate interest he takes in the Master's sad case and whets his curiosity concerning the "tragic intellectual secret," which, he is convinced, is at the heart of his recent decline.

As a dramatic character—that is, as the young *confrère* the Master wishes to save—he has to be the promising novelist he is, for since the sacrifice he is urged to make is so great, the price he is urged to pay so heavy, only the belief that he has it in him to produce a great work of art can make the Master see him as worthy of saving. The young *confrère* must also be the ideal critic in respect to Henry St. George himself; that is, he must be highly appreciative of his best work and yet acutely conscious of his recent deterioration, in order to be duly impressed, indeed shaken, by the Master's cautionary tale; and he must also, himself, be aiming very high in order to be inspired by the hard, austere doctrine of renunciation which the Master expounds.

To intensify the young writer's dilemma and make it as difficult as possible, it is not only the vision of art the Master evokes which must be alluring but also, of course, the prospects of life the young man is urged to give up. Miss Fancourt, the daughter of an English general, who has spent many years abroad and whom Paul Overt meets in the same country house in which he first comes across Henry St. George, embodies these prospects. She is presented as an idealized though very vivid specimen of the perfect woman. She is handsome, gracious, generous, vivacious, and supremely natural. She is also, and this greatly appeals to a man of Paul Overt's sensibilities, eminently modern: she is free, independent, unconventional, bold—without, however, being in the least "fast." Her having lived so many years abroad also gives her several advantages. It invests her with a certain exotic air, it serves to free her from English class-consciousness, and it makes her view England (which the young writer adores) with a fresh and admiring eye. What is even more important, Miss Fancourt possesses the Englishwoman's physical grace, without her race's inexpressiveness and insensitivity to art. Rather, she is, very much like the Jamesian American Girl at her best—curious, intelligent, sensitive, and genuinely interested in art, for which she has a great capacity of enthusiastic appreciation. We learn that she has tried to write a novel but given it up, and that she admires not only the Master's works but also Paul Overt's *Ginistrella,* with which (like the observer in *The Author of "Beltraffio")* she travels. In sum, she seems to be the ideal helpmate for a young struggling artist, and it is this which makes the necessity to give her up especially difficult.

The Master is describing to Paul Overt the insidious effects marriage has on the artist:

Again Paul was silent, but it was all tormenting. "Are there no women who really understand—who can take part in a sacrifice?"

"How can they take part? They themselves are the sacrifice, they're the idol and the altar and the flame."

"Isn't there even *one* who sees further?" Paul continued.

For a moment St. George made no answer; after which, having torn up his letters, he came back to the point all ironic. "Of course I know the one you mean. But not even Miss Fancourt." (V; 75)

And again, upon telling the young man that if he is intent on marrying Miss Fancourt he must give up the idea of "a decent perfection":

"She'd help it—she'd help it!" the young man cried.

"For about a year—the first year, yes. After that she'd be as a millstone round its [the idea's] neck."

Paul frankly wondered "Why she has a passion for the real thing, for good work—for everything you and I care for most."

" 'You and I' is charming, my dear fellow!" his friend laughed. "She has it indeed, but she'd have a still greater passion for her children—and very proper too. She'd insist on everything's being made comfortable, advantageous, propitious for them. That isn't the artist's business." (V; 75–76)

The Master, intent upon presenting to his disciple both horns of the artist's dilemma with equal impartiality, then tells him that Miss Fancourt carries *Ginistrella* with her, and joins the young writer in his admiration for the values of life (as against art) which she epitomizes in her person: "She's first-rate herself and she expends herself on the second-rate [the artist]. She's life herself and she takes a rare interest in imitations . . . Above all she exaggerates—to herself, I mean. She exaggerates you and me" (III; 42).[19]

The story progressively unfolds through a series of alternating encounters between the observer and the St. Georges and between him and Miss Fancourt. Each new encounter between the observer and either the Master or his wife further initiates him into the secrets of St. George's life, deepens his understanding of the latter's plight, and intensifies his pity for him; correspondingly, each new encounter with Miss Fancourt deepens his admiration for her and further encourages him in the belief that she might respond to his love. These two distinct lines of action, each exhibiting a growing intellectual and emotional involvement on the observer's part, finally converge in the climactic scene (chap. V) in which the Master, confessing his failure to be true to his vocation, urges his young admiring disciple to give Miss Fancourt up for art—the most monastic of vocations.

The celebrated artist's compromising position as a worshiper of false gods is first hinted at in the observer's impression of his great colleague's wife. She is a pretty, smart, aggressively elegant, self-assured *femme du monde* who, the observer feels, is eminently unsuited to the role of a life's partner to a man of letters, and he takes an immediate dislike to her. He uneasily reflects that

> he had never before seen her [the artist's wife] look so much as if her prosperity had deeper foundations than an ink-spotted study-table littered with proof sheets. Mrs. St. George might have been the wife of a gentleman who "kept" books rather than wrote them, who carried

19. Miss Fancourt represents the same values which John Berridge, the late Jamesian artist in *The Velvet Glove,* believes to be embodied in a young European princess he meets at an evening party in Paris—a belief which is rudely shattered when he finds out that this "olympian" is but another, very inferior fellow-craftswoman who "makes up" to him because she wishes him to write a "preface" to her unpublished, probably worthless book.

on great affairs in the City and made better bargains
than those that poets mostly make with publishers. With
this she hinted at a success more personal—peculiarly
stamping the age in which society, the world of conversation, is a great drawing-room with the City for its
antechamber (I; 9–10).

Paul Overt is made obscurely uneasy when he learns that
Mrs. St. George made her husband burn one of his books,
which, he immediately feels, must have been one of his best.
The outraged disciple later discovers the reason for this
auto-da-fé when his great colleague confesses that he dealt
in this book with the painful and embarrassing subject of his
own compromised position, that of the artist who has dis-
honored his profession. This uneasiness on Paul Overt's part
turns into a shocked indignation when he hears Mrs. St.
George discuss her husband's works in purely administrative
and commercial terms, complaining of his laziness and se-
renely expressing the wish that he'd produce more. Thus, as
in *The Author of "Beltraffio,"* the presentation of the wife's
philistinism through the consciousness of her husband's admirer serves most fully to bring out its enormity. In this instance, the effect is further reinforced by the sharp contrast
which is immediately established between the wife's belief
that her husband has of late produced too few works and his
disciple's belief that he has produced "too promiscuously."
Again, as in *The Author of "Beltraffio,"* the young man who
is disgusted with Mrs. St. George's "profane allusions" to the
Master's works asks himself: "Didn't she, as the wife of a rare
artist, know what it was to produce *one* perfect work of art?
How in the world did she think they were turned off?"
(I; 11–12).

The observer's initial impression of Mrs. St. George as the
wife of a gentleman who "kept" books rather than wrote
them is later fully confirmed by St. George's air of a pros-
perous gentleman:

"Ah is that he—really?" Our friend felt a certain surprise, for the personage before him seemed to be a troubled vision which had been vague only while not confronted with reality. As soon as the reality dawned the mental image, retiring with a sigh, became substantial enough to suffer a slight wrong. Overt, who had spent a considerable part of his short life in foreign lands, made now, but not for the first time, the reflexion that whereas in those countries he had almost always recognized the artist and the man of letters by his personal type, the mould of his face, the character of his head, the expression of his figure and even the indications of his dress, so in England this identification was as little as possible a matter of course, thanks to the greater conformity, the habit of sinking the profession instead of advertising it, the general diffusion of the air of the gentleman—the gentleman committed to no particular set of ideas. More than once, on returning to his own country, he had said to himself about the people met in society: "One sees them in this place and that, and one even talks with them; but to find out what they *do* one would really have to be a detective." In respect to several individuals whose work he was the opposite of "drawn to"—perhaps he was wrong—he found himself adding "No wonder they conceal it—when it's so bad!" He noted that oftener than in France and in Germany his artist looked like a gentleman—that is like an English one—while, certainly outside a few exceptions, his gentleman didn't look like an artist. St. George was not one of the exceptions; that circumstance he definitely apprehended before the great man had turned his back to walk off with Miss Fancourt. He certainly looked better behind than any foreign man of letters—showed for beautifully correct in his tall black hat and his superior frock coat. Somehow, all the same, these very garments —he wouldn't have minded them so much on a weekday —were disconcerting to Paul Overt, who forgot for the moment that the head of the profession was not a bit

better dressed than himself. He had caught a glimpse of
a regular face, a fresh colour, a brown moustache and a
pair of eyes surely never visited by a fine frenzy, and he
promised himself to study these denotements on the
first occasion. His superficial sense was that their owner
might have passed for a lucky stockbroker—a gentleman
driving eastward every morning from a sanitary suburb
in a small dog-cart. (I; 13–15)

Undoubtedly, James' own distinctive note is discernible in
this impressive piece of analysis, which, we are meant to see,
is the fruit of many previous impressions Paul Overt has
gathered in the course of his various encounters with artists,
and whose pitch of generality unmistakably foreshadows that
of the concentrated synoptic analyses in *The Ambassadors,
The Wings of the Dove,* and *The Golden Bowl.*[20]

It is noteworthy that in this passage the generalized reflections on the English artist precede the description of Henry
St. George ("St. George was not one of the exceptions"), who
emerges, as a consequence, not as an exceptional but rather
as a characteristic specimen of the English artist. What further intensifies the generality of this passage is the authorial
ironic remark about the observer who is disconcerted by St.
George's fine Sunday attire: "He [Paul Overt] forgot for the
moment that the head of the profession was not a bit better
dressed than himself." The implication that the observer is
himself a specimen of the peculiarly English race of gentle-
men-artists is of the greatest significance. The ardent, ideal-
istic young writer, who is urged to give up the "world" and
society for art, has, it transpires, very mixed feelings with
regard to the world and society. In a manner characteristic
of the artist in general and of the English artist in particular,
he views them with a mixture of repugnance and fascination,
and he both detests and respects their values. If his detesta-

20. For a discussion of this subject see Krook, *The Ordeal of Consciousness in Henry James,* pp. 199, 234.

tion of these values is dramatized in his disconcertment at St. George's wife and St. George's appearance, his respect for these very same values is dramatized in his reflection upon seeing the St. Georges leave Summersoft in a fine brougham: "and as our young man waved his hat to them in response to their nods and flourishes he reflected that, taken together, they were an honourable image of success, of the material rewards and the social credit of literature. Such things were not the full measure, but he nevertheless felt a little proud for literature" (III; 44).

St. George's confession occurs during two nocturnal talks, one in Summersoft and one in his own house in London; and in the intervening period Paul Overt falls irrevocably in love with Miss Fancourt. In the course of these two momentous talks St. George discusses his failure with his disciple in a tone which strikes the latter as supremely impartial, lucid, and bitterly self-ironical. It is during his second talk with the Master that Paul Overt learns the facts about Mrs. St. George's attitude to her husband's art. Mrs. St. George in *The Lesson of the Master* is, it appears, no less obtuse to art than Mrs. Ambient in *The Author of "Beltraffio,"* but her philistinism is expressed in a different, subtler, much more insidious fashion. She turns her husband's artistic activity into a "trade," a mere means to achieve economic and social rewards. In other words, her husband's study is to her what the City is to other women of her circle—the antechamber to the drawing room. Not surprisingly, therefore, it is she rather than the less cunning, uncalculating Mrs. Ambient who is the cause of her husband's artistic deterioration.

She is, we learn, a shrewd, highly competent administrator and disciplinarian, who has trained her husband "to produce between ten and one every morning" with a clerk's regularity. She virtually locks him up in his study, a windowless long room from which the outer world is conveniently excluded and in which, as he ironically puts it, he is "walled in to his trade." The room is furnished with "a tall desk, of great extent, at which [Paul Overt reflects], the person using it could write only in the erect posture of a clerk in a counting house." The ironic intention of the comparison of the artist's desk to that of a clerk in a counting house is of course unmistakable. The description of the room, it will be noticed, evokes not only the image of an office but also that of an artist's ivory tower, and its austere monastic air, the fact that it shuts out the outer world, makes it also an ideal writer's study. In fact, Paul Overt himself, to whom the desk momentarily appears as a clerk's desk, cannot help reflecting: "Lord, what good things I should do if I had such a charming place as this to do them in!" (V; 63, 62, 64).

The conversations between the Master and his disciple which touch on the most central issue of the artist's vocation are unparalleled in James' fiction for intellectual energy and depth, polemical vivacity, moving eloquence, and dramatic intensity. In James' full-length novel *The Tragic Muse,* in which the same theme is treated, the art conversations between Nick Dormer, the portrait painter who plans to give give up a promising political career, and Gabriel Nash, an aesthete of the nineties who combines Walter Pater's theories on life and art with Oscar Wilde's turn for paradox and aphorism, are despite their dramatic vividness, purely analytical, and they accordingly stand in contrast and opposition to the more dramatic portions of the novel in which the crucial decisions of the artist-hero are made. In *The Lesson of the Master* the art talks between St. George and his disciple are the major climactic scenes—the highest intellectual and emotional points of the story. The Master's impassioned monologues (which soon turn into heated dialogues) are the nearest James ever came to employing the device of confession, which he usually eschewed.[21] These monologues are not, however, pure confessions. Rather, they are meant to

21. It is perhaps interesting to note at this juncture that James' dislike for the confession may partly account for the fact that he was constitutionally unable to enjoy the Dostoyevskian novel. He informed Stevenson at one time that he had found himself unable to read *Crime*

serve as an exhortation, a lesson, a warning to the young writer, and are therefore of the greatest moment for both Master and disciple.

These talks are a supreme exemplification of what Austin Warren has aptly characterized as the Jamesian "dialectic."[22] Henry St. George and Paul Overt represent two opposite and irreconcilable views which they passionately defend, proceeding very much like attorneys for the defense and the prosecution. The poignant irony of the debate is that the austere doctrine of renunciation is expounded with the greatest force and vehemence by the man who has failed, as he admits, to practice it, whereas the belief in the artist's humanity, in his need to share in "all the domestic and social initiations and complications" (V; 72), is propounded by the young writer who will eventually follow the Master's advice and choose the monastic road to artistic perfection.

It should be emphasized in this connection that the Master and his disciple do not discuss an abstract matter, nor do they (like many other Jamesian characters who engage in debate) analyze other people's difficulties. Their discussion concerns the validity and the justification of the most crucial, most basic decision they have, as artists, to make. Thus, in defending the artist's humanity and the possibility of his combining artistic integrity with personal happiness, Paul Overt is not only endeavoring to justify the Master's life but is also defending his own humanity.

A significant portion of their dialogue takes the forensic form of question and answer. The Master has told Paul Overt that providing for a woman's children isn't the artist's business:

> "The artist—the artist! Isn't he a man all the same?"
>
> St. George had a grand grimace. "I mostly think not."
>
> (V; 76)

---

and Punishment to its finish. See G. Steiner, *Tolstoy or Dostoyevsky* (rev. ed. London, Penguin, 1967), p. 190.

22. On this subject see Warren, *Rage for Order,* pp. 144–45.

Again:

> "Then you don't allow him the common passions and
> affections of men?" Paul asked.
> "Hasn't he a passion, an affection, which includes all
> the rest?" [St. George replies]. (V; 77)

And again:

> "What a false position, what a condemnation of the
> artist, that he's a mere disfranchised monk and can pro-
> duce his effect only by giving up personal happiness.
> What an arraignment of art!" Paul went on with a trem-
> bling voice.
> "You don't imagine by chance that I'm defending
> art? 'Arraignment'—I should think so! Happy the so-
> cieties in which it hasn't made its appearance, for from
> the most it comes they have a consuming ache, they have
> an incurable corruption, in their breast. Most assuredly
> is the artist in a false position; But I thought we were
> taking him for granted. Pardon me," St. George con-
> tinued: " 'Ginistrella' made me!" (V; 77)

Of special interest is the dialectical development of the
concept of honor. Paul Overt, we may recall, upon seeing the
St. Georges leave Summersoft in a fine closed carriage, reflects that "they were an honourable image of success, of the
material rewards and the social credit of literature" (III; 44).
Later on, during his second nocturnal talk with the Master in
his study, he again emphasizes this "honourable" nature of St.
George's "full human life": "I see you in a beautiful fortunate
home, living in comfort and honour." But the Master immediately challenges this: "Do you call it honour?"—his host
took him up with an intonation that often comes back to him.
"That's what I want *you* to go in for. I mean the real thing.
This is brummagem" (V; 68). From the Master's point of
view there is no honor in such compromise. On the contrary,
he directs the young writer's attention to the spectacle of

himself—"a man meant for better things sunk at his age in such dishonour" (III; 36).[23]

Having exposed himself with infinite self-irony, the Master changes his tactics of persuasion and says: "And if your idea's to do nothing better [than I have done] there's no reason why you shouldn't have as many good things as I—as many human and material appendages, as many sons or daughters, a wife with as many gowns, a house with as many servants, a stable with as many horses, a heart with as many aches . . . there's no reason why you shouldn't make a goodish income—if you set about it the right way. Study me for that —study me well. You may really have horses" (V; 73).

The Master is evidently using all the resources of rhetoric to drive his point home. His derisive self-contempt is fully conveyed in the style of the passage: for instance, in his "chaotic enumeration"[24] of all the "human and material appendages," in which sons, daughters, servants, wife's gowns, and horses are lumped together with deliberate indiscrimination, with a heavy emphasis on the sheer quantity of these appendages, including the heartaches. The final ironic thrust "Study me for that—study me well. You may really have horses" is perhaps particularly significant, for, we may recall, it was the closed carriage in which the St. Georges left Summersoft which epitomized for the young destitute writer all the social amenities that contributed to the "honourable image" of the successful artist.

Up to this point I have dealt with those aspects of the tale which accord with the initial *Notebooks* conception. How-

23. The motif of the honor of artistic dedication is stated also in *The Figure in the Carpet,* another of James' literary tales, in which the critic-narrator says: "For the few persons at any rate, abnormal or not, with whom my anecdote is concerned, literature was a game of skill, and skill meant courage, and courage meant honour, and honour meant passion, meant life" (*The Figure in the Carpet,* VI; 250).

24. The expression "chaotic enumeration" was coined by L. Spitzer to characterize Walt Whitman's method of cataloguing. See his *"Explication de Texte* applied to Walt Whitman's poem 'Out of the Cradle Endlessly Rocking,' " *English Literary History, 16* (1949), 237.

ever, James in the finished tale has added certain details
which make the situation highly ambiguous. He deliberately
complicates the Master's motives by showing him as unmistakably making up to the very same woman he urges the
young writer to give up. Paul Overt accepts the Master's advice and leaves England for two years, in the course of which
he writes something highly promising and, he feels, even
better than *Ginistrella*. When he returns to England, he
learns that the Master's wife has died and that *he* is going
to marry Miss Fancourt, although he had at the time assured
his disciple that he had "given her up."

On meeting him, he cannot help noticing how well the
Master looks—everything in him "denoting the happy human being" (VI; 91). Now a terrible suspicion assails him,
the suspicion that he might have been diabolically "sold" (he
wonders twice whether the Master isn't "a mocking fiend"),
that the whole thing was planned in advance by St. George in
order to get him out of the way, and that his deference, love,
and credulity were most cynically taken advantage of (a betrayal on its more modest scale, and with a comic-ironic
rather than a tragic emphasis, matching that of Kate Croy in
The Wings of the Dove). To Paul Overt's question as to why
he had told him at the time that he had given up Miss Fancourt to his younger colleague, the Master answers that that
was before he had read *Ginistrella*, which convinced him that
the young man must dedicate himself to art. He reaffirms his
good faith, protesting that he couldn't possibly know at the
time of their nocturnal colloquy that his wife would soon die;
and to his disciple's question why he didn't at least warn him
that he was going to marry Miss Fancourt, the Master again
insists that he wished to "save" his disciple from marriage.
These protestations, however, do not alleviate Paul Overt's
suspicions; and the situation is in fact perfectly ambiguous,
seeming to allow of two perfectly consistent possibilities.
Either the Master was perfectly sincere in his passionate plea
for renunciation, advising the young writer out of the depths
of his own frustration, or he was a fraud and a humbug, only

pretending to be sincere and using all his eloquence to confuse and mystify the young man for his own purposes. The ambiguity is perhaps best expressed by the question: What *was* the (real) lesson of the Master? Thus the tale's title, too, takes on a highly ambiguous air.

The ambiguity, however, signifies something more. The young writer is suddenly not at all certain whether the Master who has lived "the full rich masculine human general life," who has renounced nothing and achieved personal happiness, might not yet recover his artistic powers and produce another masterpiece. In other words, if the Master had been self-interested rather than sincere, then perhaps he misled his disciple about the most important thing—the true way to achieve artistic perfection. Perhaps the loneliness, the monastic life, the austere self-discipline the Master had preached were not the *conditio sine qua non* of great art. This, it now transpires, is the most terrible doubt which torments Paul Overt. What it means is that his inability to decide whether the Master was sincere dramatizes on the plot level the artist's greatest predicament—namely, the difficulty of being absolutely sure not only of whether it is indeed worthwhile to renounce human felicity in order to achieve artistic perfection but, more important still, whether such a renunciation is indeed the way to achieve artistic perfection.[25] It may be noted that this most harrowing of doubts, which makes the artist's choice so much more difficult, does not torment either Nick Dormer or Miriam Rooth in *The Tragic Muse.*

The foregoing analysis has shown that in *The Lesson of the Master* the observer has become no less important for the dramatization of the art theme than the Master himself; and it is perhaps not without significance that whereas the ob-

25. Similarly, in *The Figure in the Carpet* the unsolved mystery of the figure in Hugh Vereker's carpet and the uncertainty whether George Corvick has indeed solved it dramatize the critic's predicament—namely, the impossibility fully to reproduce, in critical-analytical terms, the living concreteness of the artist's work.

servers in the other literary tales are critics, reviewers, or mere sensitive admirers, the observer in *The Lesson of the Master* is himself a distinguished writer. In this story St. George and Paul Overt each dramatizes one horn of the artist's dilemma; but it is in the last analysis the observer rather than the initial *Notebooks* artist-hero who supremely embodies the dilemma. This shift of emphasis from the central character to the observer is reflected on the plot level in the fact that this time it is not the observer who interferes with the principal character he observes in order to save him; it is rather the observed who interferes with the observer in order to save *him*.

As in many other works in which the observer is a dramatized consciousness rather than a first-person narrator, the authorial narrator's ironic voice, which is quite distinct from that of the observer himself, is heard in the closing passage, in which the situation is summed up and suitably distanced:

> His [Paul Overt's] late adviser's words were still in his ears—"You're very strong, wonderfully strong." Was he really? Certainly he would have to be, and it might a little serve for revenge. *Is* he? the reader may ask in turn, if his interest has followed the perplexed young man so far. The best answer to that perhaps is that he's doing his best, but that it's too soon to say. When the new book came out in the summer Mr. and Mrs. St. George found it really magnificent. The former still has published nothing, but Paul doesn't even yet feel safe. I may say for him, however, that if this event were to occur he would really be the very first to appreciate it: which is perhaps a proof that the Master was essentially right and that Nature had dedicated him to intellectual, not to personal passion. (VI; 96)

Although the authorial narrator does not dot his *i's* and although nothing he says resolves the ambiguity of the situation, which remains naggingly inconclusive (it is too soon to say whether Paul Overt has done his best, and there is no assurance that the Master may not recover his powers), he does seem to affirm the validity of the harsh doctrine of renunciation which, we know, James himself both preached and practiced. In *The Lesson of Balzac,* written thirteen years after *The Lesson of the Master,* James says: "Nothing counts, of course, in art, but the excellent! nothing exists, however briefly, for estimation, for appreciation, but the superlative —always in its kind."[26] And Simon Nowell-Smith in *The Legend of the Master* recounts James' advice to a young colleague:

> "My young friend," he said, "and I call you young—you are disgustingly and, if I may be allowed to say so, nauseatingly young—there is one thing that, if you really intend to follow the course you indicate, I cannot too emphatically insist on. There is one word—let me impress upon you—which you must inscribe upon your banner, and that," he added after an impressive pause, "that word is *loneliness.*"[27]

It seems therefore that on this supremely important point the reader is not meant fully to share the doubts of James' "perplexed young man" (who throughout the tale is designated with ironic familiarity as "our young man"). If the writer-observer is presented at the very end of the tale as terribly "nervous," uncertain, and tormented, the reader on his side is not supposed completely to identify himself with him but rather, sharing in this matter the authorial narrator's more omniscient viewpoint, to entertain the greatest hopes for Paul Overt. In this respect *The Lesson of the Master* may be seen as a fine example of James' capacity for transmuting his personal beliefs into a perfectly objectified literary form, and of his gift for presenting even his most cherished views in the least dogmatic, most amusing manner.

26. *The House of Fiction,* p. 79.
27. *The Legend of the Master,* comp. S. Nowell-Smith (London, 1947), p. 126.

As in *The Aspern Papers,* the effect of the dénouement of *The Lesson of the* Master is that of an open ending. I have tried to explain the thematic significance of the unresolved ambiguity in *The Lesson of the Master*. However, the inconclusiveness of James' endings, which helps to project the thematic ambiguity in such works as *The Aspern Papers, The Figure in the Carpet, The Lesson of the Master,* and *The Sacred Fount,* is present also in *The Portrait of a Lady* and *The Tragic Muse,* in which it has no such significance. Thus in *The Portrait of a Lady* we learn that Isabel Archer returns to Rome, but we are not explicitly told why and to what. Similarly, in *The Tragic Muse* we learn that Nick Dormer has indeed given up the political life for the artistic, but we are left in doubt as to whether his painting of Julia Dallow is a sign that he will be reunited with her and will become the fashionable success that Gabriel Nash predicted.

Since James' works are never naturalistic slices of life but, rather, dramatizations of very definite ideas, the reader may well demand an explanation of James' undeniable predilection for the open, inconclusive ending. There are, it seems to me, several reasons which may account for this predilection. First (and this is a point I shall discuss more fully in Chapter 8, on *The Sacred Fount*), because James virtually dispenses with the omniscient-author convention, it is inevitable that as soon as we leave the hero or heroine whose consciousness is dramatized, we should be debarred from any further information about them—information traditionally transmitted to us in the epilogue or conclusion by the omniscient author, who tidily gathers all the loose strands of the story. In fact, as I have tried to show, whenever James does resort to this traditional technique, as in *Lady Barbarina* or *The Author of "Beltraffio"* (in which the older, more mature narrator fulfills the author's function), it is invariably for ironic purposes. Second, such a tidying-up would in any case surely have seemed to James too arranged, too unsubtle, too much lacking in respect for the sensitive, intelligent reader for whom he was writing. Third, James wrote in the Preface to *Roderick Hudson:*

Really, universally, relations stop nowhere, and the exquisite problem of the artist is eternally but to draw, by a
geometry of his own, the circle within which they shall
happily *appear* to do so. He is in the perpetual predicament that the continuity of things is the whole matter,
for him, of comedy and tragedy; that this continuity is
never, by the space of an instant or an inch, broken, and
that, to do anything at all, he has at once intensely to
consult and intensely to ignore it.[28]

In the light of this, it may be argued that James' use of the
inconclusive ending was precisely his way of at once intensely
consulting and ignoring this continuity.[29]

28. Preface to *Roderick Hudson*, New York, *1*, p. vii.

29. It should be added in this connection that Viola Hopkins, who explores, in her illuminating article "Visual Art Devices and Parallels in
the Fiction of Henry James" (*PMLA*, *76*, 572–74), certain parallelisms
between James' literary style and various pictorial styles by which he was
influenced, sees the Jamesian open ending as characteristic of the Man-
nerist style, of which, she persuasively argues, James' late works are
examples.

CHAPTER 8

THE SACRED FOUNT

Having dispensed with the omniscient-author convention, James turns the observer into the drama's guiding intelligence. However, unlike the all-wise, all-knowing authorial narrator, whose vantage point transcends the fictional universe of the story, the observer is a character existing within this universe. His moral and epistemological perspectives are therefore necessarily more limited; and as a consequence of these limitations, the observer cannot simply adopt the superior explanatory tone of the authorial guide. His diverse authorial activites—the registering of impressions, projection of the drama, psychological and moral analysis, philosophical generalization—must be exhibited as the fruit of a long, complex, groping process of speculation and evaluation. In other words, the observer's interpretative commentary must be justified by being shown in the making.

The Jamesian observer, we recall, is meant to serve as a highly lucid reflector of the case he registers or, to use another Jamesian phrase, as "the most polished of possible mirrors of the subject."[1] Consequently, the subtler and more sophisticated the protagonist, and the greater the depths and complexity of his case, the greater the ingenuity the observer has to exercise in order to fulfill his role and extract from the case he analyzes its maximum of sense.[2]

---

1. Preface to *The Princess Casamassima*, p. xv.

2. F. Stanzel has placed the excessively interpretative Jamesian observer, who reflects complex mental experiences, at the opposite extreme of the turbid, sense-bound "camera-eye" in Christopher J. Sherwood's *Goodbye to Berlin* and Robbe-Grillet's *Le Voyeur*, in which a slice of

Although merely a compositional resource whose role is purely functional, the observer is interestingly the only Jamesian character who is seen from within and whose thought processes the reader is invited to watch. This means that even when his analytical activity is strictly determined by the logic of the case he registers, it cannot but become, to some extent at least, the story's second center of interest. Naturally, the more exacting and complex the observer's task, the more does the reader's interest focus on the quality of his mind, struggles, methods, and dilemmas. Pursued by James to its furthest logical limits, this process reaches its culmination in *The Sacred Fount*,[3] in which analysis turns from a subsidiary, merely instrumental activity into the story's thematic center, and the emphasis shifts from the "nominal" protagonists to their observer, who becomes "a *usurping* consciousness."[4] Furthermore, what throws the observer in *The Sacred Fount* into dramatic prominence and makes him a character of great intellectual and moral vividness is not his deviation from his analytical role but rather his fulfillment of it with the utmost zeal and devotion.

The narrating observer in *The Sacred Fount* goes to Newmarch, a country house in which he is to spend a weekend. On his way he meets Grace Brissenden and Gilbert Long, who are also going to Newmarch. He is much struck by Mrs. Brissenden's remarkably youthful appearance and by Long's remarkable growth of intelligence and newly acquired "gift of talk." These two vivid impressions provide the primary data for the sacred-fount theory which the speculative narrator eagerly begins to elaborate. According to this theory, an uncanny process of spiritual vampirism is involved in intimate love-relationships; one party constantly drains the other of

---

life is transmitted through a passive recording medium without any apparent selection, arrangement, or explanation. See F. Stanzel, *Typische Formen der Romans* (Göttingen, 1964), pp. 44–46.

3. Grove Press, New York, 1953.
4. Preface to *The Tragic Muse*, p. vii.

his inner resources or life force, and while he thrives and grows younger or cleverer, the other party inevitably grows older or stupider. The narrator attributes the rejuvenation of the plain, middle-aged Mrs. Briss to Guy Brissenden, her husband, who is not yet thirty but has come to look "quite sixty." To prove the universal applicability of his theory, however, the narrator must find the intellectually depleted woman who will, in the same way, account for Long's cleverness. While searching for "the right fool," he is much struck by the lovely May Server, another fellow guest at Newmarch, who is, he perceives, "as nervous as a cat," "all over the place," and constantly "on the rush" and "on the pounce" (V; 75). The narrator infers that May is Long's "victim" and interprets her fretful and wild flirtations as attempts to hide her pitiably "reduced state."

The two cases of spiritual vampirism are not of course identical in every respect. While in the first case the victim is depleted of physical energy and in the second of intellectual energy, the vampire, or "sacrificer," is in the first case the man, in the second the woman, and the relationship is in the first case between a husband and a wife, in the second between a pair of unmarried lovers. By introducing these variations, James not only avoids tedious repetition but also emphasizes the universality of the narrator's "law"; and it is by virtue of these very differences that the two cases function in the story as fair samples of spiritual vampirism.

Yet *The Sacred Fount,* despite its title, is not primarily a study of the phenomenon of spiritual vampirism.[5] The point is easily established by a comparison of James' handling of

5. Critics who believe that *The Sacred Fount* is the story of spiritual vampirism are bound to find it very unsatisfactory. J. W. Beach in *The Method of Henry James* (Philadelphia, 1954), p. 251, writes: "It is an extremely interesting idea from which he [James] takes his start, and one that no doubt corresponds to something profoundly true in human nature,—the idea that, between man and woman, one party to the relation is liable to pay for the happiness, the vitality, the efflorescence, of the other. . . . But true and serious as was his subject-matter, James seems for once to have but superficially conceived its possibilities."

the same theme in his two early Hawthornesque romances *De Grey-Romance* and *Longstaff's Marriage*[6] with his handling of it in *The Sacred Fount*. In the two early romances the relationship between the vampire and his victim is fully explored and developed till it comes to a head in a grim, final calamity. In *The Sacred Fount*, on the other hand, the relationship between Grace and her husband and between Long and May Server, once posited, is not further developed and never reaches an ultimate critical point. Moreover, James' evocation of psychological horror and of the sense of the ineluctibility of the dreadful law which governs the protagonists' lives is, although vivid, overshadowed by and suborinated to the epistemological question of how, conclusively, to prove its very existence. In fact, like *The Figure in the Carpet*, *The Sacred Fount* is primarily the narrator's quest-story; but unlike his predecessor, the narrator in *The Sacred Fount* has already discovered the figure in the carpet; and his is accordingly a quest not for the figure itself but for conclusive confirmation of the truth of what he has discovered. Another difference between the two quest-stories sheds additional light on the nature of the central theme of *The Sacred Fount*. The narrator in *The Figure in the Carpet* has to puzzle out a literary mystery, and his quest consists therefore of reading and rereading the works of Hugh Vereker. The narrator in *The Sacred Fount*, on the other hand, has to solve a mystery of personal relationships, and this, in turn, means that his quest consists not in any esoteric activity but in simply fulfilling the normal role of a Jamesian observer. In sum, it is best to view *The Sacred Fount* as a dramatization of *all* the characteristic and congenital problems of the Jamesian observer.[7]

6. Leon Edel has discussed James' treatment of the vampire theme in these early romances, in his Introduction to the Grove Press edition of *The Sacred Fount*, pp. xxviii–ix.

7. There are, of course, other interpretations of the central theme of *The Sacred Fount*, which is undoubtedly one of the most difficult of James' works. The variety of opinions is bewildering indeed. R. West

James deals primarily with the supreme difficulty which
any Jamesian observer is bound to some extent to face—
namely, the uncertainty as to whether he has discovered the
truth or merely succumbed to the temptation, characteristic
of a highly imaginative and speculative nature, of discovering
a meaningful pattern where there exists only the senseless
confusion of "clumsy life at her stupid work."[8] This difficulty
is shown to be an inescapable consequence of the observer's
function and position within the narrative framework. His
authorial role as the story's guiding intelligence requires that
he possess great interpretative skill, but the limitations inherent in his position inevitably makes his insights uncertain
and creates the danger of his reading too much into the
situation he is confronted with. This danger, implicit in the
interpretative activities of all the Jamesian observers, be-

in *Henry James* (London, 1916) and F. W. Dupee in *Henry James* (New
York, 1956) find the narrator's search both perverse and ridiculous. Edel
in his introductory essay to the Grove Press edition of *The Sacred Fount*,
Krook in *The Ordeal of Consciousness in Henry James*, and R. A. Ranald
in *"The Sacred Fount:* James' Portrait of an Artist Manqué," *Nineteenth-
Century Fiction, 15* (December 1960), 239–48, maintain, on the other hand,
that the search is highly significant and represents the drama of the
creative mind. R. P. Blackmur in "The Sacred Fount," *Kenyon Review,
4* (Autumn 1942), 328–52, suggests that the narrator is the hidden consciousness of the other guests; while J. K. Folsom in "Archimago's Well:
An Interpretation of *The Sacred Fount,*" *Modern Fiction Studies, 7*
(Summer 1961), 136–45, argues that he is the real vampire of the piece.
W. Follett in "The Simplicity of Henry James," *American Review, 1*
(May–June 1923), 315–25, suggests that *The Sacred Fount* is a self-parody
in which James is deliberately turning a searchlight on Henry James;
whereas R. Perlongo in *"The Sacred Fount:* Labyrinth or Parable,"
Kenyon Review, 22 (Autumn 1960), 635–48, believes that the narrator is
a modern tragic hero. Finally, P. Tyler in *"The Sacred Fount:* 'The Ac-
tuality Pretentious and Vain' *v.s.* 'The Case Rich and Edifying,' " *Modern Fiction Studies* (Summer 1963), pp. 127–38, suggests that the narrator's relation to Mrs. Briss records James' own type of experience with
élite readers (such as Mrs. Humphrey Ward and Edith Wharton), who
misunderstood the works of his late phase.

   8. Preface to *The Spoils of Poynton,* New York, *10,* v–vi.

comes the central thematic preoccupation of *The Sacred Fount*.

The narrator in *The Sacred Fount* is the quintessential Jamesian observer. To begin with, he is not only extraordinarily interested in his fellow creatures (VIII; 147)—an interest without which none of the Jamesian observers would be able to fulfill his interpretative role as a guiding intelligence—but is, in addition, acutely aware of the fact that the depth and intensity of his interest are unparalleled by anyone else: "I have more [of this extraordinary interest] than most men. I've never really seen anyone with half so much. That breeds observation and observation breeds ideas" (VIII; 147).

In the course of his intense, incessant observational and interpretative activities the narrator displays all the generic traits of the Jamesian observer on a lavish scale and in dazzling style: quickness of mind, ingenuity, subtlety, sophistication, a high lucidity, a sharp wit, an ironical sense of humor, extreme sensitivity, and obsessive scrupulosity. Moreover, he fulfills all the interpretative functions of the various types of Jamesian observer—the objective witness-narrator, the subsidiary choric commentator, and the center through whose consciousness the story is filtered. He registers impressions, serves as a source of information, contributes the element of intelligent sympathy, diagnoses the situation, predicts its outcome, distills its essence, and reflects upon it; in other words, he serves as a vehicle of observation, speculation, analysis, appreciation, and criticism.

The fact that the narrator in *The Sacred Fount* is by far the most daringly speculative, most ingenious, and wittiest of all Jamesian observers of course intensifies the danger of his having distorted reality by reading too much into it. James concentrates on this epistemological predicament to the virtual exclusion of any other interest, deliberately purifying *The Sacred Fount* of any extrinsic elements. The chief of these is the element of emotional involvement on the part of the narrator, which is minimal here. Longmore in *Madame de Mauves,* Ralph Touchett in *The Portrait of a Lady,* Lyon

in *The Liar,* and Strether in *The Ambassadors* are all at
least half in love with the women whose sad fortunes they
observe, a sentiment which accounts for their desire to save
the heroines from their plight. The narrator in *The Sacred
Fount,* however, manifests no very strong desire to rescue
the victims of spiritual vampirism, and his passion, which is
purely intellectual, is strictly confined to his analytical activity. Grace Brissenden does suggest on one occasion that
he tries to protect May Server because he is in love with
her, but it is made clear that the narrator only pities her
("the real fact was, none the less, that I was quite too sorry
for her to be anything except sorry" [VI; 95]); his compassion both for her and for Guy Brissenden is genuine indeed,
but it is an emotion which exactly fits and does not exceed
their role as victims in the scheme of his theory; in short,
his emotional response is merely the right subjective correlative of the state of affairs which he believes exists. Undeniably, the narrator does seem sorrier for May than for
Guy Brissenden (he is "far gone in pity of her," feels "tenderly compassionate" toward her, and finds her expression
"heart-rending"); but again this is because hers is objectively
"the harder case." First, unlike Guy Brissenden, who is
married, May has to conceal her illicit relationship with her
vampire lover; and second, the narrator is convinced that
the state of being intellectually depleted (in particular in
Newmarch, which is "the great asylum of the finer wit") is
much worse than that of being physically depleted:

> Guy Brissenden had, at the worst, his compromised face
> and figure to show and to shroud—if he were really,
> that is, as much aware of them as one had suspected.
> She [May] had her whole compromised machinery of
> thought and speech, and if these signs were not, like
> his [Guy's], external, that made her case but the harder,
> for she had to create, with intelligence rapidly ebbing,
> with wit half gone, the illusion of an unimpaired estate.
> (VI; 96–97)

As a means of dramatizing the observer's inability to decide whether his interpretations are or are not in excess of the facts, James creates with great skill a perfectly ambiguous situation (a device he has already exploited for different thematic purposes in *The Lesson of the Master* and *The Figure in the Carpet),* in which every piece of evidence is double-edged and there is no way of determining whether it is the reality or the appearance, the face or the mask, truth or delusion. Moreover, in order to make the reader experience this epistemological uncertainty as a real, inescapable difficulty and not merely as a result of the narrator's intellectual myopia or, as in *The Liar,* of a lapse in imaginative perception due to excessive emotional involvement, James is careful not to make the reader superior in knowledge to the narrator. The reader never experiences dramatic irony; the situation always seems to him as puzzling and as ambiguous as it does to the narrator, and the ironies which work against the narrator are worked as fully against him. Moreover, *The Sacred Fount* consists (like *The Awkward Age* written two years earlier) of large stretches of dialogue, the dramatic objectivity of which reinforces the effect of ambiguity.

James created the effect of ambiguity by various means. To begin with, it appears on closer inspection that the narrator has not simply been struck by the initial "facts" on which the sacred-fount theory is based, but that they have been, each time, pointed out to him by other people: Mrs. Briss' miraculous rejuvenation has been pointed out to the narrator by Long, who made much of the so-called discrepancy between her youthful looks and her actual age; Long's remarkable growth of intelligence has been pointed out to the narrator by Mrs. Briss; and May Server's "nervousness" has been suggested to the narrator by Ford Obert, who insisted that May was conspicuously different from what she had been when she had sat for her portrait the previous year. This, of course, casts a doubt even on the bare factuality of these "facts." As for the theory to which they give rise, it is deliberately so contrived as to be absolutely unverifiable. The narrator, who is on the look out for what he calls significant "relations," "conjunctions," "combina· tions," and "juxtapositions," continually watches the social activities of the guests at Newmarch. But what he observes (or seems to observe) is always maddeningly inconclusive, for practically every relation lends itself to two equally plausible interpretations, and may be either the "real thing" or a red herring, either a "significant relation" or a mere "screen."

The unverifiability of the narrator's theory, which makes his intellectual task both impossible and Quixotic, is partly the product of the social milieu in which he moves. Thus in the brilliant, sophisticated, society of Newmarch it is un-likely indeed that anyone will ever give himself away un-awares, and it is clear that only ambiguous and hence unsatis-factory "proofs" are to be expected where self-control is a highly valued virtue and where the cultivation of a smooth surface has become an integral part of the social mores. In fact, the highly lucid narrator is fully conscious of the nature of the society of Newmarch and loses himself in admiration for *"the beauty and the terror* of conditions so highly or-ganized that under their rule her [May's] small lonely fight with disintegration could go on without the betrayal of a gasp or a shriek" (IX; 167; my italics). However, the am-biguous nature of the proofs has its source in the investi-gating subject as well as in the investigated object and is partly due to self-imposed restrictions. Owing to the high-minded view the narrator takes of the intellectual enquiry he is conducting, the range of evidence he is willing to accept is restricted to what his suspects choose to reveal and to his methods of discovery and speculation upon it. The idea of the search as an intellectual game of skill, enjoyable only to the extent that it is played according to the rules, whose diffi-culties merely contribute to the intensity of the amusement it yields, is dominant in *The Sacred Fount*. On one occasion the narrator explicitly characterizes his activity as "the high sport of intelligence" (IX; 164). In his talk with Ford Obert, the painter, it is made perfectly clear that not only will he not use "the detective and the keyhole" (in the manner of the narrators in *The Aspern Papers* and in *The Private Life*) but that a material clue would actually spoil everything for him. He desires not simply to arrive at the truth but to arrive at it in the right way, and in this respect he resembles George Corvick in *The Figure in the Carpet,* who refuses to ask for another tip from Vereker in order not to spoil "the delight and the honour of the chase," and because he wants "to bring down the animal with his own rifle" (V; 245):[9]

> "We ought to remember," I pursued, even at the risk of showing as too sententious, "that success in such an inquiry may perhaps be more embarrassing than failure. To nose about for a relation that a lady has her reasons for keeping secret—"
>
> "Is made not only quite inoffensive, I hold"—he immediately took me up—"but positively honourable, by being confined to psychologic evidence."
>
> I wondered a little. "Honourable to whom?"
>
> "Why, to the investigator. Resting on the *kind* of signs that the game takes account of when fairly played —resting on psychologic signs alone, it's a high application of intelligence. What's ignoble is the detective and the keyhole."
>
> "I see," I after a moment admitted. "I did have, last night, my scruples, but you warm me up. Yet I confess also," I still added, "that if I do muster the courage of my curiosity,[10] its a little because I feel even yet, as I think you also must, altogether destitute of a material clue. *If I had a material clue, I should feel ashamed; the fact would be deterrent*" (IV; 65–66; my italics).

The impasse to which the observer has come is therefore due

9. New York, *15.*

10. The phrase occurs in *The Aspern Papers,* in which Mrs. Prest says to the narrator: "Certainly you've the courage of your curiosity" (I; 13).

to a large extent to his preoccupation with method—the kind of method which by its nature combines intellectual, aesthetic, and moral scrupulousness.

The relevant critical questions to be asked at this point are: What is the narrator's attitude toward his theory? Is he aware of the ambiguous nature of his proofs, or does he mistakenly suppose that he had, in fact, conclusively proved his theory? Is his analytical fury a form of madness or does he preserve his sense of reality? Some critics (for instance, Oscar Cargill) cut the Gordian knot and brand the narrator as mad and utterly deluded on the ground that, regardless of the nature of his "proofs," his sacred-fount theory is too whimsical and fantastic to be the product of a sane imagination. It seems to me, however, that such a view of the theory of spiritual vampirism is due simply to the critics' failure to take into account that, like Poe and Hawthorne, James, who never committed himself to the premises of naturalism, liked at times to work by means of the unusual, the extravagant, and the supernatural. In *The Sacred Fount* a Jamesian idea—that of spiritual vampirism—has taken the form of an elaborate, semifanciful, almost parable-like conceit (this is made quite explicit in the narrator's reflection: "There was really a touching truth in it, the stuff of—what did people call such things?—an apologue or a parable" [II; 29]); and there is no doubt that James believed it to correspond to something profoundly true in human nature. Once this point is conceded it becomes clear that the sacred fount theory which the narrator entertains should not be viewed as a delusion merely by reason of its fancifulness and supernaturalism. Indeed, the idea of spiritual vampirism had preoccupied James for a long time: it appears twice in his *Notebooks;*[11] it is treated

11. (a) "The notion of the young man who marries an older woman and who has the effect on her of making her younger and still younger, while he himself becomes her age. When he reaches the age that *she* was (on their marriage), she has gone back to the age that *he* was.—Mightn't this be altered (perhaps) to the idea of cleverness and stupidity? . . . The two things—the two elements—beauty and 'mind,' might be corres-

in two of his apprentice works, *De-Grey Romance* (1869) and *Longstaff's Marriage* (1878); and it is elaborated in a psychological vein in *The Bostonians* and *The Ambassadors*.[12]

Apart from this external evidence, there is ample internal evidence to show that James did not wish the reader to believe that the narrator was simply spinning out a "crazy" theory. To begin with, his speculations are not (at first) met with a raising of the eyebrows, nor are they ridiculed by his two confidants, Ford Obert and Mrs. Briss. On the contrary, these two are clearly stimulated and intrigued by his suggestion and are very eager to participate and to contribute both facts and insights. Ford Obert, for example, openly confesses that he is charmed: "It's a jolly idea—a torch in the darkness . . . You've given me an analogy, and I declare I find

---

pondingly, concomitantly exhibited as in the history of two related couples—with the opposition in each case, that would help the thing to be dramatic" *(Notebooks,* pp. 150–51).

(b) "Don't lose sight of the little *concetto* of the note in former vol. that begins with the fancy of the young man who marries an old woman and becomes old while she becomes young. Keep my play on idea: the *liaison* that betrays itself by the *transfer* of qualities—qualities to be determined—from one to the other of the parties to it. They *exchange.* I see 2 couples. One is married—this is the *old-young* pair. I watch *their* process, and it gives me my light for the spectacle of the other (covert, obscure, unavowed) pair who are *not* married" *(Notebooks,* p. 275).

12. The idea of vampirism crops up even in James' personal writings. James writes to his brother William upon the death of Minny Temple, his beloved cousin: "Among the sad reflections that her [Minny's] death provokes for me, there is none sadder than this view of the gradual change and reversal of our relations: I slowly crawling from weakness and inaction and suffering into strength and health and hope: she sinking out of brightness and youth into decline and death" (Quoted in F. O. Matthiessen, *The James Family* [New York, 1947], p. 260). The terms in which James expresses the irony of the fact that he was getting better (recovering from his spinal disorder) while his young and lively cousin was getting worse are strikingly similar to those he uses in his descriptions of the fictional vampire-situation—a fact which betrays his obscure, perhaps unacknowledged sense of guilt at his cousin's untimely death.

it dazzling" (IV; 64). Moreover, he clearly makes use of the narrator's tip: "You gave me the pieces. I've but put them together . . . I've blown on my torch, in other words, till, flaring and smoking, it has guided me, through a magnificent chiaroscuro of colour and shadow, out into the light of day" (XI; 222). (One notices the painter's use of pictorial imagery to express his intellectual detective-work.) In other words, since the other guests at Newmarch are not only appreciative of the narrator's ingenuity but display an ingenuity almost equal to his own, it is clear that his own activity, despite its superior quality, is not meant to appear—at least not in the opening sections of the story—as hopelessly and ridiculously perverse.

The narrator is as ferociously logical as he is imaginative and as boldly speculative as he is observant, and these two aspects of his remarkable intelligence are fully reflected in his narrative style. First, his narrative abounds, to an extent unparalleled in any other Jamesian works (not even the Prefaces and the last novels) in logical and legal phraseology. The narrator discusses his activities in terms of articulate axioms, postulates, fallacies, grounds, inductions, inferences, implications, hypotheses, principles, confirmations, demonstrations, corroborations, attestations, and justifications, as well as in terms of warrants, collations, collateral evidence, and verdicts. The words "logic" and "logically" constantly recur in his narrative, emphasizing the intensely ratiocinative turn of his mind: "in that case the thing we're looking for ought logically to be the person, of the opposite sex, giving us the maximum sense of depletion for his benefit?" (III; 38); "whoever she was [the woman depleted by Long], she must logically have been idiotised" (VIII; 138); "she [May] hadn't a glimmering of the real logic of Brissenden's happy effect on her nerves" (VIII; 145); "I still don't see the logic of her [May's] general importunity" (V; 79); it wasn't for me definitely to image the logical result of a verification by the sense of others of the matter of my vision" (IX; 174). Moreover, apart from his abundant—indeed, obsessive—use of logical terms, the narrator constantly expounds his conjectures in subjunctive conditionals, implications, and disjunctive and hypothetical syllogisms. For instance: "Why, since she [Grace] was bold, should she be susceptible, and how, since she was susceptible, could she be bold?" (XII; 254); "If it was [his old feeling of pity for May] not the result of what I had granted to myself was the matter with her, then it was rather the very cause of my making that concession" (VI; 95); "If she [May] was "nervous" to the tune I had come to recognise, it could only be because she had grounds" (VI; 96).

Second, his style is not only excessively logical but also intensely figurative. Indeed, the imaginative narrator frequently seems to be carried away by the sheer momentum of his own image-making, and the rapid succession of a variety of metaphors, poetic and homely, witty and droll, colloquial and recherché, enables him to convey with poignant vividness the mystery and the complexity of the case he is investigating. For example, James' image for the vampire relationship is the poetic "sacred fount," but he is perfectly capable of rendering it also in the homely, humorous image of the turkey: "But the sacred fount is like the greedy man's description of the turkey as an 'awkward' dinner dish. It may be sometimes too much for a single share, but it's not enough to go round" (II; 29). The metaphors used to convey his impression of May Server's predicament are equally rich and varied:

> She reminded me of a sponge wrung dry and with fine pores agape. Voided and scraped of everything, her shell was merely crushable.

> She was the absolute wreck of her storm, accordingly, but to which the pale ghost of a special sensibility still clung, waving from the mast, with a bravery that went to the heart, the last tatter of its flag.

> To take up again the vivid analogy [the narrator is shown

to be fully conscious of his use of recurrent imagery],
she had been sailing all day, though scarce able to keep
afloat, under the flag of her old reputation for easy response.

What made the difference with *me*—if any difference had
remained to be made—was the sense of this sharp cessa-
tion of her public extravagance. She had folded up her
manner in her flounced parasol, which she seemed to
drag after her as a sorry soldier his musket.

This [the oddest thing which occurred] was neither more
nor less than the revival of her [May Server's] terrible
little fixed smile. It came back as if with an audible click
—as a gas-burner makes a pop when you light it. (VIII;
136, 137, 139, 131, 148)

In spite of the frequency, variety, and brilliance of the narrator's "tropes and figures" (XIII; 285), they do not create an
effect of concrete sensuousness. Rather, the overwhelmingly
rapid succession of metaphors, drawn from the most hetero-
geneous sources and evoked by every fleeting impression,
seem to be another expression of intellectual virtuosity and
reinforce rather than diminish the dominant effect of the
rarified abstractness, tenuousness, preciosity, and excessive
intellectuality of the narrative—an effect which is admirably
appropriate to the treatment of the epistemological theme.

The narrator takes the highest view of his analysis, which
he considers not only as "a high sport" but also as an artistic
activity. Thus he tells Ford Obert, who has praised his insight
into the relationship between Grace and her husband: "I only
talk . . . as you paint; not a bit worse!" (II; 30); (one is reminded of James' conception of the writer as "the painter of
life"). On another occasion, when the narrator reviews during
a Chopin concert the four terms of his equation, he cannot
help conceiving of himself as a virtuoso in his own line: "and
so it was that, while our pianist played, my wandering vision

played and played as well" (X; 169); and again when particularly pleased with the outcome of his speculations, the
narrator confesses: "I positively found myself overtaken by
a mild artistic glow" (VI, 104).

In fact, not only does the narrator treat his analytical
activity as a creative art of the highest order, he also exults
in his intellectual superiority over all the other uninitiated
guests. Thus, in describing his impression of Long's newly
acquired cleverness, he positively affirms his "supernatural
acuteness." When he perceives that Lady John has no inkling
of what he is talking about, he unashamedly confesses:

> It's a matter as to which the truth sounds priggish, but
> I can't help it if—yes, positively—it affected me as hope-
> lessly vulgar, to have made any induction at all about
> our companions [May and Guy Brissenden] but those I
> have recorded, in such detail, on behalf of my own
> energy. It was better verily not to have touched them
> —which was the case of everyone else—than to have
> taken them up, with knowing gestures, only to do so
> so little with them. (IX; 185)

These frequent congratulations which the narrator be-
stows upon his own ingenuity are the expression not only of
a boundless intellectual arrogance but also of imaginative
zest and exuberance, intellectual high-spirits, and sheer delight in the brilliance, boldness, and beauty of his "prodigious" insights and inferences. In fact, the humorously exaggerated self-praise and the use of so many superlatives to
characterize one's own achievements are strongly reminiscent
of James' own style in the Prefaces, and it is in this respect
that *The Sacred Fount* may well be called "a [Jamesian]
critical Preface in action."[13] (In this connection it is interesting to note that in the *Notebooks* entry to *The Sacred
Fount* James refers to the narrator who is to be the author
of the sacred fount theory as "I": "I watch *their* [the old-
young couple's] process, and it gives me my light for the

13. N. Lebowitz, *The Imagination of Loving* (Detroit, 1965), p. 78.

spectacle of the other [overt, obscure, unavowed] pair who are not married." [*Notebooks,* 275]) If this analysis is correct and the narrator's style is indeed a faithful reproduction of the author's own stylistic idiosyncrasies, it surely refutes Wilson Follett's view that *The Sacred Fount* is "a stupendous self-parody," "James's lampoon on his own fictional methods."[14] Further, it is, in a sense, a faithful, nonparodic projection of James himself. The intense intellectual passion which possesses the narrator informs his narrative style down to the minutiae of verbal idiosyncrasy. The frequent coupling of an emotionally charged adjective with an abstract logical noun which it qualifies is one instance: he talks of "a *haunting* principle," "an *immense* confirmation," "a *dreadful* [or *ferocious*] logic," "a *frenzied* fallacy." When the intellectual passion rises to a high pitch, the narrator (again, not unlike the James of the Prefaces) describes these moments of intensity in the language of mystical ecstasy. Thus, on beginning to perceive the sacred-fount pattern, he feels a "mystic throb" (VIII; 127), and later experiences "an undiluted bliss, in the intensity of consciousness that I had reached" (IX; 177). With Lady John he feels "a rare intellectual joy, the oddest secret exultation, in feeling her begin instantly to play the part I had attributed to her in the irreducible drama" (VI; 102). And on still another occasion he recalls "the joy of intellectual mastery of things unnameable, that joy of determining, almost creating results, which I have already mentioned as an exhilaration attached to some of my plunges of insight" (XI; 214), and rejoices in "the intensity of amusement I had at last enabled my private madness to yield me" (IX; 162). The narrator is clearly afflicted with what might be called "divine madness," which is admirably reflected in the story's narrative technique. Thus *The Sacred Fount* concentrates on the narrator's analysis, conducted in the form either of inner reflections or of a discussion with other fellow guests, to the exclusion of everything else. There is never

14. W. Follett, "Henry James's Portrait of Henry James," *New York Times Book Review* (August 23, 1936), p. 16.

any change of either scene or subject, only a maddening persistence in this single line and direction, powerfully reflecting the obsessive character of the narrator's activity. This is reinforced by the highly conversational narrative idiom, so different from that of "the tales of the literary life," which creates the further effect of an interminable, obsessive garrulity on the narrator's part.

The narrator's divine madness is, however, to be distinguished from insanity in the sense of a loss of a sense of reality. The fact is that the narrator's skepticism and self-doubt are no less intense than his hubristic exaltation, and his self-criticism no less acute than his self-congratulation. (In this respect, too, he differs from the self-deceived narrator in *The Aspern Papers.*) The narrator is perfectly aware of the dangers to his sanity of his speculative excesses and of their obsessive character, and what he terms at one point his "private amusement" and his "private triumph" he terms at other times "his private madness." Indeed, he decides at one point to give up his analytical activity and flee from the fascinations of Newmarch—a resolve which he of course fails to carry out: "I remember indeed that on separating from Mrs. Brissenden I took a lively resolve to get rid of my *ridiculous obsession*. It was absurd to have consented to such immersion, intellectually speaking, in the affairs of other people" (VI; 89; my italics). And again: "I *would* go, I was going; if I had not had to accept the interval of the night I should already have gone. . . . It was on my way to the place [Newmarch], in fine, that my obsession had met me, and it was by retracting those steps that I should be able to get rid of it" (X; 201).

Having put the narrator of the story inside its frame as a fictional character, a demand arises for a justification, either implicit or explicit, of his knowledge of the narrated material. Since confession is ruled out, a certain amount of prying on the narrator's part is necessarily required.[15] Normally, the

15. On the various channels of information open to the observer see Friedman, *PMLA*, 70, 1174: "What the witness may legitimately transmit to the reader is not as restricted as may at first appear: he can talk

reader whose interest focuses on the protagonists accepts prying as part of the convention of a first-person narrative. In *The Sacred Fount* the reader's interest shifts from the nominal protagonists to the narrator's interpretative activity. It is therefore hardly surprising that the psychological and moral aspects of prying assume in this work the greatest importance. In exploring the moral aspects of prying, James reechoes in his own manner the predominant Hawthornesque theme—the violation of the sanctity of another's individuality.

The narrator in *The Sacred Fount* clearly perceives the danger to his moral integrity of prying into affairs which are "none of his business" (an expression which constantly recurs in his narrative). In the early flush of his excitement at having discovered "the right fool," he discusses May Server with Grace Brissenden. Later on, however, he realizes to his horror that he has "dreadfully talked about her" and thus "compromised" the poor lady. The repentant narrator instantly decides to "protect" May and save her from "the peril of the public ugliness" (IX; 177) to which she has become exposed by henceforth pretending to Grace that May was not the woman depleted by Long. Thus the Jamesian motif which runs through so many of his works, that of the narrator as savior, acquires a new ironic twist in *The Sacred Fount:* the narrator resolves to save the heroine from a situation into which he himself has plunged her.

But the prying motif is elaborated in an even subtler way. The narrator presently discovers, to his great moral discomfiture, that the mere act of thinking about affairs which are none of his business is a form of prying no less insidious than

---

to the various people within the story and can get their views on matters of concern (notice how carefully Conrad and Fitzgerald have troubled to characterize Marlow and Carraway as men in whom others feel compelled to confide); particularly he can have interviews with the protagonist himself; and finally he can secure letters, diaries, and other writings which may offer glimpses of the mental states of others. At the utmost limit of his tether, he can draw *inferences* as to how others are feeling and what they are thinking."

that of using the detective and the keyhole: "I meddled with them almost more in thinking them over in isolation than in hovering personally about them. Reflection was the real intensity; reflection, as to poor Mrs. Server in particular, was an indiscreet opening of doors" (VI; 89–90). Moreover, the narrator suspects that in having pried he has endangered not only May, the sacrificed, but even Grace Brissenden and Gilbert Long, the sacrificers. He begins to suspect that "the sacrificing couple," hitherto blissfully unconscious of their predatory role, have begun, as a result of his prying, to be aware of it:

> Mrs. Brissenden and Long had been hitherto magnificently without it [consciousness, perception], and I was responsible perhaps for having, in a mood practically much stupider than the stupidest of theirs, put them gratuitously and helplessly *on* it. To be without it was the most consistent, the most successful, because the most amiable, form of selfishness; and why should people admirably equipped for remaining so, people bright and insolent in their prior state, people in whom this state was to have been respected as a surface without a scratch is respected, be made to begin to vibrate, to crack and split, from within. Wasn't it enough for *me* to pay, vicariously, the tax on being absurd? Were we all landed, without an issue or a remedy, in a condition on which that tax would be generally levied? (IX; 184)

The narrator, it transpires, is a man whose deepest impulse is to probe the depths but who is at the same time extremely reluctant to break the surface. He practices "a religion of consciousness" (Matthiessen's expression in *Henry James: The Major Phase*), but is at the same time fully conscious of the price which has to be paid and feels guilty of having infected the innocent vampires with the "disease" of consciousness and thus caused their "fall."

The narrator goes on pursuing his theory with ever greater gusto and refinement. But in default of an objective proof to clinch matters and unequivocally determine the truth or falsity of his theory, he grows more and more eager to secure at least a measure of intersubjective agreement. The significance of his emphasis on the "privacy" of his perceptions ("my private elation," "my private joy," "my private amusement," "my private triumph," and "my private madness") is twofold. On the one hand, it expresses an exultation in his being the only initiated person at Newmarch; on the other, it indicates his dangerous solipsistic position. Ironically, however, his fellow detectives appear to desert him precisely at the moment of his direst need. The impression one may well receive is that, being after all mere amateurs, the fellow guests' interest gradually slackens and finally peters out; feeling that the narrator goes too far and persists too much, their initial (superficial) curiosity at last turns into annoyance. Moreover, not only do they cease to participate in the narrator's game, they even repudiate their earlier contributions to his theory. Thus Long, who had made so much of Mrs. Briss' miraculous rejuvenation, now insists that she is plain and middle-aged; Obert, who had told the narrator that May was different from what she had been a year ago, now says that she is not changed or, rather, that she has "changed back"; and Mrs. Briss, who was so struck with Long's unusual cleverness, now contends that he is nothing but "a prize fool."

Mrs. Briss takes the most radical measures against the narrator during the final showdown between the two (a nocturnal meeting strongly reminiscent of similar occasions in *The Lesson of the Master* and *The Figure in the Carpet*). She attempts to impress upon the narrator that he is totally deluded and that his imaginative activity is a form of madness. She tells him that he is "an intelligent man gone wrong" (XIII; 292), that he likes the "horrors" he perpetrates, and finally, point blank, that he is "crazy," insisting that his only "cure" is to stop, absolutely to stop, exercising his imagination: " 'But isn't the interest of this occasion, as I've already suggested,' she propounded, 'simply that it makes an end, bursts a bubble, rids us of an incubus [here Mrs. Briss intimates that the narrator is himself a vampire] and permits us to go to bed in peace?' " (XIV; 299, 310).

Were Mrs. Briss only the representative of common sense and of what Bertrand Russell has called "a robust sense of reality," she might well be considered to have gained the victory. But Mrs. Briss is, we recall, not only a fellow detective but also a term in the narrator's equation—possibly a vampire thriving upon her husband's physical resources—and, as such, everything she says may easily be construed as an attempt on her part to defend the very source of her astonishing vitality. Her rudeness, brutality, buoyant vulgarity—indeed, the sheer force of her vitality—may be viewed not only as the expression of commonsensical tough-mindedness but, just as plausibly, as the qualities belonging by definition, so to speak, to the "vampire" type.

Mrs. Briss' final tactic is to come out with new "facts." She informs the narrator that his Long-May Server theory is wrong and that she has had it from her husband that Long was having an affair with Lady John and that May Server was all the time making love to him, Guy Brissenden. Had Mrs. Briss not been a term in the narrator's equation, his theory might very well have collapsed under the pressure of these meaningless "conjunctions," which express what James has elsewhere called "the muddle of fact," the sheer brute force of a recalcitrant reality, which is "all inclusion and confusion," as opposed to art which is "all discrimination and selection."[16] But again, Mrs. Briss' final disclosures fit into the self-defense hypothesis as smoothly as all her previous bold moves. Indeed, if the narrator's theory is right, Mrs. Briss' last tactic acquires a still deeper significance. For by cleverly extricating herself and by presenting May, whom she knows the narrator cares about most, as the most "horrid" of the culprits, she sacrifices her all over again (presumably with Long's approval), reenacting, this time consciously, her initially unconscious "sin."

16. Preface to *The Spoils of Poynton,* pp. v–vi.

Viewed in the light of this analysis, the narrator's last cryptic statement does not mean that he confesses he has been beaten. He says: "I *should* certainly never again, on the spot, quite hang together, even though it wasn't really that I hadn't three times her method. What I too fatally lacked was her tone" (XIV; 319). Since Mrs. Briss' behavior is amenable to two consistent and equally plausible interpretations, neither of which is definitive and conclusive, there is surely no good logical reason why he *should* feel himself beaten. In mock-modestly confessing that he "too fatally" lacked Mrs. Briss' "tone," all the narrator admits is that he cannot match her brashness, insolence, and effrontery—of which, it seems, he is not only temperamentally incapable, but which he would clearly scorn to use. The final effect is therefore (as in *The Lesson of the Master, The Aspern Papers,* and *The Figure in the Carpet*) again that of an open ending; the initial ambiguity has not been dispelled, there is no final *éclaircissement,* and the riddle has not been solved. The narrator, caught in his solipsistic trap, is doomed to go on wrestling alone with his epistemological dilemma.

If the account I have given of *The Sacred Fount* is correct, James' decision to omit such a preeminently experimental and technically sophisticated work from the New York Edition calls for an explanation, in particular if one has in mind his remarkable capacity for self-criticism, as well as his interest in problems of technique, which led him to accord the highest praise to, of all his works, *The Awkward Age* and *The Ambassadors.*

Some insight into the reasons for James' rejection of *The Sacred Fount* may be gained from his letter to Howells on December 11, 1909:

> [The Sacred Fount] is one of several things of mine in these last years that have paid the penalty of having been conceived only as the 'short story' that (alone, apparently) I could hope to work off somewhere (which I mainly

failed of) and then *grew* by a rank force of its own into something of which the idea had, modestly, never been to be a book. This is essentially the case with the S.F., planned, like *The Spoils of Poynton, What Maisie Knew, The Turn of the Screw,* and various others, as a story of '8 to 10 thousand words'!! and then having accepted its bookish necessity or destiny in consequence of becoming already, at the start, 20,000, accepted it ruefully and blushingly, moreover, since, *given the tenuity of idea,* the larger quantity of treatment hadn't been aimed at. I remember how I would have chucked the whole thing at the 15th thousand word, if in the first place I could have afforded to 'waste' 15,000, and if in *the second* I were not always ridden by a superstitious terror of not finishing, for finishing's and for the precedent's sake, what I have begun.[17]

James' main criticism of *The Sacred Fount* is, it appears, that its treatment is in excess of its "tenuous" idea. My principal argument has been that the idea of *The Sacred Fount*—the epistemological and moral dilemma of the quintessential observer—constitutes a major Jamesian theme, and that the excessively reflective and lengthy first-person narrative is a perfect reflection of the central character's analytical obsession. It seems to me, therefore, that in branding the idea of *The Sacred Fount* as "tenuous," James is referring to the original idea of spiritual vampirism, which, as his *Notebooks* entry shows, he intended to treat in the semifanciful, supernatural vein of *The Private Life, The Friends of the Friends, The Third Person, Sir Edmund Orme,* and *Maud-Evelyn.* Viewed as belonging to this genre, which developed out of the Romantic tradition of supernaturalism and romance, the emphasis placed on the observer's quest is bound to appear incomprehensible, and the nervous intensity and long-windedness of his narrative grossly in excess of his limited

17. *The Letters of Henry James, 1,* ed. P. Lubbock (2 vols. New York, 1920), 408–09.

role as an authorial narrator. What emerges is that, in this instance, James judged the finished work not on its own merits but rather in terms of the extent to which it was a successful realization of his initial design, apparently unaware of the radical shift of emphasis, from the observed to the observer, which occurred in the process of its composition.

Although James wrote some very fine short stories like *The Two Faces, The Abasements of the Northmores, The Tree of Knowledge, Broken Wings,* and *Julia Bride,* in which, to use his own phrase, he managed successfully "to dissimulate his capital," the hard-and-fast rule of the "from six to eight thousand words" imposed on him by editors always irked him. His genius was for the more leisured forms—"the beautiful and blest *nouvelle"* and the long novel. The length of his works is an expression of his dramatic inventiveness and analytical temper—of his urge to elaborate all the dramatic possibilities inherent in any germinal situation, and to explore most exhaustively, minutely, and painstakingly the characters' consciousnesses. However, unlike Tolstoy, Balzac, Zola, the Goncourts brothers, and Proust, who gloried in the epic breadth of their many-volumed chronicles, James, who was writing in the dramatic rather than the epic mode, was forever struggling to restrict the length of his novels in the interests of narrative brevity and intensity, and at the same time forever failing to stop the "rank growth" of his initial subjects.[18] In *The Sacred Fount* (in contrast to *What Maisie Knew, The Ambassadors, The Wings of the Dove,* and *The Golden Bowl,* all of which were initially conceived of as short works and then grew beyond their intended scope), it was not the original *Notebooks* idea of spiritual vampirism which manifested the "unforeseen principle of growth," but a new idea, that of the observer's predicament. This may have prevented James from recognizing, as he did in all the

18. On the conflict between James' expansive and economical urges see J. A. Ward, "James' Idea of Structure," *PMLA, 80* (September 1965), 419–26.

other cases, the inner logic and the appropriateness of the expansion.[19]

Yet, in view of the self-conscious craftsmanship of *The Sacred Fount,* it is extremely difficult to believe that James was entirely unaware of what he had accomplished in the finished work. Is it possible, one cannot help wondering, that in describing the idea of *The Sacred Fount* as "tenuous" James was, after all, referring to the epistemological theme and not to the initial *Notebooks* theme of spiritual vampirism; and that what he meant was that the pure epistemological theme, when not embedded in a richly human fable (as it was, for instance, in *The Golden Bowl),* was too abstract, too thin an affair, to justify the elaborate, ingenious treatment he accorded it?

19. For a similar account of the reasons for James' rejection of *The Sacred Fount* see J. Raieth, "Henry James' Rejection of *The Sacred Fount,*" *Journal of English Literary History, 16* (1949), 308–24.

CHAPTER 9

THE GOLDEN BOWL

The Golden Bowl[1] is perhaps James' most subtle, most complex, and at the same time most intensely international domestic drama. Its personal and generic elements are most felicitously combined, and its four principal dramatis personae, who are all supremely representative of their respective nationalities and social classes, are the most fully dramatized and the most intimately "known" individuals in James' fiction.

The drama revolves about two closely related international marriages, representing, according to James' international "myth," the union of American wealth and innocence with European nobility and sophistication. The first marriage is that of Maggie Verver, the daughter of an American multimillionaire and art collector, to Prince Amerigo, an impecunious Italian aristocrat, a distinguished *galantuomo,* sophisticated, well-bred, possessing natural grace and elegance, and accomplished in all the social virtues, who is virtually collected by Maggie's father. The second marriage is that of Adam Verver, Maggie's father, and Charlotte Stant, his daughter's much admired former schoolmate, a beautiful, brilliant, strong-minded, grand but penniless American-born cosmopolite. Prior to the Prince's engagement to Maggie, he and Charlotte have been very much in love, but because neither of them had the means to marry (and there was in this case no Aunt Maud to "square," as in *The Wings of the Dove,* which turns upon the same germinal situation), they had—courageously and honorably by their standards—

1. New York, 23–24.

broken off their relationship. Although they marry the Ververs in perfect good faith, the Prince and Charlotte are
gradually driven, by their spouses' mutual absorption in each
other, to resume their illicit relationship. Maggie discovers
the true state of affairs and succeeds in winning back her
husband's love without directly exposing the adulterers and
without wrecking the marriages.

This simple, melodramatic, internationally emphasized
plot supports the most searching, most penetrating analysis
of character and motive, anticipating in its minuteness, depth,
and clinical precision the Proustian analysis. The extreme
paucity of the novel's overt action contrasts sharply with the
richness of the inner, psychological adventures which it
dramatizes. In fact, one of its distinctive features is the high
tension engendered by the contrast between the internal
turmoil, the terror and the desperation which beset the
drama's "bleeding participants," and its smoothness of surface resulting from their strict, undeviating observance of
"high decorum."

The Prince's and Maggie's motives for marrying each other
are characteristically international. The Ververs' money is an
immense inducement to the impecunious Prince, a fact which
he gracefully and self-deprecatingly acknowledges. Nonethe-
less, his marriage is far from being merely a marriage of convenience. He sincerely wishes to escape from the tradition
of decadent Roman immorality and to throw in his lot with
the representatives of what he is pleased to call the New
World's "science." Moreover, he genuinely "likes" his pros-
pective wife, and finds her American innocence and simplicity touchingly "funny" and immensely appealing. In
short, he undertakes the marriage in perfect good faith and
is determined to fight down the "arrogance and greed" of
which his national (if not his personal) past is full, and cultivate the virtues of humility and gratitude. He sincerely
wishes to do the right thing, and feeling somewhat at sea with
regard to the American moral code, he seeks help and guidance on this point from Mrs. Assingham, an American ex-

patriate and a devoted friend of both the Ververs and the Prince, whom she has actually brought together.

As for Maggie, what, she candidly admits, appealed to her American imagination was not the Prince's "personal self" but rather his "public quantity," which she sees as "made of the history, the doings, the marriages, the crimes, the follies, the boundless *bêtises*" of his aristocratic and immoral ancestors—precisely the "quantity" of which he wishes, by aligning himself with the Ververs, to disburden himself. At the same time, Maggie "adores" the Prince in a way which has absolutely nothing to do with a collector's attitude toward a precious and expensive *morceau de musée*.

The marriage between Adam Verver and Charlotte Stant is more of a marriage of convenience; but again, both Adam and Charlotte make the reasons which have determined them to marry perfectly plain to each other. Adam Verver admits that he marries primarily in order to put his child—who feels uneasy for having, since her marriage, neglected him—at peace, and Charlotte, on her side, confesses that she wants above all to be married, and married to a rich person, for it is the only "condition" or "state," as she calls it, possible for a woman of her type. In spite of all this mutual frankness all round, there is one crucial fact—the Prince's past relationship with Charlotte—about which, for obvious reasons, neither of the two enlightens the Ververs; and it is, as we shall see, this initial deception which corrodes and vitiates from the very start the relationship of the four protagonists.

A distinctive feature of James' treatment of the theme of the betrayal of the innocent American in *The Golden Bowl* is, I suggest, its perfect international impartiality. The European adulterers are not the heartless, cruel, callous, unscrupulous, cynical villains of James' earlier tales, and the betrayed Americans are not simply their blameless victims. Rather, *The Golden Bowl* is remarkable for the subtle complications of the protagonists' motives, whose proceedings are characterized by an extraordinary mixture of sincerity and bad faith, extreme conscientiousness and blind egotism.

The novel's chief irony is that although the four protagonists behave in ways which they believe to be most "beautiful" and "magnificent," and go to the greatest lengths to "spare" the others, their actions ineluctably give rise to the falsest, ugliest, most painful of situations.

Thus we are expected to see that in not telling Maggie anything about her past relationship with the Prince in order to make his marriage possible, Charlotte has acted beautifully and generously. As for the Prince, when Charlotte unexpectedly returns from America on the eve of his nuptials and asks for an "hour" with him in memory of their past intimacies, he cannot as a *galantuomo* but comply with such a seemingly modest request in return for her past generosity. Then, when Charlotte's chance to marry Mr. Verver comes, she again behaves grandly in asking the Prince's permission to marry his father-in-law, and of course he, on his part, repays her considerateness by courageously giving his consent. Charlotte acts boldly and "magnificently" when she offers to show Mr. Verver the Prince's rather ambiguous telegram (which reads: "*À la guerre comme à la guerre* then. We must lead our lives as we see them, but I am charmed with your courage and almost surprised at my own" [III, IV; *23, 290*]), and he, on his side, shows great delicacy in tactfully declining her offer.

As for Maggie and her father, they too, no less than the Prince and Charlotte, manifest a meticulous consideration for each other. As soon as Maggie marries the Prince, she begins to feel that she must "make up" to her father for neglecting him. Mr. Verver, who is quick to understand his daughter, marries Charlotte mainly in order to allay her anxieties (and not, interestingly, for the reason James suggested in his *Notebooks* entry, "in order to console himself for the loss of the daughter to whom he has been devoted").[2] Maggie, in her turn, immediately sets out to prove to him by constantly keeping him company that his marriage (which she knows has been undertaken primarily for her sake) is not go-

2. *Notebooks*, p. 130.

ing to make any difference in their relationship. Then—and
this is the beginning of what Fanny Assingham, the novel's
central choric commentator, terms "the vicious circle"—
Maggie perceives that by being so much with her father she
neglects her husband, to whom she must now "make up,"
and this she does by allowing him the use and enjoyment of
Charlotte. Thus, as Mrs. Assingham puts it, "before she knew
it at any rate her little scruples and her little lucidities,
which were really so divinely blind—her feverish little sense
of justice, as I say had brought the two others together as her
grossest misconduct couldn't have done" (III, XI; *23, 396*).

In staying with her father Maggie manifests not only "a
feverish sense of justice" but also a certain unconscious
egotism. Being by nature a domestic creature (F. W. Dupee
calls her and her father *"devotées* of the private life and
addicts to it"),[3] Maggie likes to stay with her father, letting
the Prince and Charlotte, whom she and her father have
"acquired" to "do the 'worldly'" for them, represent the
two households at all the season's social events.

The Prince and Charlotte, on their side, are equally responsible for this unusual "arrangement," in which they too
acquiesce for reasons both moral and egotistical. They decide to take the most generous and accommodating view of
their domestic use and consider it a point of honor faithfully
and uncomplainingly to fulfill their part of the bargain. At
the same time, being by nature particularly suited to the
public life, the "funny arrangement" enables them to enjoy
with impunity each other's company without their feeling
that they are being unfair to the Ververs.

The same emphasis on the beauty of everybody's intentions
persists in James' presentation of the adulterous liaison into
which the Prince and Charlotte finally enter. The adulterers
are shown neither as mere pleasure-seeking opportunists nor
as young people carried away by an uncontrollable passion
but rather as people who believe that they are acting in accordance with "a higher and braver propriety" than the

3. Dupee, *Henry James, His Life and Writings,* p. 227.

merely moral (III, VII; *23, 334*). In fact, they consider their being systematically thrown together as a justifying and not merely as an extenuating reason for their adulterous relationship—a European view of the matter which James projects with the utmost cogency and persuasiveness. This is how Charlotte analyzes the situation: "Nothing stranger surely had ever happened to a conscientious, a well-meaning, a perfectly passive pair: no more extraordinary decree had ever been launched against such victims than this of forcing them against their will into a relation of mutual close contact that they had done everything to avoid" (III, IV; *23, 289*). And this is how the Prince is shown to feel about the matter:

> Deep in the bosom of this falsity of position glowed the red spark of his inextinguishable sense of a higher and braver propriety. There were situations that were ridiculous but that one couldn't help, as for instance when one's wife chose, in the most usual way, to make one so. Precisely here however was the difference; it had taken poor Maggie to invent a way so extremely unusual—yet to which none-the-less it would be too absurd that he should merely lend himself. Being thrust, systematically, with another woman, and a woman one happened, by the same token, exceedingly to like, and being so thrust that the theory of it seemed to publish one as idiotic or incapable—this was a predicament of which the dignity depended all on one's own handling. What was supremely grotesque in fact was the essential opposition of theories—as if a *galantuomo,* as *he* at least constitutionally conceived galantuomini, could do anything *but* blush to "go about" at such a rate with such a person as Mrs. Verver in a state of childlike innocence, the state of our primitive parents before the Fall. The grotesque theory, as he would have called it, was perhaps an odd one to resent with violence, and he did it—also as a man of the world—all merciful justice. (III, VII; *23, 334–35*)

What the Prince, as a Roman *galantuomo* feels is that it would be ungracious, undignified, grotesque, and positively unintelligent not to take advantage of the situation. His European conception of what constitutes dignity and propriety is of course totally different from the American, exclusively moral conception of these phenomena. But given his conception, he can only see as "stupid" the American "grotesque theory" that it is actually possible, without being ashamed of one's obtuseness, "to 'go about' at such a rate with such a person as Mrs. Verver in a state of childlike innocence, the state of our primitive parents before the Fall." This conviction on the Prince's part is coupled with and reinforced by the irritation, contempt, and impatience an intelligent, sophisticated European man-of-the-world is bound to feel toward the Ververs' American "innocence," which seems to him in this mood indistinguishable from sheer "stupidity."

> They [the Ververs] knew, it might have appeared in these lights, absolutely nothing on earth worth speaking of—whether beautifully or cynically; and they would perhaps sometimes be a little less trying if they would only once for all peacefully admit that knowledge wasn't one of their needs and that they were in fact constitutionally inaccessible to it. They were good children, bless their hearts, and the children of good children; so that verily, the Principino [Maggie's and the Prince's child] himself, as less consistently of that descent, might figure to the fancy as the ripest genius of the trio. (III, VII; *23,* 333–34)

The Prince and Charlotte find no reason to regard their renewed liaison as a betrayal of their respective partners, of whom they remain genuinely solicitous. Since, as we saw, they have persuaded themselves both of the inevitability and the propriety of their relationship, and since they are convinced that their spouses are innocent "good children" constitutionally inaccessible to knowledge, they argue that the only way to protect and "take care" of such "poor lambs" is carefully to hide the truth from them, its always being, as the Prince puts it in one of his earliest conversations with Charlotte, "a question of doing the best for one's self one can—without injury to others" (I, III; *23, 58*).

A characteristically ambiguous scene in *The Golden Bowl* is, accordingly, that in which the Prince and Charlotte seal their pledge to make the Ververs' security and well-being "sacred" with a passionate lovers' kiss—the only one throughout the novel to which the reader is a witness. It is of course not at all difficult to regard the adulterers' pledge as a blasphemous Machiavellian sophistry or as a huge piece of self-deception. But this, it seems to me, would be too limited, one-sided, external an interpretation of their action. Instead, it is perhaps best to consider this scene as a characteristic instance of the ironic law which governs the relationships in *The Golden Bowl,* according to which the "beautiful intentions" on everybody's part perversely produce the most tragic consequences. In this instance it is precisely the sincerity of the Prince's and of Charlotte's mutual decision to treat the Ververs' with infinite tenderness and kindness which draws them more closely together. And when Maggie begins, at a later stage, to suspect the Prince and Charlotte, it is these very "ingenuities of pity," this intense consideration for her, and the alacrity with which they accept all the little changes in the arrangement she suggests that make her feel she is being "treated"—and thus confirm her suspicion, deepen her malaise, and intensify her feeling of loneliness and abandonment. Later on, during the crucial showdown between her and the Prince in the scene with the golden bowl, Maggie makes this point very emphatically: " 'Oh the thing I've known best of all is that you've never wanted together to offend us. You've wanted quite intensely not to, and the precautions you've had to take for it have been for a long time one of the strongest of my impressions. That, I think,' she added, 'is the way I've best known' " (IV, X; *24,* 199–200).[4]

4. On the syntactical misplacing of "together" as an effective way of making Maggie's point, see R. W. Short, "The Sentence Structure of Henry James," *American Literature, 18* (1946), 79.

A brief examination of the essentially similar though, of course, far less complex situation in the story called *The Path of Duty* may shed further light on James' treatment of it in *The Golden Bowl*. In *The Path of Duty* Lord Ambrose Tester has been for years in love with Lady Vandeleur but has no expectation of marrying her. Yielding to family pressure, he at last rather reluctantly becomes engaged to Jocelind Bernardstone, who is young, charming, and innocent. Then Lady Vandeleur's husband unexpectedly dies, and the lovers' union becomes possible. But to throw poor Jocelind over seems so wrong—so "beastly awkward," in Lord Ambrose's own idiom—that he and Lady Vandeleur decide that he ought, as a gentleman and a man of honor, to marry the poor girl. However, and this is the little tale's chief irony, it is precisely this noble decision which brings the two lovers more closely together. This ironic point is shrewdly made by the tale's narrator:

> Yes, they [Lord Ambrose and Lady Vandeleur] are certainly in felicity, they have trod the clouds together, they have soared into the blue, and they wear in their faces the glory of those altitudes. They encourage, they cheer, inspire, sustain each other; remind each other that they have chosen the better part. Of course they have to meet for this purpose, and their interviews are filled, I am sure, with its sanctity. He holds up his head, as a man may who on a very critical occasion behaved like a perfect gentleman. It is only poor Jocelind that droops. Haven't I explained to you now why she doesn't understand.[5]

One basic difference in James' treatment of the almost identical donnée in *The Path of Duty* and in *The Golden Bowl* immediately imposes itself. The relationship between Sir Ambrose and Lady Vandeleur is presented from the out-

5. *The Path of Duty*, Edel, *6*, 193–94.

side—that is, from the point of view of an observer-narrator who, in her role of the tale's guiding intelligence, gives expression to James' own amused and ironic view of the "sanctity" of the relationship. By contrast, the relationship between the Prince and Charlotte is presented exclusively from the adulterers' point of view, rather than filtered through the consciousness of some detached and skeptical observer. In fact, in *The Golden Bowl* James is particularly careful not to impose his own moral perspective and refrains from incorporating into the Prince's inner monologues any external authorial insinuations. This extreme moral reserve on James' part is completely consistent with his purpose at this stage in the novel. It is to make the reader see and thoroughly understand, though not necessarily unreservedly accept, the European's sense of the matter—an understanding which rules out the kind of detached critical irony manifested by the narrator in *The Path of Duty*. In fact, James meant the reader to form his final opinion of the quadrangular case only through gaining the fullest, finest, most comprehensive understanding of both the European and the American points of view, without the aid of guiding authorial comments, however oblique.

The novel's second part, which begins with Maggie's awakening from her deluded condition, is recorded entirely through her "American" consciousness. Maggie begins at last vaguely to feel that something has gone wrong, and this vague feeling finally crystallizes into a definite suspicion when the Prince and Charlotte, who have gone together as usual to a grand house-party at Matcham, stay there longer than is proper. With this suspicion, which causes her great anguish, Maggie is at last rudely jolted out of the state of paradisal innocence in which she was previously submerged. This state is symbolized by her relationship with her father —"he peculiarly paternal, she intensely filial"[6]—a relationship which is intimate, cosy, natural, guileless, and entirely

6. *Notebooks,* p. 131.

uncomplicated, and which in the end Maggie has to give up. Since this daughter-father relationship is meant to embody the state of innocence from which Maggie is eventually to emerge, it is surely wrong to interpret it as Matthiessen does, in psychoanalytical terms, as a "pathological fixation."[7]

From the moment the truth dawns on Maggie, she ceases to be the "funny," "quaint" little American girl she was. Having become acutely aware not only of the wrong done to her but also of the degree to which she herself has unwittingly contributed to the false situation, she determines to cast off the role of Mr. Verver's little daughter and to prove to the Prince that she has not been too stupid to have arrived at knowledge. In other words, she decides to *be* a changed creature and to make her husband recognize that she is. At the same time, she is resolved to do this in the most civilized manner possible, as befits *"her* husband's wife" and *"her* father's daughter"—that is to say, not to play the part of the wronged wife and to avoid at all costs anything as crude, sordid, ugly, and tedious as open accusation and exposure. This plan forces Maggie to dispense with what she thinks of as "any of the immediate, inevitable, assuaging ways, the ways usually open to innocence outraged and generosity betrayed"; it involves overcoming the grave temptation to complain, to cry out, to take "the straight vindictive view" of the matter, and to exercise "the rights of resentment." Instead, it imposes on her the constant paradoxical effort "never by a hair's breadth to deflect into the truth" (V, II; *24, 236, 250*).

Maggie must move very cautiously between the Scylla of failing to make the others see what they have to see and the Charybdis of insisting too much—a task requiring intelligence, self-possession, a high degree of self-control, courage, tenacity, and infinite patience. More important still, Maggie's "lucid little plan" is not only the most sensible, the most intelligent, and the most civilized, but also the most considerate with respect to the others. Any crude unmasking of the

7. See Matthiessen, *Henry James, The Major Phase,* p. 93.

adulterous relationship would irrevocably have shattered the two marriages and destroyed both the Prince and Charlotte, whereas Maggie means to "spare" them and to "save" them—in short, to make it as easy for each of them "as the case permitted" and yet, in particular, with respect to her rival, not less easy than the case permitted. And most important and most interesting: her lucid little plan spares and saves not only them but also herself—indeed, saves herself *by* saving them.

We have already discussed the Prince's and Charlotte's earlier decision to be "tender" to the Ververs, to do the best for themselves without, as far as possible, injury to their *sposi*. By one of those ironic symmetrical reversals in which James delighted, Maggie, the innocent American Girl, outdoes in this respect the sophisticated Europeans. She behaves even more "magnificently" than they; she preserves appearances even more "beautifully" than they; she evinces an even "higher considerateness" for them than they evinced for her; and she considers their "safety" as even more "sacred" than they considered hers.

In spite of the ironic parallelism of these two situations, there are several respects in which Maggie's conspicuously differs from Charlotte's. Charlotte is "grand," splendid, hard, worldly, strong-minded, aggressive, and naturally bold; she thrives on dangers and has, as James puts it, "an easy command, a high enjoyment, of her crisis" (III, I; *23*, 246). She has had a hard life and is used to fighting. By contrast, Maggie is a timid, open, artless, domestic person, as well as a perpetual worrier, and unlike her rival, she has never up till now had to struggle in order to get what she wanted. Consequently, all her actions, inconspicuous but done "with an infinite sense of intention" (IV, I; *24*, 9), go against her grain and do violence to her nature. But there are other important differences between Charlotte's and Maggie's respective situations which make Maggie's much more difficult to bear. Charlotte, we may recall, was in collusion with the Prince, with whom she worked for the "safety" of the Ververs. Maggie, on her

side, does not wish to "sacrifice" her father by telling him the
truth; she is therefore unutterably alone, and her fear lest
her father find out the truth only adds terror to the anguish
of her loneliness. Again, Charlotte is not in the least afraid of
Maggie, whereas Maggie is constantly harrassed by her fear
of Charlotte. Finally, Charlotte is convinced that Maggie
knows nothing and is therefore, in her "quaint" little way,
perfectly happy. Maggie, on the other hand, is acutely aware
of her rival's intense suffering, a suffering she cannot allay
save by giving up the Prince—the only thing she is not prepared to do.

Maggie's efforts are at last crowned with success. The
Prince gradually becomes aware of her intelligence, courage,
and high consideration for everyone; and simultaneously
with his growing interest in and appreciation for her, he
devastatingly pronounces Charlotte "stupid"—for having
failed to understand his wife. The first, most important sign
of the Prince's change of heart is his not telling Charlotte
that he knows that Maggie knows, thus disrupting their
former "exquisite complicity" which held them together in
the past. Indeed, an ironic reversal of positions has now been
effected. First, Charlotte turns out to be, as the Prince recognizes, much more "stupid" than Maggie ever was, and being
an intelligent *femme du monde* as well as an American, more
inexcusably so. Second, the quality of the Prince's new feeling
for Maggie is deeper and finer than that of his feeling for
Charlotte, which was a combination of the commercial and
the aesthetic.[8] Third, if Maggie had "to stuff [her] pocket-
handkerchief into [her] mouth . . . so as not to be heard too
indecently moaning" (IV, VI; *24,* 110), the mystified and confounded Charlotte is doomed to an even more agonized
silence, for, as Maggie recognizes, in her case "to confess to
wretchedness was by the same stroke to confess to falsity" (V,
V; *24,* 312). Charlotte must be separated from the Prince and

8. Dorothea Krook elaborates this point in her analysis of what she
calls the fatal taint in the relationship of Prince Amerigo and Charlotte
Stant. (See her *The Ordeal of Consciousness,* pp. 280–99.)

has no ground on which to object to her husband's plan to go back to American City. The only thing she can do, and does, is to save her pride by boldly pretending that it is she rather than her husband who wants to leave Europe, and that she does it in order to separate her husband from Maggie and have him at last to herself. Thus, perhaps the subtlest and cruelest scene in *The Golden Bowl* is that in which the mutual humbugging of the two women reaches its peak of irony. In a scene which is the very opposite of the traditional showdown between the two feminine rivals, Charlotte accuses Maggie of having planned to take Adam Verver from her, and Maggie admits that since Charlotte has persuaded him to go to American City, she has failed—a magnanimously perfidious confession of "failure" which marks her complete success both in winning back the Prince and in sparing Charlotte by preserving her dignity and pride—qualities Maggie genuinely admires and respects.

One of the most effective ways in which James emphasizes the ironic parallelism of the reversed situations in *The Golden Bowl* is by describing Maggie's and the Prince's or Maggie's and Charlotte's situations in terms of the same basic images, a device characteristic of the narrative style of *The Golden Bowl,* which is as rich in metaphor and symbol as that of poetry.[9] James' elaboration of the images of the bath, the cage, and the cup offers an excellent illustration of this technique.

At the beginning of the novel the Prince develops the bath conceit to express his view of his position vis-à-vis the Ververs. He feels as if he were sitting in a bath of gold, and Maggie's words

9. A. Rose analyzes the novel's poetic texture in his "The Spatial Form of *The Golden Bowl*," *Modern Fiction Studies, 12* (Spring 1966), 103–06, in terms of Joseph Frank's famous distinction between the temporal, linear narrative progression and the "spatial" simultaneous and cross-referencing elements of the novel. See "Spatial Form in the Modern Novel" in M. Schorer, J. Miles, G. McKenzie, eds., *Criticism, The Foundations of Modern Literary Judgment* (New York, 1958), pp. 379–92.

sweetened the waters in which he now floated, tinted them as by the action of some essence, poured from a gold-topped phial, for making one's bath aromatic. No one before him, never—not even the infamous Pope—had so sat up to his neck in such a bath . . . into which Maggie scattered, on occasion, her exquisite colouring drops. They were of the colour—of what on earth? of what but the extraordinary American good faith? They were of the colour of her innocence, and yet at the same time of her imagination, with which their relation, his and those people's, was all suffused (I, I; *23,* 10).

This same bath image, playfully elaborated by the Prince, takes on a tragic and sinister note when it is used at a later stage by Maggie to express her sense of being "treated" by the Prince and Charlotte:

So that she sat there in the solid chamber of her help-lessness as in a bath of benevolence artfully prepared for her, over the brim of which she could but just manage to see by stretching her neck. Baths of benevolence were very well, but at least, unless one were a patient of some sort, a nervous eccentric or a lost child, one wasn't usually so immersed save by one's request. [But] it wasn't in the least what *she* had requested. (IV, II; *24,* 44)

The cage image undergoes a similar development. During the first half of the novel it is Maggie who feels like a caged bird. "She had flapped her little wings as a symbol of desired flight" but, she thinks with bitterness, it was interpreted by the Prince and Charlotte as "a plea for a more gilded cage and an extra allowance of lumps of sugar" (IV, II; *24,* 44). In the second half of the novel Maggie, quite conscious of the analogy, sees Charlotte tormented by uncertainty as, in her turn, a bird in a similarly gilded cage:

Even the conviction that Charlotte was but awaiting some chance really to test her trouble upon her lover's wife left Maggie's sense meanwhile open as to the sight

of gilt wires and bruised wings, the spacious but sus-
pended cage, the home of eternal unrest, of pacings,
beatings, shakings, all so vain, into which the baffled
consciousness helplessly resolved itself. The cage was
the deluded condition, and Maggie, as having known
delusion—rather!—understood the nature of cages. She
walked round Charlotte's—cautiously and in a very
wide circle; and when inevitably they had to communicate she felt herself comparatively outside and on the
breast of nature: she saw her companion's face as that
of a prisoner looking through bars. So it was that
through bars, bars richly gilt but firmly though discreetly
planted, Charlotte finally struck her as making a grim
attempt; from which at first the Princess drew back as
instinctively as if the door of the cage had suddenly
been opened from within. (V, I; *24, 229-30*)

The elaboration of the cup image (which is closely related
to the novel's central symbol of the golden bowl) is the
subtlest and most complex of the three. It first occurs when
the Prince at Matcham reflects on the irritating innocence
of the Ververs:

He felt at moments as if there were never anything to do
for them that was worthy—to call worthy—of the personal relation; never any charming charge to take of
any confidence deeply resposed. He might vulgarly have
put it that one had never to plot or to lie for them; he
might humorously have put it that one had never, as by
the higher conformity, to lie in wait with the dagger or
to prepare insidiously the cup. These were the services
that by all romantic tradition were consecrated to affection quite as much as to hate. But he could amuse himself with saying—so far as amusement went—that they
were what he had once for all turned his back on. (III,
VI; *23, 314-15*).

Ironically, the Prince is quite wrong in his belief that he has

turned his back upon his ancestors' tradition of the dagger
and the cup, for he is soon to betray Maggie by drinking,
together with Charlotte, the cup of pleasure and happiness.
The Prince's and Charlotte's great moment at Matcham,
where they most fully enjoy all "the ingenuities and im-
punities of pleasure" (III, VII; 23, 332), is also conveyed in
terms of a cup image: "So therefore while the minute lasted
it passed between them that their cup was full; which cup
their very eyes, holding it fast, carried and steadied and
began, as they tasted it, to praise" (III, IX; 23, 356). Later
Maggie experiences her great need of the Prince (to which she
never confesses) in terms of the cup image which stood earlier
for the Prince's and Charlotte's happiness: "It's all very well,
and I perfectly see how beautiful it is [the constant humbugging on everybody's part], all round: but there comes a
day when something snaps, when the full cup, filled to the
very brim, begins to flow over. That's what has happened to
my need of you—the cup, all day, has been too full to carry.
So here I am with it, spilling it over you—and just for
the reason that's the reason of my life" (IV, I; 24, 18).
Toward the end, after her reconciliation with the Prince, it is
Maggie who, in her turn, experiences happiness in terms of
the image of the full cup: "Some day at some happier season
she would confess to him that she hadn't confessed [her need],
though taking so much on her conscience; but just now she
was carrying in her weak stiffened hand a glass filled to the
brim, as to which she had recorded a vow that no drop
should overflow" (V, V; 24, 298).

I have tried to show that each of the four participants in
the international drama is a highly complex person and that
James has been careful to make none of them either an un-
mitigated villain or a perfect saint. A comparison of James'
first *Notebooks* entry about *The Golden Bowl* (written
twelve years before its actual composition) with the finished
novel shows that James introduced into the finished novel
precisely those elements which make it the morally complex and internationally impartial drama it is. James sug-

gests in the *Notebooks* that "the subject [of the 'little tale'] is really the pathetic simplicity and good-faith of the father and daughter in their abandonment."[10] There is no trace in this initial sketch of the idea which is of central importance in the novel—that such simplicity on the part of the American father and daughter is not merely pathetic but actually a species of "stupidity." Similarly, there is no indication of the idea that by being completely absorbed in each other, and by systematically throwing their European spouses together, the father and the daughter contribute their share to the false situation. Lastly, James does not mention in the *Notebooks* the American girl's awakening, her struggle to win back her husband, and her final victory over the Europeans.

James leaves out in the *Notebooks* entry not only the complexities of the American characters, who are sketched as mere victims of European villainy, but also all the redeeming features of the European husband, who is conceived of as a typical European villain: "The young husband may be made a Frenchman—*il faut,* for a short tale, *que cela se passe à Paris.* He is poor, but has some high social position or name —and is, after all, morally only the pleasant *Français moyen* —clever, various, inconstant, amiable, cynical, unscrupulous —charming always, to 'the other woman.' "[11] Prince Amerigo is obviously a much more complex, subtler, and finer character. There are indeed vestigial traces in him of the *Français moyen* of James' original conception: one remembers the way he looks at—"appreciates"—Charlotte at their first meeting in Fanny Assingham's house (I, III; 23, 42–43, 45–46), and the way he thinks of her as he waits for her in the terrace at Matcham (III, IX; 23, 319–20). Yet it is a main part of his good faith, good will, and determination to be as "good" as possible in respect of the Ververs, his benefactors, that he should wish to curb, suppress, and if possible to exorcise those

10. *Notebooks,* pp. 130–31.
11. *Notebooks,* p. 131.

vestiges of his *galantuomo* past. Accordingly, he is shown to
be as charming to his wife as he is to "the other woman"
and the whole point of the Maggie-Amerigo story is that
Amerigo betrays his wife not because, or not mainly, because
he is "inconstant" or "promiscuous," but rather because
this, according to his European code, is the only "right"
response to the extraordinarily "funny" situation in which
the Ververs have placed him.

Since James does not present the husband as an unre-
deemable villain, it is not surprising that he should have
made him an Italian prince rather than a profligate French
aristocrat (like, for instance, the Baron in *Madame de
Mauves*). As Oscar Cargill rightly points out, James meant
the Prince (like his cruder forerunner, Count Valerio in *The
Last of the Valerii*) to represent a modern, nonmythological
Donatello—that is to say, a person who has remained, in
spite of his worldly sophistication and cosmopolitan background, a child of nature innocent of morality—a view which
James' comments upon the original Donatello in Hawthorne's *The Marble Faun* seem to support:

> The idea of the modern faun was a charming one; but I
> think it a pity that the author should not have made him
> more definitely modern, without reverting so much to his
> mythological properties and antecedents, which are very
> gracefully touched upon, but belong to the region of
> picturesque conceits, much more than to that of real
> psychology. Among the young Italians of today there are
> still plenty of models for such an image as Hawthorne
> appears to have wished to present in the easy and natural
> Donatello.[12]

Many critics have failed to appreciate the novel's international impartiality. By ignoring half of the evidence, by
dwelling exclusively on only one of its aspects, and by insist-

12. Cargill, *The Novels of Henry James*, p. 390.

ing on a consistently ironic reading of only one of its two parts, they have lost sight of its moral complexity and arrived at what Walter Wright appropriately terms "two types of oversimplification."[13] The first type of oversimplification consists in viewing Maggie as a saintly character, the innocent, tender, mild, magnanimous, and compassionate wronged wife, who takes the adulterers' sins upon herself and redeems them through the exercise of universal love. It also therefore views Charlotte as a hard, cruel, ruthless Machiavellian opportunist who takes advantage of Maggie's innocence and whose sufferings are the inescapable wages of her sin.[14] The second type of oversimplification consists in viewing Charlotte as the tragic, passionate woman who entertains for the Prince a "decent passion"[15]—a free spirit who suffocates in the cramping atmosphere of the rich, acquisitive, provincial, puritanical Ververs. It views Maggie as a sinister anti-Christ figure who merely plays at being Christ, as the "crafty-innocent, smugly virtuous Princess"[16] who wallows in self-righteousness and gloats over the suffering of her rival, whom she controls through her financial power.[17]

13. W. Wright, "Maggie Verver: Neither Saint nor Witch," *Nineteenth-Century Fiction, 12* (June 1957), 60.

14. The exponents of this view are: Anderson, *The American Henry James;* R. P. Blackmur, Introduction to *The Golden Bowl* (New York, 1952); J. Barzun, "Henry James, Melodramatist," in *The Question of Henry James, A Collection of Critical Essays,* ed. F. W. Dupee (New York, 1945); E. Stevenson, *The Crooked Corridor, A Study of Henry James* (New York, 1959).

15. See Leavis, *The Great Tradition,* p. 178.

16. F. Nuhn, *The Wind Blew from the East, A Study in the Orientation of American Culture* (New York, 1942), p. 133.

17. The exponents of this view are: P. Edgar, *Henry James, Man and Author* (Boston, 1927); Leavis, *The Great Tradition;* Nuhn, *The Wind Blew from the East;* J. J. Firebaugh, "The Ververs," *Essays in Criticism, 4* (October 1954), 400–10; J. Kimball, "Henry James's Last Portrait of a Lady: Charlotte Stant in *The Golden Bowl,"* American Literature, *28* (January 1957), 449–68. The writers who emphasize the moral complexity of the drama are: Matthiessen, *Henry James, The Major Phase;*

On the view proposed in this chapter Maggie is neither a Christ-figure nor an anti-Christ. Undeniably, she is surrounded with images linking her with Christ,[18] but these are on a par with many other images (the little trapezist girl, the caged bird being given an extra allowance of lumps of sugar, the small erect commander of a siege, the timid tigress, the actress improvising on a stage) through which Maggie experiences her situation at different moments in the drama. The significance of each is therefore limited to the situation in which it occurs; thus, when she experiences the anguished difficulty of carrying the burden of "knowledge" she cannot impart to others, Maggie sustains herself by a religious analogy:

> They [the other three participants in the drama] thus tacitly put it upon her to be disposed of, the whole complexity of their peril, and she promptly saw why: because she was there, and there just *as* she was, to lift it off them and take it; to charge herself with it as the scapegoat of old, of whom she had once seen a terrible picture, had been charged with the sins of the people and had gone forth into the desert to sink under his burden and die. (V, II; *24, 234*)

In spite of the force of this analogy, however, Maggie's drama as a whole lacks certain elements required to make her a Christ-figure in any proper sense. First, the love which is the spring of all her actions is the love of a woman for a particular man; it is by no means the universal *agape* of the Christian ideal. Second, in spite of her consideration for others, she yet fights for her rights as a wife by using all the resources

---

F. C. Crews, *The Tragedy of Manners, Moral Drama in the Later Novels of Henry James* (New Haven, 1957); Krook, *The Ordeal of Consciousness;* and Wright, *Nineteenth-Century Fiction, 12,* 59–71.

18. The two writers who first drew attention to the Christian imagery in *The Golden Bowl* are: Anderson, *The American Henry James,* and Crews, *The Tragedy of Manners.*

of worldly wisdom. Finally, her suffering is not expiatory, she does not die a sacrificial death like Milly Theale in *The Wings of the Dove;* and although Maggie spares Charlotte and helps her preserve her "pride," the idea of forgiveness does not assume in *The Golden Bowl* the same central thematic importance it has in *The Wings of the Dove* and *The Altar of the Dead.*

The perfect international impartiality which characterizes *The Golden Bowl* is achieved, it should be emphasized, not by an equal detachment from the European and American conflicting viewpoints but rather by an equally intense immersion in the consciousnesses of both the European and the American "bleeding participants" (the Prince and Maggie), whose experiences James registers with a sensitivity, a delicacy, a vividness, and a completeness he has never before attained.

James presents the first half of the international domestic drama exclusively from the Prince's point of view and its second half exclusively from Maggie's point of view, with as few oblique authorial interpolations as possible. "It is," he explains in the Preface to *The Golden Bowl* (p. viii), "the Prince who opens the door to half our light upon Maggie, just as it is she who opens it to half our light upon himself; the rest of our impression, in either case, coming straight from the very motion with which the act is performed." There is, as a consequence, no one ultimate objective viewpoint which unequivocally imposes itself. Rather, and this is what makes *The Golden Bowl* such a disturbing work ("the large problem child among James's writings," as F. W. Dupee has called it),[19] both points of view are so intimately, so exhaustively, so persuasively presented that neither imposes itself as the only valid one.

James does not use in *The Golden Bowl*—as he did, for instance, in *Lady Barbarina*—the method of regular alternations of the European and American centers. Instead, he uses

19. Dupee, *Henry James*, p. 225.

the method of successive centers which he employed in *An International Episode,* in which the first half of the little drama is registered exclusively from the point of view of Lord Lambeth, the English nobleman, and its second half exclusively from the point of view of Bessie Alden, the young American girl.[20] One reason for this choice of method in *The Golden Bowl* is structural: by building "two sufficiently solid *blocks* of wrought material"[21] he is able to develop uninterruptedly and unhurriedly, in the epic manner, the complex dramatic situation of the book. As for the order in which the successive centers are dramatized, it is by dramatizing the Prince's consciousness in the first part and Maggie's in the second that James is able to extract the maximum of sense out of the complex international drama he projects.

Thus, in the first half of the novels, in which James focuses on the Prince's consciousness, it is he rather than Maggie who is both the more active dramatic agent and the more perceptive, more intelligent, more sensitive observer. It is the Prince who communicates to the reader the impression of Maggie's stupidity," irritating simplicity, and "divine blindness." Precisely the same reasons which justify James' choice of the Prince as the center of consciousness of the first half of the novel justify his choice of Maggie as the center of consciousness of its second half. From the moment of her awakening it is she whose inner life is the more intense, who is the more important, more active dramatic agent of the two. And since it is she who now manipulates the situation, it is also she who possesses the clearest, deepest, and most penetrating view of it. However, the fact that the beginning of Maggie's activity as a center of consciousness coincides with the beginning of her awakening from the state of innocence serves to emphasize the dramatic significance of this awakening—a

20. Oscar Cargill points out the possible influence on James of Maupassant's *Pierre et Jean* and *Forte comme la morte,* in which the French writer experimented with the method of successive centers. See his *The Novels of Henry James,* p. 438.

21. Preface to *The Wings of the Dove,* New York, *19,* p. xii.

technical device James used before in *The Portrait of a Lady*, in which Isabel becomes the novel's center of consciousness precisely at the point at which she begins her European career.

In spite of the meticulous fullness and intensity with which James dramatizes the inward vision of the novel's two principal vessels of consciousness, and in spite of the dramatic explicitness of the great scenes in which they confront each other, he nevertheless introduces two observers, Fanny and Bob Assingham, who view the quadrangular situation from without, and function, somewhat in the manner of the Freers in *Lady Barbarina*, as its choric commentators. As the dramatic situation in *The Golden Bowl* is immeasurably more complex and subtle than that in *Lady Barbarina*, the Assinghams' role is, not surprisingly, correspondingly more complex than that of their forerunners in the early international comedy.

The "inimitable" and "world-worn" couple is introduced almost at the very beginning of the novel (in chapter II), and the wife's and husband's respective qualifications to perform their analytic function are immediately clarified. Fanny Assingham, the novel's central choric commentator, is an American by birth but a European by discipline—a combination which makes her, not unlike Mrs. Freer, perfectly acquainted with the international scene and keenly aware of the dangers and the splendid possibilities of the international marriage. Like all Jamesian observers, she is passionately interested in personal relationships, being, as she admits, "a person for whom life was multitudinous detail, detail that left her, as it at any moment found her, unappalled and unwearied," that gave her "plenty to do" and made her perpetually "sit up." Her avid interest in people, though purely functional, is nevertheless accounted for in terms of her personal predicament. It springs, we learn, from her need to compensate herself for her "want of children" and her "want of wealth"—the two great "gaps in her completeness" (I, II; *23, 35*). It is her want of children which accounts for her filial feelings toward the Prince, and her (comparative) want of wealth which accounts for the attraction the Prince and the Ververs—her social and economic superiors—have for her.

In contradistinction to Mrs. Freer, an uninvolved though an acutely interested observer of the international experiment, Mrs. Assingham is a meddling observer who has actually assisted in bringing about the double international marriage. Again, it is her personal history which accounts, to some extent at least, for her meddling in such a risky affair. She is herself, we are told, one of the first American women to have married a European at a time when this was considered a bold and original venture on both sides; we are also informed that her marriage to the English Colonel is considered by all her friends as "the happiest of its kind." Bearing in mind that Fanny has virtually invented the international "combination," her interest in promoting another combination of this kind, though on a much grander scale, is made understandable.

It is made clear that Fanny Assingham fully appreciates all the dangers which threaten the marriage of an innocent American heiress to an impoverished, sophisticated Roman Prince, who has known many women and who was, not so very long ago, in love with a woman like Charlotte. What, however, prompts the well-intentioned cosmopolitan lady to take these risks is her firm belief that the marriage will work—a belief based on the exhibition, on the Prince's part, of humility, good faith, and a willingness to adapt himself to the Ververs, to whom he is sincerely grateful.

However, in her eagerness to bring such a beautiful international union about, Mrs. Assingham becomes guilty of a serious oversight. She does not take into account the possibility of Charlotte's reappearance. Therefore, as soon as the latter does turn up, Mrs. Assingham becomes extremely worried; and when, upon noticing her "nervousness," the Prince asks her whether she believes that Charlotte's return is going to constitute a complication, she promptly retorts:

"a handsome clever odd girl staying with one is always a complication" (I, II; *23, 43*). In order to remedy the situation, Mrs. Assingham gets involved in an even more risky experiment—the marriage of Adam Verver and Charlotte, which again she helps to bring about. She takes the view that since Adam Verver wants to get married principally for Maggie's sake, Charlotte would make the best of wives for him; for besides the other qualifications she possesses, she is the only kind of woman Maggie would wholeheartedly accept as her stepmother. Mrs. Assingham is convinced that only the right kind of marriage—and Charlotte's marriage to Adam Verver is the right kind—will "cure" Charlotte of her dangerous attachment to the Prince. She also believes that by marrying Maggie's father Charlotte will become no less grateful to the Ververs than the Prince, and her gratitude will prevent her—as it will prevent him—from ever abusing their confidence. She therefore persuades herself that by arranging this second marriage she is "working" not only for Adam Verver and Charlotte but also for Maggie and the Prince. Only after the Matcham episode does Mrs. Assingham realize that her calculations were all wrong, and is forced to admit that her having (not unlike the narrator in *The Sacred Fount*) fallen in love with "the beautiful symmetry" of her plan (III, XI; *23, 389*) had prevented her from correctly assessing the dangers of the double marriage. Thus, in her own minor way, Mrs. Assingham is also a victim of the ironic law which governs the action in *The Golden Bowl*—the law according to which the most honorable intentions bring about the most painful consequences. Especially significant in this connection is Mrs. Assingham's share in the initial deception of the Ververs. Charlotte's motive for not telling Maggie about her past relations with the Prince was, we saw, "honourable." Mrs. Assingham's acquiescence in this deception is, we are made to see, no less "honourable." "There are things, my dear—" she tells her husband, "haven't you felt it yourself, coarse as you are?—that no one could tell Maggie. There are things that, upon my word, I shouldn't care to attempt to tell her now . . . she'd be so frightened. She'd be, in her strange little way, so hurt. She wasn't born to know evil. She must never know it" (I, IV; *23*, 77–78).

Naturally, by arranging this second international marriage, the load of responsibility Mrs. Assingham carries grows heavier than before. Once she perceives the turn events have taken, her greatest fear is that, in spite of having "worked" for everyone, the Ververs will accuse her of having taken advantage of their American innocence in order to provide her two "grand," "interesting," flamboyant European friends with financial security, and (more horrible still) in order at the same time to place them in a situation in which they will be able to carry on their former liaison with impunity.

Like all the Jamesian passionate observers, Fanny Assingham is sensitive, subtle, intelligent, and imaginative. It is she who expresses some of the novel's most important *aperçus,* both diagnostic and prognostic, who gives expression to some of its most crucial generalizations, who illuminates obscure points, and who fulfills a variety of expository, explanatory, and anticipatory functions. Thus it is she who is the first to perceive the change in Maggie and to realize that it is Maggie who will "see everybody through." It is she who propounds the perceptive vicious-circle theory and who makes the point that Maggie has never, before her awakening, really "had" the Prince. Again, it is she who comes to see that, all appearances to the contrary, the Prince doesn't really "care" for Charlotte because, as she shrewdly puts it, "men don't, when it has all been too easy" (III, XI; *23*, 399). As the author's deputy, she expresses the view that morality is nothing but high intelligence and that "the forms . . . are two thirds of conduct" (I, IV; *23*, 88, 390). Again, it is she who insists that initially there were "beautiful intentions all round" and that all the four "bleeding participants" are equally, though in different senses, mere helpless victims of fate. (III, XI; *23*, 392)

At the same time, however, Fanny Assingham makes many fatal mistakes and cannot therefore, in spite of the quantity

of illumination she provides, be considered without qualifications as the novel's guiding intelligence. Thus, upon
Charlotte's sudden arrival on the eve of the Prince's marriage,
she propounds the extravagant and improbable hypothesis
that Charlotte has come to be "magnificent" and to "see
Maggie through"—that is to say, that since Maggie doesn't
know the Prince, whereas she does, Charlotte must believe
her presence is going to be "an element of *positive* safety"
(I, IV; *23, 85*). Later, when she meets the Prince and Charlotte, she is reluctant, in spite of the disquieting impression
she has received, to admit that the Prince, who has in the
past demonstrated his good faith and asked her for moral
guidance, is no less "shaky" than Charlotte, and refuses to
understand his "quintessential wink." In the analytical session with her husband which follows this episode, she still
argues (ingeniously but wrongly) that the Prince and Charlotte will not form an adulterous liaison; for Charlotte must
be grateful to the Prince for not having objected to her marriage with his father-in-law and she must therefore—by every
dictate of moral delicacy—leave the Prince alone and not
interfere with him. She also argues (again ingeniously but
wrongly) that precisely because the Ververs leave the Prince
and Charlotte so much together, they are bound in honor not
to abuse Ververs' confidence and that this is what saves them.
(III, X; *23, 368*)

In sum, far from being, like Maria Gostry in *The Ambassadors,* wholly "the reader's friend," Mrs. Assingham is often
likely to confuse the reader, who in addition to the strenuous
efforts he has to make to interpret the motives of the novel's
highly complex characters, for whom the maintenance of
forms is almost equivalent to morality, must also thread his
way through the labyrinth of Mrs. Assingham's ingenious
and supersubtle theories, which are, we saw, as often wrong
as they are right. Thus the introduction of a choric commentator who, though generally profoundly perceptive and
intelligent, is yet also often confused and fallible is, I suggest,
of the greatest thematic significance in *The Golden Bowl.* It

contributes, in its minor way, to the effects of moral complexity and ambiguity, which I have tried to show, are at the core of the novel. In fact, by denying the choric observer the usual degree of functional clairvoyance, James pushes the authorial self-effacement he practices in *The Golden Bowl* in order to achieve complete objectivity.

Fanny Assingham's grossest, most blatant mistakes concern the Prince's and Charlotte's motives, whereas her best insights and most accurate choric prophecies concern Maggie's. Bearing in mind the personal stake she has in the matter, this is hardly surprising. Since she wishes the marriages she has arranged to work, she systematically refuses to understand those actions on the part of the Europeans which undermine them, whereas for the same reason she is correspondingly quick to perceive those actions on Maggie's part which, she hopes, will save them. In general, Fanny Assingham is less perceptive with regard to the Europeans because she is inclined to attribute to them a greater degree of American moral delicacy than the case warrants. Thus it transpires that, in spite of her cosmopolitan background and long acquaintance with European mores, she too exhibits some vestiges of the American innocence, simplicity, and "stupidity" which characterize the Ververs. Indeed, Fanny Assingham is shown as, in her way, no less of a worrier than Maggie and as completely devoid of the Prince's aristocratic composure and of Charlotte's hard imperturbability. So that, apart from her analytical role, she clearly constitutes a second, minor case of the American's failure to understand the European code of behavior. In fact, the analytic chapters in which she develops her mistaken theories with regard to the Prince and Charlotte are succeeded by dramatic chapters which immediately falsify them. For instance, the early session of the choric pair, in which Mrs. Assingham propounds the theory that Charlotte has returned to America on the eve of the Prince's marriage in order to be "magnificent" and "see Maggie through" (I, IV), is immediately followed by the shopping expedition of the Prince and Charlotte, their talk in

Hyde Park, and their visit to the antiquary's shop (I, V). Another discussion (III, III), in the course of which Mrs. Assingham reaches the conclusion that precisely because the Ververs leave the Prince and Charlotte so much together they are bound in honor not to abuse the Ververs' confidence, is followed by the scene (III, V), retrospectively evoked by the Prince, in which he and Charlotte seal with a lovers' kiss their pledge to make the Ververs' security sacred to themselves; and this in turn is followed by the scene at Matcham (III, VII) which is the high point of the Prince's and Charlotte's illicit affair. Thus, as the interpreter of the European protagonists, Fanny Assingham appears as almost a parody of the traditional infallible choric commentator.

In contrast to Mrs. Freer, the earlier choric commentator whose unerring prophecies, based almost exclusively on her knowledge of the protagonists' national psychology, require no actual participation in the action, Mrs. Assingham, the much more privileged observer, actually assists at the novel's three most crucial scenes. These are the Prince's first meeting with Charlotte after her unexpected return from America, the grand house-party at Matcham, at which the Prince and Charlotte stay fatally behind, and the golden bowl episode, the crucial encounter between Maggie and the Prince during which she confronts him with the proof of his betrayal. The first two scenes bristle for Mrs. Assingham with innumerable contradictory significances and give her plenty to think about. Indeed, she is humorously described by James as eagerly "bottling" her impressions for future preservation, in order chemically to analyze them later on "in the snug laboratory of her afterthought" (III, II; *23, 271*). Not surprisingly, Mrs. Assingham's first two encounters with the European protagonists are followed by long, intense analytical sessions with her husband, in which she dissects, anatomizes, and appraises what she has observed, testing at her leisure a great many possible theories which would account for it. Appropriately enough, only the golden bowl scene, which is free of the ambiguity and subtle elusiveness of the

two earlier crucial scenes, is not followed by such a supple-
mentary choric discussion.

Apart from their interpretative and thematic value, the
analytical conversations between Mrs. Assingham and her
husband are highly amusing and provide, like a Shakespearian comic subplot, comic relief. They are conducted in
a lucid, direct, colloquial style which contrasts sharply with
the elaborate, syntactically complex, and richly metaphorical
style of the novel's dramatic parts. Moreover, since the four
protagonists avoid at all costs any open discussion of their
situation, and since as a consequence their conversations are
designed to cover up rather than reveal the truth, Mrs.
Assingham's more explicitly stated speculations, however
extravagant and oversubtle, serve to break up the unbearable
tension the protagonists' sustained mutual humbugging en-
genders.

As in *Lady Barbarina,* the marked differences between the
two choric commentators ensure the dramatic vividness, the
dialectical intensity, and the comic tension of their colloquies.
Like the narrator in *The Sacred Fount,* Mrs. Assingham is of
a highly imaginative and speculative nature and has a passion
for analysis. She is teeming with innumerable "ideas" with
which she constantly experiments, and none of them, as she
tells her husband, is ever her "whole" idea. She takes a very
high-minded view of her analytical task, is very high-strung,
and carries on her interpretative activity at a high pitch of
intellectual and emotional exaltation. Like the narrator in
The Sacred Fount, she tends to read too much rather than
too little into the situation she observes; and this tendency
takes, in her case, the form mainly of attributing to the Prince
and Charlotte a too great moral delicacy. Because of her
uneasiness and her unwillingness to admit her mistakes, her
reasoning, though subtle, is often inconsistent, and her view
of the situation is, in spite of her shrewdness and perspicacity,
frequently vitiated by wishful thinking.

Mrs. Assingham's military husband is a far less involved
and a far less intense observer and commentator. He takes
only a mild interest in the quadrangular international case,

and even this interest depends mainly on the fact that his wife has become involved in it. Moreover, by pretending, like Mr. Freer in *Lady Barbarina,* to care only for the "fun" of observing the situation—an attitude which his wife angrily brands as grossly immoral—he brings into high relief her sense of being deeply involved and seriously responsible. On the whole, the Colonel enjoys watching his wife's extraordinary performances "very much as he had sometimes watched at the Aquarium the celebrated lady who, in a slight, though tight, bathing-suit, turned somersaults and did tricks in the tank of water which looked so cold and uncomfortable to the non-amphibious" (I, IV; *23,* 65). At the same time, he never follows very closely all the involutions of her tortuous reasoning and is in the habit of editing her play of mind just as he edits her redundant telegrams. (I, IV; *23,* 67)

The Colonel's participation in the discussions consists in his constantly punctuating his wife's interminable speculations with laconic questions and comments, which serve to point the issues at stakes, force her to enlarge on her cryptic prophetic pronouncements, and indirectly criticize them. Mrs. Assingham, on her side, is in the habit of ruthlessly pursuing her own independent line of thought regardless of her husband's interruptions, which she characterizes as "his short cuts, always across her finest flower-beds" (III, X; *23,* 367).

The obtuseness, dullness and coarse-mindedness which Mrs. Assingham attributes to her husband are of course more assumed than real and serve obliquely to deflate her intensities and exaltations. Moreover, by pretending to obtuseness and an exasperating literal-mindedness, the Colonel manages to point out to his wife those inconsistencies in her reasoning which spring from her refusal to face the truth concerning the Prince and Charlotte—a strategy the following passage conveniently illustrates:

> "It *is* always the Prince [says Mrs. Assingham], and it *is* always, thank heaven, marriage. And these are the things, God grant, that it will always be. That I could help

[Maggie and the Prince], a year ago, most assuredly made me happy, and it continues to make me happy."

"Then why aren't you quiet?"

"I *am* quiet," said Fanny Assingham.

He looked at her, with his colourless candour, still in his place; she moved about again a little, emphasising by her unrest her declaration of her tranquillity. He was as silent at first as if he had taken her answer, but he wasn't to keep it long. "What do you make of it that, by your own show, Charlotte couldn't tell her [Maggie] all [about her past relationship with the Prince]? What do you make of it that the Prince didn't tell her anything? Say one understands that there are things she can't be told —since, as you put it, she is so easily scared and shocked." He produced these objections slowly, giving her time, by his pauses, to stop roaming and come back to him. But she was roaming still when he concluded his enquiry, "If there hadn't been anything there shouldn't have been between the pair before Charlotte bolted—in order, precisely, as you say, that there *shouldn't* be: why in the world was what there *had* been too bad to be spoken of?"

Mrs Assingham, after this question, continued still to circulate—not directly meeting it even when at last she stopped. "I thought you wanted me to be quiet." (I, IV; 23, 81–82)

Being an Englishman, the Colonel takes a less exalted and more cynical view of the international situation than his wife does. He correctly appraises the dangers of the international marriages and is not at all surprised by the turn events take. Believing from the very first that the marriage of the innocent American heiress with the penniless sophisticated Roman Prince, which is based on a lie, will not work, it is he who, after the Matcham episode, forces upon his wife the recognition of the Prince's "shakiness." At the same time he is much slower than his wife to understand Maggie's heroism and admits that he finds it difficult to see in her more than "the American young girl with a million a year." Thus, apart from its purely "dialectical" significance, the Assinghams' disagreement about the correct interpretation of the international drama they observe is itself an exemplification, though in the light, comic vein, of those very misunderstandings which are at its root.

By emphasizing the more sordid and ugly aspects of the case, the Colonel systematically deflates his wife's excessively exalted, "American" view of it. She, on her side, irritated by such insinuations and afraid lest they may prove to be true, vehemently accuses him of coarseness, cynicism, and vulgarity—accusations which it seems leave him unperturbed:

> "Her [Charlotte's] marrying will prove the truth" [says Mrs. Assingham].
>
> "And what truth?"
>
> "The truth of everything I say."
>
> "Prove it to whom?"
>
> "Well, to myself, to begin with. That will be enough for me—to work for her. What it will prove," Mrs. Assingham presently went on, "will be that she's cured. That she accepts the situation."
>
> He paid it the tribute of a long pull at his pipe. "The situation of doing the one thing she can that will really seem to cover her tracks?"
>
> His wife looked at him, the good dry man, as if now at last he was merely vulgar. "The one thing she can do that will make new tracks altogether." (I, IV; 23, 87)

Again:

> "That creates for her [Charlotte], upon my word," Mrs. Assingham pursued, "a duty of considering him [the Prince] of honourably repaying his trust, which— well, which she'll be really a friend if she doesn't make the law of her conduct. . . . "
>
> He [the Colonel] literally asked in short an intelligent,

well-nigh a sympathising, question. "Gratitude to the Prince for not having put a spoke in her wheel—*that,* you mean, should, taking it in the right way, be precisely the ballast of her boat?"

"Taking it in the right way." Fanny catching at this gleam, emphasized the proviso.

"But doesn't it rather depend on what she may most feel to *be* the right way?" [the Colonel suggests].

"No—it depends on nothing. Because there's only one way—for duty or delicacy."

"Oh—delicacy!" Bob Assingham rather crudely murmured. (III, III; *23,* 282–83)

And again:

"Their [the Prince's and Charlotte's] situation"—this was what he didn't see—"is too extraordinary."

" 'Too'—?" He was willing to try.

"Too extraordinary to be believed, I mean, if one didn't see. But just that, in a way, is what saves them. They take it seriously."

He followed at his own pace. "Their situation?"

"The incredible side of it. They make it credible."

"Credible then—you do say—to *you?*"

She looked at him again for an interval. "They believe in it themselves. They take it for what it is. And that," she said, "saves them."

"But if what it 'is' is just their chance—?"

"It's their chance for what I told you when Charlotte first turned up. It's their chance for the idea that I was then sure she had."

The Colonel showed his effort to recall. "Oh your idea, at different moments, of any one of *their* ideas!" . . . "Are you speaking now of something to which you can comfortably settle down?" (III, X; *23,* 368)

In addition to her role as the novel's intelligent but fallible choric commentator, there is yet another way in which Fanny

Assingham's presence contributes to our understanding of the international drama she observes. The protagonists' attitudes toward her are highly instructive and enrich our understanding of their temper, point of view, and basic character traits.

In the course of the Matcham house party in which Charlotte and the Prince conspicuously stay together, Fanny—worried, restless, uneasy, anxious—has two successive talks with Charlotte and with the Prince, in the course of which they try to make her see the situation from their point of view and secure her collaboration. Precisely because Charlotte's and the Prince's aims are identical, their distinct ways of handling the woman who has made both their marriages possible most effectively bring out the differences between them. Charlotte is shown as hard, unaccommodating, extremely clear-headed, and not in the least nervous or uneasy on account of Fanny's suspicions, which she means to confirm rather than allay. In fact, she is eager to make her situation clear and proceeds boldly and very pointedly with what she is pleased to call her "demonstration." She is quite indifferent to Fanny's secret torments, and when the poor woman tells her that she does not want to upset her, Charlotte coolly replies that she simply couldn't even if she thought it necessary. As for the Prince, we are made to see that he genuinely likes Fanny, and being amiable and good-natured, tries to make his point as painlessly and blandly as possible. He is much less intense and much less insistent than Charlotte, and justifies his being together with her by the fact that they are, in a sense, "in the same boat" and that this inevitably creates a link between them. When Fanny points out to him that Charlotte is in Mr. Verver's "boat," he agrees with alacrity, adding, with disarming self-depreciation, that he too is, for that matter, in Mr. Verver's "boat." Proceeding to elaborate the boat metaphor, he cunningly assures Fanny that she needn't worry, for the boat is after all tied to the dock and all he and Charlotte might, at the worst, do is take "harmless little plunges" (III, II; *23*, 270). In short, the Prince's way of making the same point as Charlotte is subtle, humorous, sly, and highly ambiguous, and it is precisely this ambiguity which Fanny, despite her European "discipline," finds so disquieting and sinister.

The same difference between the Prince's and Charlotte's attitudes is even more pointedly exhibited in their own discussion of whether Fanny is "squared." The Prince, who would have liked to persist in considering Fanny as his "kind instructress," is disappointed in her and judges her failure to collaborate with him as "the failure of courage, the failure of friendship and the failure of wit." However, although Fanny has not lived up to his expectations, he is not vindictive and very soon persuades himself that, having taken her time to think it all out, she has come to "trust" them. He tells Charlotte: "But her [Mrs. Assingham's] tone and her whole manner means nothing at all unless they mean that she trusts us to take as watchful, to take as artful, to take as tender care, in our own way, as she so anxiously takes in hers. So that she's—well . . . what you may call practically all right" (III, VIII; *23*, 338–39).

Charlotte, on the other hand, promptly dismisses the Prince's suggestion that Fanny "trusts" them, and insists that the point is rather that she has become powerless to hurt them because, being responsible for the marriages, she would be the first to be "dished" by telling the truth to the Ververs. Coolly and precisely, making no attempt to hide her satisfaction in Fanny's discomfiture, she tells the Prince: "I only say that she's *fixed,* that she must stand exactly where everything has, by her own act, placed her . . . She's condemned to consistency; she's doomed, poor thing, to a genial optimism. That, luckily for her however, is very much the law of her nature. She was born to soothe and to smooth. Now then therefore . . . she has the chance of her life!" (III, VIII; *23*, 341).

Although Charlotte has a better insight into Fanny than the Prince, she too, it should be noted, is mistaken about her. For what keeps Fanny quiet is, we are soon to learn, neither

her "trust" in the Prince's and Charlotte's method of "caring" for the Ververs, nor merely her fear of being exposed to the Ververs. It is, rather, her penetrating realization, which she promptly communicates to her husband, that Maggie has her own "idea" of how to tackle the situation and that the only way they can help her carry it out is by pretending to be "absolute idiots."

In the second half of the novel Fanny serves mainly as Maggie's confidante. After a highly dramatic and very moving scene (IV, VI; *24*, 100–20) in which Mrs. Assingham repudiates any knowledge of the Prince's and Charlotte's betrayal and Maggie pretends to believe her, she explains to her husband that pretending to believe her is Maggie's way of kindly "letting her off" and "sparing" her, just as she spares all the others. She adds, with characteristic perceptiveness, that the fact that Maggie does not accuse her of anything is particularly extraordinary in view of the fact that innocent "lambs" like her are, on the whole, more deeply hurt by a betrayal of this kind than more sophisticated, blasé "lions" and tend as a consequence to be more resentful and unforgiving (IV, VI; *24*, 128).

In view of the exceedingly complex role the Assinghams fulfill in *The Golden Bowl* it is somewhat surprising that, in the growing volume of James criticism, they should have hardly ever have received the full critical treatment they invite,[22] or that when they have been discussed, they should usually have been severely criticized. A characteristic instance of the prevailing attitude toward them is Edith Wharton's:

> In "The Golden Bowl," still unsatisfied, still in pursuit of an impossible perfection, he felt he must introduce a sort of *co-ordinating consciousness* detached from, but including, the characters principally concerned. The same attempt to wrest dramatic forms to the uses of the

22. The only exception is Sister Corona M. Sharp's discussion in *The Confidante in Henry James: Evolution and Moral Value of a Fictive Character* (Notre Dame, Ind., 1963), pp. 214–46.

novel that caused "The Awkward Age" to be written in
dialogue seems to have suggested the creation of Colonel
and Mrs. Assingham as a sort of Greek chorus to the
tragedy of "The Golden Bowl." This insufferable and
incredible couple spend their days in espionage and
delation, and their evenings in exchanging the reports
of their eavesdropping with a minuteness and precision
worthy of Scotland Yard. The utter improbability of
such conduct on the part of a dull-witted and frivolous
couple in the rush of London society shows that the
author created them for the sole purpose of revealing
details which he could not otherwise communicate without lapsing into the character of the mid-Victorian
novelist chatting with his readers . . . The Assinghams
[are] forced into [the story] for the sole purpose of acting
as spies and eaves'-droppers.[23]

Edith Wharton's strictures indicate that she has completely failed to grasp the complex role of this Jamesian
choric couple. It is surely wrong to view the Assinghams as
characters created "for the sole purpose of revealing details
which he [James] could not otherwise communicate without
lapsing into the character of the mid-Victorian novelist chatting with his readers," for, as I have tried to show, the couple's
central function is interpretative and evaluative rather than
expository and informative. In fact, as merely a purveyor of
information, Mrs. Assingham could easily be dispensed with,
for such expository material as she does supply (it is through
her discussions with her husband that we learn about Charlotte's past relationship with the Prince) could easily have
been made accessible through the Prince's consciousness.
Moreover, the characterization of the Assinghams as the
Greek chorus of the tragedy of *The Golden Bowl* is inaccurate
and apt to be misleading, for it leaves out of account those
aspects of the Assinghams' choric activities which distinguish

23. E. Wharton, *The Writing of Fiction* (New York, 1925), pp. 90–92;
quoted in *The Confidante in Henry James,* p. 222.

them from the traditional choric commentators. Again, it is certainly unjust to describe the Assinghams as "a dull-witted and frivolous couple," for, as I have tried to show, Mrs. Assingham is if anything supersubtle and excessively solemn. One is forced to conclude that Mrs. Wharton has entirely missed the Jamesian humor which pervades the analytical exchanges of the Assinghams and has mistaken it for frivolousness.

As for her dislike of the "insufferable" meddling couple who exchange the reports of their eavesdropping "with a minuteness and precision worthy of Scotland Yard," this is strikingly similar to Edmund Wilson's dislike of the obsessively curious and supersubtle narrator in *The Sacred Fount*. However, if Edmund Wilson's dislike of the narrator in *The Sacred Fount* can be accounted for (if not justified) by the fact that the narrator's interpretative activity is indeed in excess of the meager facts before him, Edith Wharton's dislike of the Assinghams cannot similarly be explained, since the Assinghams' supersubtlety is not at all in excess of the complexity of the quadrangular case they observe and comment upon.

Unlike Edith Wharton, I think it can fairly be claimed that the Assinghams are the most perfectly realized choric couple in James' fiction. They are finely and delicately drawn characters in their own right, and highly amusing as conversationalists. More important still, far from being expendable they perform a greater variety of interpretative functions, and their analytical activity is, I have tried to show, of the greatest thematic importance. In particular, the fact that Mrs. Assingham, though super subtle, is yet often fallible contributes substantially to the moral ambiguity of the international case she observes and analyzes.

There are, we have seen, two major types of Jamesian observers: the observer whose personal perspective completely controls the story, and whose complex, intense, and exacting analytical activity tends to become the work's true center of interest; and the observer who appears only intermittently

in the subsidiary role of choric commentator, and who therefore never becomes a truly "*usurping* consciousness," however subtle and ingenious his (or her) analysis. If the narrator
in *The Sacred Fount* is the finest specimen of the first type of
Jamesian observer, Mrs. Assingham in *The Golden Bowl* is
undoubtedly the most striking, most refined instance of the
second type.

CHAPTER 10

THE BEAST IN THE JUNGLE

In *The Beast in the Jungle*[1] James treats the existential
themes of isolation and frustration, spiritual emptiness and
emotional barrenness, and explores the problems of personal
fate and self-identity. Not surprisingly, therefore, its themes
—like those of *The Altar of the Dead* and *The Bench of
Desolation,* two other late *nouvelles*—are not projected in an
international drama; nor does it contain any of the social
comedy and delightful analysis of manners in which James'
middle works excel. In contrast to the intensely international
late novels—*The Ambassadors, The Wings of the Dove,* and
The Golden Bowl—its drama is abstracted from the social
and national frameworks and is almost completely internalized: James virtually strips its protagonist of all exter-
nalities and concentrates wholly on the inward life.

In *The Beast in the Jungle* James treats in the *nouvelle*
form the "too late" theme which he explores in the larger
international drama of *The Ambassadors.* But although these
two works (which were probably written simultaneously)[2]
have close thematic affinities, they differ radically in conception, mood, and technique, and belong to altogether different Jamesian genres. *The Beast in the Jungle* is a structurally
compressed, intensely poetic, tragic-ironic tale; its mood is
that of ferocious pessimism and profound sadness; and it
completely lacks the epic leisureliness, breadth of canvas,
and humor of *The Ambassadors.* The poetic element is con-

1. New York, *17*, pp. 61–127.
2. On this point see *Krook, The Ordeal of Consciousness,* p. 333.

spicuously present in its use of the beast-in-the jungle motif
as a means of defining its theme, and in this respect the tale
is comparable to the best works of Marcel Proust and Virginia Woolf. At the same time, it possesses, like *The Figure
in the Carpet* and *The Sacred Fount,* many of the features of
a tightly knit, well-made intellectual detective story, in which
the protagonist's case is presented as a riddle. However, the
quest of the protagonist in *The Beast in the Jungle* differs
radically from that of the critic in *The Figure in the Carpet*
and the narrator in *The Sacred Fount* in being an inner-
directed quest for self-definition, for the "figure" in one's
own carpet. *The Beast in the Jungle* also differs from these
two earlier stories in being a closed rather than an open
parable.[3] For while the puzzle in *The Figure in the Carpet*
and *The Sacred Fount* remain unresolved and perhaps un-
resolvable, the riddle in *The Beast in the Jungle* is fully
answered in the climactic recognition scene. Indeed the
definitiveness and finality of the answer brings out the fable's
affinities with *Ethan Brand* and *Young Goodman Brown,*
Hawthorne's parables of human isolation, to which, however, James' parable is superior by virtue of its greater philosophical depth, finer psychological penetration, and subtler
irony.

John Marcher—like Spencer Brydon, Stransom, White-
Mason, Mark Monteith, and Herbert Dodd, the protagonists
of James' other late *nouvelles*—is a lonely, self-absorbed,
middle-aged man of cultivated sensibilities, the melancholy,
timid, morbidly cautious New Englander of James' apprentice works grown old. He is the quintessential Jamesian
character *manqué,* or, to appropriate Clifton Fadiman's
phrase, the un-Faustian man, the epitome of the unlived
life.[4] It is Marcher's deep, unshakable conviction—which

3. On open and closed parables see R. M. Eastman, "The Open
Parable: Demonstration and Definition," *College English,* 22 (October
1950), 15–18.

4. See C. Fadiman's headnote to *The Beast in the Jungle* in his edition of Henry James' short stories (New York, 1945), p. 599.

May Bartram, his confidante, comes to share with him—that he is peculiarly marked for some great and overwhelming event. This conviction makes him feel that the trivial activities of his humdrum life, the motions of which he goes through daily, are nothing but acts of dissimulation which mask rather than express his true self. He is aware that his conviction may appear to others perverse and ridiculous, and considers it to be a curse, a burden, something that marks him in the same way in which the hump marks the hunchback. At the same time, he cannot help feeling that it is the greatest of privileges: it ensures his uniqueness, distinguishes him from the common run of humanity, and makes his life worth living. Ironically, it is precisely the intensity with which Marcher believes that he is destined for something "rare and strange, possibly prodigious and terrible" (I; 71), which makes him insensible to the beauties and excitements of ordinary human experience, including of course the supreme experience of love. After living for years in futile expectation of this event, Marcher at last discovers that it has already occurred: it was his failure to respond to May Bartram's love when this was offered to him. In the final great recognition-scene Marcher realizes that the prophecy of his "inner oracle" has come true, though in the most unexpected way: the prodigious event for which he had been waiting for so many years turns out to have been something which failed to happen. One is reminded in this connection of the significance which the "negative relation" of never having met assumes in *The Friends of the Friends*.

Marcher has always thought of the advent of the great, unprecedented event as of the leap of a beast in the jungle, and in the last scene this metaphor powerfully expresses the violence with which it has failed to happen: "The Beast had lurked indeed, and the Beast, at its hour, had sprung; it had sprung in that twilight of the cold April when, pale, ill, wasted, but all beautiful, and perhaps even then recoverable, she [May] had risen from her chair to stand before him and let him imaginably guess. It had sprung as he didn't guess; it had sprung as she hopelessly turned from him, and the mark, by the time he left her, had fallen where it *was* to fall" (VI; 126).[5]

In projecting the theme of the unlived life a writer like Chekhov would probably have made his antihero only half-conscious in the end of the aridity and sterility of his life. James, however, does not hesitate to make Marcher—"the man of his time to whom nothing on earth was to have happened"—as "finely aware" and as "richly responsible" as any of his other heroes. In making Marcher recognize "the real truth" about himself, James makes him transcend the fate of the man who has never lived; for his acute consciousness of what he has missed, his bitter realization of his life-long inadequacy, his tragic sense of the cruel mockery of his fate make Marcher (though belatedly) "live," feel and vibrate with the greatest intensity a Jamesian vessel of consciousness is capable of. It can therefore be claimed that the great event in Marcher's life takes, in the end, not the form of something which happened to him without his being aware of it (his failure to respond to May's love) but rather that of waking up to the terrible consciousness of this great, irrevocable failure. The beast therefore springs twice, and its second leap is even more violent than its first:

> This horror of waking—*this* was knowledge, knowledge under the breath of which the very tears in his eyes seemed to freeze. Through them, none the less, he tried to fix it and hold it; he kept it there before him so that

5. Though not the tale's key metaphor, the Beast appears also in *The Jolly Corner*. As Spencer Brydon roams his house in search of his alter ego he reflects: "It had been the theory of many superficially-judging persons, he knew, that he was wasting that life in a surrender to sensations, but he had tasted of no pleasure so fine as his actual tension, had been introduced to no sport that demanded at once the patience and the nerve of this stalking of a creature more subtle, yet at bay perhaps more formidable, than any beast of the forest . . . he found himself holding his breath and living in the joy of the instant, the supreme suspense created by big game alone" (*The Jolly Corner*, New York, *17*, II, 456–57.)

he might feel the pain. That at least, belated and bitter, had something of the taste of life. But the bitterness suddenly sickened him, and it was as if, horribly, he saw, in the truth, in the cruelty of his image, what had been appointed and done. He saw the Jungle of his life and saw the lurking Beast; then, while he looked, perceived it, as by a stir of the air, rise, huge, and hideous, for the leap that was to settle him. His eyes darkened—it was close; and, instinctively turning, in his hallucination, to avoid it, he flung himself, face down, on the tomb. (VI; 126–27)

James strikes in *The Beast in the Jungle* a strong fatalistic note. Marcher, we are told, has always felt that he was destined for a great event, that this was "in the lap of the gods," and that there was, accordingly, nothing in the world he could do either to bring it about or to avoid it. This feeling is shared by May Bartram, who tells Marcher at the end of their crucial meeting that what *was* to be had happened. When the truth finally dawns on Marcher, he comes to recognize that "he had failed, with the last exactitude, of all he was to fail of" (VI; 126). The significance of this unmistakably fatalistic note should not, however, be misunderstood. The ineluctability of Marcher's fate is of a purely internal nature. If Marcher is doomed, it is his character which is his doom; and if things happen (or rather do not happen) to him as they were bound to happen, they do so only in the sense of his having acted out his nature. This is surely the implication of the reference to the fulfillment of the prophecy of what might be called Marcher's inner oracle. The prophecy is as vague as the prophecies of oracles traditionally always are: *any* event which Marcher considered sufficiently "prodigious" would have, so to speak, filled the bill. Therefore the "rare

---

Perhaps the most significant difference between the two metaphors is that in *The Beast in the Jungle* Marcher passively waits for the spring of the Beast, whereas in *The Jolly Corner* Spencer Brydon is actively engaged in stalking him.

and strange" experience for which Marcher supposed himself
reserved could have been the experience of love; and that it
turned out to be the failure to love is no more surprising than
the fact that given Isabel Archer's background, character,
and aspirations, she ended by marrying Gilbert Osmond.

In his late *nouvelles* James ceases to use the observer as the
center through whose consciousness the protagonists are projected, and instead directly dramatizes the protagonist's consciousness. But even in these instances James does not dispense with the observer as an intelligent interpreter of the
case he witnesses. This function May Bartram (like Ralph
Touchett in *The Portrait of a Lady* and Maria Gostrey in
The Ambassadors) fulfills through her analytical conversations with the protagonist. May Bartram's point of view pervades, however, not only the analytical but also the reflective
portions of the tale—those in which Marcher's consciousness
is dramatized. James achieves this effect by making Marcher
constantly reflect upon May's view of him, so that her lucidity
about him is constantly shown through the haze of his self-
deception. Moreover, the impression of May's lucidity about
Marcher is reinforced by his own frequent admissions that
he believes her to have a better insight into his case than he
himself has. For instance: "He allowed for himself, but she,
exactly, allowed still more; partly because, better placed for
a sight of the matter, she traced his unhappy perversion
through reaches of its course into which he could scarce
follow it. He knew how he felt, but, besides knowing that,
she knew how he *looked* as well" (II; 81). Again:

> It had come up for him then that she "knew" something
> and that what she knew was bad—too bad to tell him
> . . . She had no source of knowledge he hadn't equally—
> except of course that she might have finer nerves. That
> was what women had where they were interested; they
> made out things, where people were concerned, that the
> people often couldn't have made out for themselves.
> Their nerves, their sensibility, their imagination, were

conductors and revealers, and the beauty of May Bartram was in particular that she had given herself so to his
case. (III; 92–93)

The presentation of the observer's point of view as mir-
rored in the protagonist's consciousness—a reversal of James'
usual method of seeing "through"—seems particularly appropriate to the treatment of Marcher's case. *The Beast in
the Jungle* is not merely an anecdote about Marcher's personal singularity. It dramatizes a fundamental aspect of the
human condition; its significance is universal. And by focus-
ing on Marcher's consciousness and dramatizing his inward
vision of the futility and barrenness of his life, James makes
the reader identify himself with him. Moreover, although
James meant the reader not to lose sight of Marcher's subtle
egoism and blindness, he yet wished above all to emphasize
the pitifulness and sadness of his case. James achieves this
effect by a constant interfusion of May's point of view with
Marcher's own. May is aware of Marcher's egoism and sees
through his self-deception (though she is never explicit about
them); at the same time, she refrains from judging him
harshly, and treats him with the greatest tenderness and the
deepest compassion—attitudes the reader is meant fully to
share.

The observer-protagonist relationship undergoes in the
late *nouvelles* a radical change. The observer in James' early
and middle works is in most cases prying and inquisitive, and
once his interest in the protagonist's case is aroused, he frequently becomes guilty of some form of meddling. The protagonist, on his part, usually resents the observer's interference, is irritated by his occasional indelicacies, and is reluctant to confide in him—a reluctance which reaches its
highest point in *The Sacred Fount*. The observer in the late
nouvelles is generally not inquisitive or meddlesome. The
protagonist, a lonely, middle-aged bachelor, generally appeals
to the woman who plays the role of his observer to enter
imaginatively into his case and to become the responsive

recipient of his confidences. Far from resenting the interest she takes in his case, the protagonist is grateful to the confidante for her generous sympathy, trusts her implicitly, and is to a great extent emotionally dependent on her.[6] That the lonely man's desperate need to share his burden with someone becomes the central thematic issue of *A Round of Visits,* another late *nouvelle,* proves that the changes James introduced in the observer-protagonist relationship reflect a change in his thematic preoccupations.

The confidential relationship follows in most of the late *nouvelles* a similar pattern. The confidante is generally an elderly spinster, sensitive, refined, generous, self-denying, and compassionate, who is in love with the protagonist, whereas he, on his side, is either incapable or unwilling to reciprocate her love and is instead perfectly content with mere companionship. Significantly, only in *The Beast in the Jungle* does the protagonist's constitutional failure to reciprocate the confidante's love—elsewhere of subsidiary, functional importance—becomes the tale's central issue, in terms of which James projects its existential theme of the unlived life. May stands for the life Marcher could have had, and his inability (common to other Jamesian "poor, sensitive gentlemen") to see his relationship with May as more than merely confidential and to make his affection for the woman who is the devoted recipient of his confidences flower into real passion constitutes his failure to "live." In making May Bartram fulfill two roles, the analytical and the dramatic, James achieves a fresh triumph of economy and compression, and reaches a perfect solution of the double-focus problem which arises in such transitional works as, for instance, *The Liar,* in which the two interests—that of the initial *Notebooks* marital drama of the Capadoses and that of the conflict between Mrs. Capadose and Lyon, the observer of her marital troubles—remain to the very end quite distinct.

6. On the motherly qualities of the women in James' late *nouvelles* see J. W. Shroeder, "The Mothers of Henry James," *American Literature,* 22 (January 1951), 424–31.

Since the full significance of Marcher's fate is to be re-
vealed only at the very end, *The Beast in the Jungle* is, not
surprisingly, particularly rich in preparatory and anticipatory
elements. This is especially true of the introductory chapter.
It opens with Marcher's renewal of an old acquaintance with
May at Weatherend, an English country house he visits,
where May is staying on the footing of a poor relation.
Spencer Brydon and White-Mason, two other late Jamesian
protagonists, have, like Marcher, lived for many years away
from the confidante and have almost forgotten her. John
Marcher pushes this "generic" forgetfulness to its furthest
extreme. He is entirely unaware, until May reminds him of
it, that he had met her ten years back, a lapse of memory on
his part particularly remarkable in view of the fact that he
had on that past occasion imparted to May his innermost
secret—his expectation of the leap of the beast. Moreover,
even when he does manage vaguely to recall, after May's
gentle reminders, that he had in fact met her ten years ago,
he still fails to remember what it was that had passed between
them and is convinced that it couldn't have been more than
"trivialities of youth, simplicities of freshness, stupidities of
ignorance" (I; 66). At the same time, as is always the case
with such suppressions and repressions (and here James seems
indeed to have anticipated Freud with the last exactitude),
Marcher's feelings for May are in excess of what he is able to
remember about her—an excess about which he wonders
and which begins to make sense to him only after she sup-
plies him with the missing link. As he at last remembers everything, Marcher realizes that this new knowledge entirely
transforms the meaning of his past: "He had thought of himself so long as abominably alone, and lo he wasn't alone a
bit. He hadn't been, it appeared, for an hour—since those
moments on the Sorrento boat. It was *she* who had been, he
seemed to see as he looked at her—she who had been made
so by the graceless fact of his lapse of fidelity" (I; 71). What
Marcher characterizes as "the graceless fact of his lapse of
fidelity" is symptomatic—indeed, prophetic, of his subse-

quent tragic failure to assign to his relationship with May its appropriate weight and significance. His early retrospective realization that he hadn't in fact been alone similarly foreshadows his final moment of recognition.

The introductory scene is rich in still other anticipatory notes, the full significance of which is to dawn on the reader only when he reaches the end of the story. Thus May suggests that perhaps Marcher's expectation of the dangerous "rare and strange" event which is to befall him is simply a sensitive man's anticipation of falling in love—a suggestion which Marcher brushes aside with a certainty foreshadowing of his ultimate shrinking from emotional commitment—so that May's penetrating view of Marcher is unobtrusively indicated at the very outset.

James presents Marcher's reflections in a kind of quasi-narrative, consecutive order while preserving their meditative rather than narrative tone. In the course of these intensely foreshortened, reflective parts of the tale, Marcher's inner drama slowly unfolds and his view of his relationship with May is fully registered. Marcher considers it a "rare luck" and a great "luxury" to have met May. He is keenly aware and fully appreciative of her unselfish and wholehearted dedication to his case and is humbly grateful for her "mercy, sympathy, seriousness, [and] her consent not to regard him as the funniest of the funny" (II; 77). He views the relationship as a very "special" friendship, in the beauty and perfection of which he constantly delights and takes a very high-minded view. Thus, for instance, he is careful to discuss with May the great "subject" with precisely the right kind of restraint and is anxious to sustain such discussions at exactly the right pitch: "The thing to be, with the one person who knew, was easy and natural—to make the reference rather than be seeming to avoid it, to avoid it rather than be seeming to make it, and to keep it, in any case, familiar, facetious even, rather than pedantic and portentous" (II; 80). Marcher also tries not to impose himself too much on May and to remember that "she had also a life of her own, with things that might happen to *her,* things that one should likewise take account of" (II; 77), believing that "his point was made . . . by his not eternally insisting with her on himself" (III; 90). These periodic qualms about egotistically imposing himself on May are particularly ironic in view of his active exploitation of her. Most ironic of all appears the reason Marcher gives for not consummating his "beautiful" relationship with May by marriage:

> The real form it [their relationship] should have taken on the basis that stood out large was the form of their marrying. But the devil in this was that the very basis itself put marrying out of the question. His conviction, his apprehension, his obsession, in short, wasn't a privilege he could invite a woman to share; and that consequence of it was precisely what was the matter with him. Something or other lay in wait for him, amid the twists and the turns of the months and the years, like a crouching beast in the jungle. It signified little whether the crouching beast were destined to slay him or to be slain. The definite point was the inevitable spring of the creature; and the definite lesson from that was that a man of feeling didn't cause himself to be accompanied by a lady on a tiger-hunt. (II; 79)

The full ironic force of Marcher's self-characterization as "a man of feeling" emerges only at the end. But even at this point in the story one cannot help asking whether the friendship Marcher offers May—which he so carefully refrains from consummating by marriage—does not amount to the very thing "a man of feeling" should in his view avoid. What else does it signify but his asking the lady to accompany him on a tiger hunt?

Marcher's excessive scrupulousness is, too evidently, only a disguise for his fear of the deeper emotional involvement. As such, it appears to be a subtler manifestation of the same deep-rooted fear of the business of life from which the young men of James' apprentice works suffer. In them it takes the

cf. Winterborne

form of morbid suspiciousness: they suspect the women they love of artificiality, levity, heartlessness, and mercenary motives, and they hasten to give them up upon the flimsiest confirmation of these vague suspicions. They often even congratulate themselves on the "tremendous escape" from the bondage of marriage and settle down to a life of celibacy, unhappy but with a "tidy conscience."[7] Significantly, this sense of relief is to be detected again in one of the latest of James' late stories, *Crapy Cornelia,* in which the elderly, cautious hero, White-Mason, who has been rejected three times and is on the point of giving up the idea of proposing to the rich but vulgar Mrs. Worthingham, enjoys the thought of "how right he had been, right, that is, to have put himself forward, always, by the happiest instinct, only in impossible conditions."[8]

7. The phrases quoted occur in *The Diary of a Man of Fifty,* Edel, *4,* 390, 389.

8. *Crapy Cornelia,* Edel, *12,* 337–38.

The early stories abound in examples of such withdrawals. Lieutenant Ford in *The Story of a Year* and Colonel Mason in *A Most Extraordinary Case,* who have been wounded in the Civil War, feel that their illness makes them unfit for the women they love. They scrupulously renounce all claim to them and inevitably lose them to more robust and determined young men, whereupon they die, frustrated and disappointed. John Lennox in *The Story of a Masterpiece* suspects his fiancée of heartlessness and shallowness—suspicions which are (not surprisingly) confirmed by a portrait of her painted by a previous rejected lover. Gordon Wright in *Confidence,* uncertain about the woman he loves, asks his friend's opinion of her character and is quick to act upon the latter's unfavorable verdict, thus losing the woman to this very friend. Again, the diarist in *The Diary of a Man of Fifty* gives up the Italian countess with whom he is in love because he suspects her of being a coquette capable of trifling with a man's affections (this being the cardinal feminine sin according to these Jamesian young men).

That the young men's suspicions are groundless and are the expression of their fear of "life" is clearly intimated in all these stories, and most emphatically in *Osborne's Revenge* and *The Diary of a Man of Fifty.* In *Osborne's Revenge* the friend of the young man who has committed suicide because he was cruelly jilted learns that the former's version of his relationship with the young woman had been wildly dis-

The Beast in the Jungle advances by a regular alternation between Marcher's foreshortened meditative spells and the analytical discussions he conducts with May. The dialogues do not here constitute independent compositional units, but appear to grow out of the reflective parts. Nor are they presented "scenically"—as, for instance, in *The Awkward Age* —but are registered wholly from Marcher's point of view. They also establish more directly May's point of view, furnish the reader with valuable clues to the solution of the riddle of Marcher's fate, and function as ironic commentaries on his own view of his case, as it is presented in the reflective parts of the fable.

One of the distinctive features of May Bartram's analytical task (like that of Maria Gostrey in *The Ambassadors*) is that it is not restricted to providing the reader with an interpretative commentary, but is primary that of trying to help the self-deceived protagonist see the truth about himself. This new educative aspect of the analysis is of the greatest thematic significance in *The Beast in the Jungle*—a quest story of man in search of himself. What makes the analytical discussions so much more dramatic than any of their counterparts is the fact that May, the confidante, is more deeply involved with the protagonist than any previous Jamesian observer and that she is engaged in the most difficult and delicate task of making a man who is affectionate and grateful but lacking in passion see that she loves him. May's attempts repeatedly fail, and Marcher does not show the slightest inkling of what, in her gently circuitous way, she is driving at. For instance:

------

torted and that she is not to blame. More subtly, in *The Diary of a Man of Fifty* the middle-aged diarist tries to dissuade a young man, who seems to him to be a reincarnation of his younger self, from marrying the daughter of a woman he has once given up, because she bears a striking resemblance to her fickle mother. The young man disregards the diarist's warnings. When the latter learns after some years that the young man is happily married, he begins to suspect the wisdom of his past decision, of which he has up to that moment been extremely proud.

"I judge, however," he [Marcher] continued, "that you see I'm not afraid now."

"What I see, as I make it out, is that you've achieved something almost unprecedented in the way of getting used to danger. Living with it so long and so closely you've lost your sense of it; you know it's there, but you're indifferent, and you cease even, as of old, to have to whistle in the dark. Considering what the danger is," May Bartram wound up, "I'm bound to say I don't think your attitude could well be surpassed."

John Marcher, faintly smiled. "It's heroic?"

"Certainly—call it that."

It was what he would have liked indeed to call it. "I *am* then a man of courage?"

"That's what you were to show me." [Note the past tense, which indicates May's despair that Marcher is ever going to show her.]

He still, however, wondered. "But doesn't the man of courage know what he's afraid of—or *not* afraid of? I don't know *that,* you see. I don't focus it. I can't name it. I only know I'm exposed."

"Yes, but exposed—how shall I say?—so directly. So intimately. That's surely enough." (II; 87–88)

The crucial meeting between Marcher and May takes place at a time when May is already mortally ill (she suffers, as James ambiguously puts it, from "a deep disorder in her blood" [III; 94]). The illness, we are made to see, is an expression of despair and resignation, a form of giving up and of "turning one's face to the wall." Marcher, on his side, is at that time deeply distressed by the thought that it is now overwhelmingly late for anything to happen to him, a distress coupled with the fear that his "admirable friend" would die and leave him to cope alone with the unanswered riddle. The description of this crucial encounter as it is experienced by Marcher is one of James' greatest triumphs: it is done with supreme power and delicacy, with the poetic and dramatic elements combined in a manner hardly surpassed in James' entire fiction. This is how James describes Marcher's impression of May:

> Then it was that, one afternoon, while the spring of the year was young and new she met all in her own way his frankest betrayal of these alarms. He had gone in late to see her, but evening hadn't settled and she was presented to him in that long fresh light of waning April days which affects us often with a sadness sharper than the greyest hours of autumn. The week had been warm, the spring was supposed to have begun early, and May Bartram sat, for the first time in the year, without a fire; a fact that, to Marcher's sense, gave the scene of which she formed a part a smooth and ultimate look, an air of knowing, in its immaculate order and cold meaningless cheer, that it would never see a fire again. Her own aspect—he could scarce have said why—intensified this note. Almost as white as wax, with the marks and signs in her face as numerous and as fine as if they had been etched by a needle, with soft white draperies relieved by a faded green scarf on the delicate tone of which the years had further refined, she was the picture of a serene and exquisite but impenetrable sphinx, whose head, or indeed all whose person, might have been powdered with silver. She was a sphinx, yet with her white petals and green fronds she might have been a lily too—only an artificial lily, wonderfully imitated and constantly kept, without dust or stain, though not exempt from a slight droop and a complexity of faint creases, under some clear glass bell. The perfection of household care, of high polish and finish, always reigned in her rooms, but they now looked most as if everything had been wound up, tucked in, put away, so that she might sit with folded hands and with nothing more to do. She was "out of it," to Marcher's vision; her work was over. (IV; 98–99)

James achieves in this passage one of those rich, pictorial effects of which the impressionist, Lambinet-like picture in *The Ambassadors* of Chad and Madame de Vionnet on the river is perhaps the most famous instance.[9] The somber, ominous note of impending death suggested by the extinguished fireplace and the cold, immaculate order which reigns in May's room is reinforced by the cold colors with which the whole picture is suffused—the whiteness of May's pale, wax-like face, and of her transparent draperies, the greenness of her faded scarf, the soft silver of her hair. The image of the artificial lily "constantly kept without dust or stain under some clear glass bell" strikes the note of *her* wasted, unlived life. May looks to Marcher not only ill and wasted but also old. He perceives that "the marks and signs on her face were as numerous and as fine as if they had been etched by a needle," and sees the artificial lily to which he compares her as "not exempt from a slight droop and a complexity of faint creases." The fact that May has grown old evidently only makes her in Marcher's eyes look even more delicate, refined, and spiritual than before; and in this James shows himself to be again the poet of the beauty of old age, which he celebrated elsewhere in such works as *The Wheel of Time, The Beldonald Holbein, Flickerbridge,* and *The Bench of Desolation.*

Touched by Marcher's anguish, his fear that he has been "sold," and his heart-rending appeal to her not to abandon him, May tries, for the last time, to help him "baffle his doom." The fact that she has just been shown as having given up her "work" and despaired of Marcher lends special poignancy to this last effort to which she rouses herself:

> "The door isn't shut. The door's open," said May Bartram.
>
> "Then something's to come?"
>
> She waited once again, always with her cold sweet eyes

9. Interestingly, this is one of the three scenes selected by Demuth for his illustrations to *The Beast in the Jungle.* See J. L. Sweeney, "The Demuth Pictures," *Kenyon Review* (Autumn 1943), pp. 522–32.

on him. "It's never too late." She had, with her gliding step, diminished the distance between them, and she stood nearer to him, close to him, a minute, as if still charged with the unspoken. Her movement might have been for some finer emphasis of what she was at once hesitating and deciding to say. He had been standing by the chimney-piece, fireless and sparely adorned, a small perfect old French clock and two morsels of rosy Dresden constituting all its furniture; and her hand grasped the shelf while she kept him waiting, grasped it a little as for support and encouragement. She only kept him waiting, however; that is he only waited. It had become suddenly, from her movement and attitude, beautiful and vivid to him that she had something more to give him; her wasted face delicately shone with it—it glittered almost as with the white lustre of silver in her expression. She was right, incontestably, for what he saw in her face was the truth, and strangely, without consequence, while their talk of it as dreadful was still in the air, she appeared to present it as inordinately soft. This, prompting bewilderment, made him but gape the more gratefully for her revelation, so that they continued for some minutes silent, her face shining at him, her contact imponderably pressing, and his stare all kind but all expectant. The end, none the less, was that what he had expected failed to come to him. Something else took place instead, which seemed to consist at first in the mere closing of her eyes. She gave way at the same instant to a slow fine shudder, and though he remained staring—though he stared in fact but the harder—turned off and regained her chair. It was the end of what she had been intending, but it left him thinking only of that. (IV; 105–06)

Marcher registers with the greatest sensitivity every detail of the scene. He perceives May's attempt to approach him as if "for some finer emphasis," he notes the delicacy (like that of the Dresden china of the fireless chimney-piece) of her face;

he is aware of her momentary hesitation and of the way in which she grasps the shelf for support. He notes her subdued eloquence, feels that "she has something more to give him," and sees this intention shining in her wasted face. And yet— and this is the stroke of the profoundest irony—though he is shown to be a man of such superfine sensibilities, and though he appears to be alive to the subtlest shades in May's behavior, he yet utterly fails to read her urgent and desperate message or to understand what she is trying to communicate to him.

The disparity between Marcher's idea of the form his "great accident" is to take and the form of May's appeal to him partly accounts for Marcher's tragic failure of perception. He is waiting for something violent and brutal to happen, whereas what May offers him is something "inordinately soft"; he expects to see the "glare" of the Beast, whereas May's intention shines at him with a white luster; he is prepared for the sudden spring of the Beast, whereas May merely "diminishes the distance between them."

This great negative adventure into which Marcher's career finally resolves itself is preceded by a long series of minor negative adventures. Over the years the idea that May Bartram may have something to do with his "great affair" repeatedly occurs to Marcher, but only to be dismissed. In this respect he resembles "the blinded seeker in the old-fashioned game [who] 'burns' on occasion, as with the sense of the hidden thing near—only to deviate again however into the chill."[10] Marcher mentions the idea playfully when he writes to May Bartram that "perhaps the great thing he had long felt as in the lap of the gods was no more than this circumstance, which touched him so nearly, of her acquiring a house in London" (II; 80). The jocular tone of the letter, however, leaves no doubt about his real feeling—that the great thing which he feels "as in the lap of the gods" cannot possibly have anything to do with May. When May falls ill, Marcher begins

10. Preface to *The Altar of the Dead*, New York, *17*, x.

to feel "what, oddly enough, he had never felt before, the growth of a dread of losing her by some catastrophe—some catastrophe that yet wouldn't at all be *the* catastrophe" (III; 93). Then, as May's condition grows worse, the idea that her death is *the* catastrophe begins to seem less absurd to Marcher, who catches himself *"really* wondering if the great accident would take form now as nothing more than his being condemned to see this charming woman, this admirable friend, pass away from him. He had never so unreservedly qualified her as while confronted in thought with such a possibility; in spite of which there was small doubt for him that as an answer to his long riddle the mere effacement of even so fine a feature of his situation would be an abject anticlimax" (III; 95–96).

These reflections express a deep, genuine appreciation of May, to whom Marcher pays full tribute, whom he handsomely describes as "this charming woman," "this admirable friend," and as "so fine a feature of his situation." Yet they also possess a certain curiously dispassionate quality, showing itself in his inability to view her impending death as sufficiently catastrophic not to be thought of as "an abject anticlimax" to his long wait.

Only after his fateful interview with May—that is, too late —does Marcher's attitude undergo a radical change:

> What could the thing that was to happen to him be, after all, but just this thing that had begun to happen? Her dying, her death, his consequent solitude—*that* was what he had figured as the Beast in the Jungle, that was what had been in the lap of the gods. He had had her word for it as he left her—what else on earth could she have meant? It wasn't a thing of a monstrous order; not a fate rare and distinguished; not a stroke of fortune that overwhelmed and immortalised; it had only the stamp of the common doom. But poor Marcher at this hour judged the common doom sufficient. It would serve his turn, and even as the consummation of infinite wait-

ing he would bend his pride to accept it . . . He had lived
by her aid, and to leave her behind would be cruelly,
damnably to miss her. What could be more overwhelming than that? (V; 108–09)

For the first time Marcher joins the ranks of ordinary humanity; he "bends his pride" and humbly accepts the idea
that though what "happens" to him is not something vin-
dicating his belief in "a fate rare and distinguished," it is yet
sufficiently overwhelming and painful to "fill the bill" and
serve as "the great accident" for which he had been reserved.
There is of course intense irony in the timing of this change
in Marcher's view, for it occurs immediately after he has
forfeited his last opportunity to "live" by failing to understand May's urgent message.

When May dies, after having told Marcher that the thing
which was to have happened had at last happened, the period
of his worst suffering begins. Knowing by now that his great
adventure has already come to pass, and having nothing
more to look forward to, his life is drained of significance.
This feeling of "hollowness" is powerfully evoked through
the transformation of the jungle image into a kind of waste-
land image:

> This was what closed his mouth now—now that the
> Jungle had been threshed to vacancy and that the Beast
> had stolen away . . . What it presently came to in truth
> was that poor Marcher waded through his beaten grass,
> where no life stirred, where no breath sounded, where
> no evil eye seemed to gleam from a possible lair, very
> much as if vaguely looking for the Beast, and still more
> as if acutely missing it. (V; 116)

Although in refraining from telling Marcher what had happened May had meant to spare him, her "merciful fraud"[11]
affects him quite differently. By telling Marcher that the

11. The expression "merciful fraud" is taken from E. Honig's article
"The Merciful Fraud in Three Stories of Henry James," *The Tiger's
Eye, 9 (October* 1949), 91–98.

thing which was to have happened had happened, without, however, letting him into the secret of what the thing was, May had unwittingly condemned him to wander helplessly in the limbo of half-ignorance—the most unendurable torment which could be inflicted on a Jamesian vessel of consciousness. Incapable of enjoying the bliss of ignorance, Marcher begins to be haunted by his past with the same obsessive intensity with which he was previously haunted by his future, trying desperately "to win back by an effort of thought the lost stuff of consciousness" (V; 117). Marcher had defined himself by reference to the great adventure which was to befall him; therefore his failure to find out what it was amounts not only to the loss of his special distinction ("he was in the dust, without a peg for the sense of difference" [VI; 119]) but, more important still, to the loss of his self-identity. Since May was the only person who had known of Marcher's "great adventure," it is clear that his claim to its existence rested exclusively on the fact of its having once been reflected in her consciousness. Marcher had thus become totally dependent on May not only for comfort, sympathy, and encouragement but for the preservation of his self-identity. He now goes on a long, desolate pilgrimage in search of his past, only to return to May's grave, which becomes "the center of his desert" (VI; 120):

> It was as if, being nothing anywhere else for any one, nothing even for himself, he were just everything here, and if not for a crowd of witnesses or indeed for any witness but John Marcher, then by clear right of the register that he could scan like an open page. The open page was the tomb of his friend, and *there* were the facts of the past, there the truth of his life, there the backward reaches in which he could lose himself. (VI; 121)

At this point James seems to have anticipated Sartre's view that there is an aspect of ourselves which exists exclusively in the consciousness of the Other. The differences between Sartre's and James' views of this "being-for-others" are, how-

ever, more important than the similarity. According to
Sartre, the fact that the Other possesses an aspect of oneself
is a source of perpetual conflict. To be seen by the Other is to
be deprived of freedom by becoming a fixed and unchanging
object. Therefore one always tries—though the attempt is as
futile as that of Tantalus—to recapture this aspect of oneself from the Other. James reverses the emphasis. The fact
that an aspect of himself exists in May's consciousness is precisely what preserves Marcher's identity and makes it a source
of hope (however meager) rather than of despair. Moreover,
to appropriate one's "being-for-others" turns out not to be an
impossible task, for Marcher does in the end capture and
fully appropriate the "lost stuff" of his consciousness. This,
significantly, occurs only when he ceases to press on and insist
on finding out what had happened, and instead accepts with
humility the condition of living entirely by the knowledge
that May had known what his "great adventure" was. When
the truth finally breaks on him, his desert turns again into a
jungle and the Beast which has been lurking there at last
pounces.

Unlike Marcher, the self-deceived tragic hero of *The Beast
in the Jungle,* the mature reader does sense the significance
of the crucial scene in which May offers herself to Marcher.
Consequently, the truth which dawns on Marcher in the final
recognition scene does not come entirely as a surprise to him;
it is rather a confirmation of what he has been invited all
along to guess. May's disclosure, however, is far from being
explicit: she is only, as James puts it in the *Notebooks,* "un-
expressedly lucid."[12] Therefore Marcher's tragic discovery of
the truth, though partly expected, has the effect of appeasing
the reader's intellectual curiosity and relieving the high suspense created by all the unexpressed lucidities. Everything
now becomes intelligible; everything "fits and fits"; all the
events which have led up to the dénouement, and in particular May's enigmatic pronouncements, unfold their full
meaning.

12. *Notebooks,* p. 311.

CONCLUSION

Having dispensed with the omniscient-author convention of the fiction of Trollope, Thackeray, Dickens, and George Eliot, James makes the observer fulfill most of the basic authorial functions. As a central intelligence—either a first-person narrator or a dramatized center of consciousness—the Jamesian observer presents the reader with the story; but even where the story is not presented exclusively from his point of view, he still performs, with varying degrees of infallibility, many interpretative functions. He diagnoses the situation, predicts its customs, provides moral and psychological analysis, and gives expression to the work's most crucial *aperçus*. And this is equally true of him when he actually assists at the drama's most crucial scenes, or forms his judgments merely by intelligent conjecture; when, obsessed by his curiosity, he "meddles" with the protagonists, or when he is appealed to by them to become the recipient of their confidences.

The Jamesian observer is a fictional character whose vantage point, unlike that of the authorial narrator, does not transcend the fictional universe of the story. He is not omniscient, and his moral and epistemological perspectives are necessarily limited. This enables James to show his two main authorial activities—narration and interpretation—in the making, that is, to present them as complicated, groping processes of observation and evaluation. Narration thus ceases to be the expression of authoritative omniscience. Instead, the story generally progresses by means of a series of encounters between the observer and the protagonist, in the course of which the former gradually achieves a comprehensive view of the case. *(Four Meetings,* one of James' early international tales, exemplifies this procedure.) James' predilection for showing observation in process may be seen in his increasing use of the method of dramatizing the observer's consciousness. I have tried to show in my analysis of *The Aspern Papers* (Chap. 5) that even when James does employ first-person narrative he makes it as similar as possible to dramatization of consciousness. He systematically declines to make any use of the "privileges" of the retrospective narrator, who may possess (like the omniscient authorial narrator) a full, rounded-off view of the case he narrates; he prefers to reproduce, with vivid dramatic immediacy, the adventures of the experiencing self.

Interpretation or "analysis" undergoes a similar change. The reader witnesses the gradual evolution of the observer's view of the meaning of the case. Because the analytical commentary is shown in process, it appears as tentative and conjectural only; and thus, though the observer's analysis is generally meant to be no less definitive than that of the Victorian omniscient narrator, it is free of the latter's pontifical, moralizing tone. At times, indeed, as in *The Sacred Fount* and *The Golden Bowl,* where the thematic ambiguity necessarily precludes definitiveness, the reader is actually invited to doubt the validity. Moreover, interpretation (like narration) is fully dramatized in the famous scenes of analysis in which the protagonist's case is dissected either by the observer and himself or by a pair of fellow observers.

James views the observer as the right reflector or perfect mirror of the case he observes and interprets. As I have pointed out, this is confirmed by a perusal of his *Notebooks,* in which James first sketches the case he intends to dramatize and only afterward proceeds to determine what kind of observer will best bring out its full value. The "right reflector," says James, is "the person most capable of feeling in the given case more than another of what is to be felt for it, and so serving in the highest degree to *record* it dramatically and objectively, is the only sort of person on whom we can count not to betray, to cheapen or, as we say, give away, the value and beauty of the thing."[1] Significantly, James gives the term "objectivity," which belongs to the vocabulary of French naturalism, a new meaning. He does not equate objectivity with impersonality—that is, a clinical, unimpassioned presentation of the facts. For James objectivity does not necessarily preclude emotional involvement. What it means for him is the most sensitive, imaginative, and finely appreciative record of the facts, a record which, as he puts it, does not give away their value and their beauty, and extracts from them their maximum of sense.

James meant the observers to serve as perfect mirrors of the cases they witness. Accordingly, they all possess certain necessary generic traits, without which they could not fulfill this function. These are a passionate interest in their fellow men, imagination, sensitivity, a high lucidity, and a developed power of analysis. Apart from these common generic characteristics, however, most of them are perfectly individualized. Their age, sex, and nationality, as well as the kind and degree of their involvement in the cases they observe, depend on the nature of the donnée of the work in which they act their part. Thus the observer may be another "passionate pilgrim," as in the story of that name, or he may be a critic, as in the tales of the literary life, or an innocent American who burns with the sacred rage in a story about American Puritanism, or a Europeanized expatriate in a study of the American Girl, or a sophisticated cosmopolite in an international drama.

I have tried to show that though he is the author's deputy, the Jamesian observer is never (except in some of James' apprentice works) a disembodied narrative or interpretative voice. He is a fully imagined fictional character, whose background James usually sketches before launching him, and whose curiosity, keenness of observation and intensity of interpretative activity James carefully accounts for in terms

1. Preface to *The Princess Casamassima*, pp. xii–xiii.

of his personal drama. Consequently, the Jamesian observer generally acquires a significance which goes beyond that of his primary function as interpreter. Thus in *Madame de Mauves* and *The Golden Bowl* he serves as a second, more low-pitched exemplification of the case he observes; in *The Portrait of a Lady* and *The Liar* he (Ralph Touchett, Lyon) acts as a foil to the male protagonist (Osmond, Colonel Capadose) who is the object of his critical observation; and in *The Madonna of the Future, Lady Barbarina, The Author of "Beltraffio,"* and *The Turn of the Screw* he or she precipitates and clinches the crisis.

James frequently postulates some kind of an intimate relationship between the observer and the protagonist. The observer may be helplessly in love with the protagonist, as in *The Portrait of a Lady* and *The Beast in the Jungle*, or about to marry her (or him), as in *The Two Faces* and *The Friends of the Friends;* or he may be a rejected suitor, as in *Louisa Pallant* and *The Liar.* James posits such relationships in order to render the observer's interest in the protagonist more intense, thus sharpening his critical insight into his case. Once he has done this, James frequently proceeds to make use of this relationship to reinforce the work's moral or point. For instance, in *The Two Faces* the observer, who is engaged to be married to the protagonist, gives her up upon seeing how meanly and vindictively she has treated the wife of her previous lover who had preferred the other woman to herself; by giving her up, the observer expresses his judgment of her. Similarly, in *The Friends of the Friends* the female observer, who is the protagonist's fiancée, gives him up on realizing the depth of his feelings for the woman he has never met—an action which brings home to the reader the power of the protagonist's unnatural attachment to the dead woman. These renunciations on the part of the observers are not, of course, meant to further the plot. Rather, in both cases the fact that the interpretative observer is a fictional character existing within the fictional universe enables him to express his view of the case he witnesses in terms of real action.

Sometimes James finds the observer-protagonist relationship, initially posited for functional reasons, highly interesting in its own right, and cannot resist the temptation to develop its dramatic potentialities, thus initiating an entirely new thematic interest. For instance, in *The Liar* James adds to the initial *Notebooks* subject—the marital drama of the Capadoses—a quite distinct subject, that of the conflict between Mrs. Capadose and the observer of her marital troubles. Such a development, where it occurs, raises the double-focus problem of how to combine the work's two distinct interests: a problem James satisfactorily solves in such works as *The Lesson of the Master* and *The Beast in the Jungle,* in which the observer-protagonist relationship acquires, over and above its purely analytical value, a thematic centrality. In *The Lesson of the Master* James meant to dramatize in the person of St. George, the Master, the greatest predicament of the artist, namely, the necessity to renounce all forms of human felicity in order to achieve artistic perfection. As the *Notebooks* entry to the tale shows, James chose a writer as his observer in order to enable him to function as the perfect mirror of the artist's predicament. In the finished tale, however, it is the observer rather than the protagonist who supremely embodies the true artist's spirit of renunciation, practicing what the great Master has merely preached. In *The Beast in the Jungle* the theme of the unlived life is presented in terms of the observer-protagonist relationship, and it is precisely the protagonist's failure to treat his relationship with the observer, who functions as his confidante, as more than merely confidential which constitutes his failure to live.

It will be remembered that the observer is in many of James' shorter works the central intelligence whom the reader knows from within, whose thought processes he is invited to watch. Since the observer's analytical activities are shown in action, the more exacting and complex these are, the more does the reader focus on the observer's mind; and the interest shifts from the observed, who dwindle into nominal protagonists, to the observer, who grows into a character of great intellectual and moral vividness. The governess in *The Turn of the Screw* is one striking instance, the narrator in *The Sacred Fount* is another. Nor does the observer achieve this growth by deviating from his analytical function; he achieves it here rather by exercising it to the full. That is, it is qua observer that he becomes interesting; and where this happens, certain fundamental analytical traits or activities or dilemmas become the work's central thematic issues and acquire psychological, moral, and philosophical significance.

Thus the observer's curiosity, in most cases a purely functional trait, becomes in *The Aspern Papers, The Figure in the Carpet,* and *The Sacred Fount* an obsession which is psychologically interesting. Similarly, "prying" and "interfering"—two other functional activities—turn in *The Aspern Papers, The Liar, The Turn of the Screw, The Sacred Fount,* and *The Golden Bowl* into moral issues of central importance. Finally, the theme of the observer as the protagonist's savior can also be seen to grow out of an initially functional narrative situation. The observer witnesses the protagonist's predicament, and because he is not a disembodied narrative voice but a fully imagined fictional character who has a definite personal relationship with the protagonist, and because the predicament is not the subject of retrospective narration, the question of what the observer, qua human being, is going to do about it becomes at times the story's center of interest. The Jamesian observer's attempt and final failure to save the protagonist acquire in such works as *The Pupil* and *The Turn of the Screw* a central thematic significance. The same is true, though in a subtler sense, of *The Beast in the Jungle,* in which it is the analytical activity of the confidante that constitutes her attempt to save the self-deceived protagonist by helping him to see the truth about himself.

The most conspicuous instance of this transformation of a functional activity into a thematic issue is *The Sacred Fount,* which I have called a fable about the predicament of the quintessential observer. In this work, James deals with the supreme difficulty which every observer in some degree has to recognize and face, namely, the uncertainty as to whether he has discovered the truth or has merely succumbed to the temptation peculiar to highly imaginative and speculative natures, that of discovering a meaningful pattern where none exists. In *The Sacred Fount* the recognition of this dilemma reaches a quintessential fullness of intensity, and thus the observer's epistemological limitation, which is a consequence of his position within the fictional universe, becomes in this story the subject of a philosophical drama. Significantly, such transformations of functional activities into central thematic issues are never mentioned in James' *Notebooks* entries. This means that they never form a part of his initial conception of the fictional work and are, as such, major cases of what James called "the triumph of intentions never entertained."

SELECTED BIBLIOGRAPHY

PRIMARY TEXTS BY JAMES
(other than the fiction listed in the Note on Citations, p. xv)

The Future of the Novel, Essays on the Art of Fiction, ed. with intro. by Leon Edel, New York, Vintage Books, 1956.

Notes on Novelists, with Some Other Notes, New York, Scribner, 1914.

English Hours, ed. with intro. by Alma Louise Lowe, London, Heinemann, 1960.

Parisian Sketches: Letters to the New York Tribune 1875–1876, ed. with intro. by Leon Edel and Ilse Dusoir Lurd, New York, New York University Press, 1957.

The Complete Plays of Henry James, ed. Leon Edel, Philadelphia, Lippincott; London, Rupert Hart-Davis, 1949.

Henry James: Autobiography, ed. with intro. by Frederick W. Dupee, New York, Criterion Books; London, W. H. Allen, 1956.

The Notebooks of Henry James, ed. F. O. Matthiessen and Kenneth Murdock, New York, Oxford University Press, 1947, 1961; George Braziller, 1955.

The Letters of Henry James, ed. Percy Lubbock, New York, Scribner, 1920.

Henry James and H. G. Wells: A Record of Their Friendship, Their Debate on the Art of Fiction and Their Quarrel, ed. with intro. by Leon Edel and Gordon N. Ray, Urbana, University of Illinois Press, 1958.

Henry James and Robert Louis Stevenson: A Record of Friendship and Criticism, ed. with intro. by Janet Adam Smith, London, Rupert Hart-Davis, 1948.

BIBLIOGRAPHY OF JAMES

Leon Edel and Dan Laurence, *A Bibliography of Henry James,* 2d rev. ed. London, Rupert Hart-Davis, 1957.

CRITICAL AND BIOGRAPHICAL WORKS

GENERAL

Allott, Miriam, "Symbol and Image in the Later Work of Henry James," *Essays in Criticism, 3* (July 1953), 321–36.

Anderson, Quentin, *The American Henry James,* New Brunswick, Rutgers University Press, 1957.

Andreas, Osborne, *Henry James and the Expanding Horizon, A Study of the Meaning and Basic Themes of James's Fiction,* Seattle, University of Washington Press, 1948.

Barzun, Jacques, "Henry James, Melodramatist," *Kenyon Review, 5* (Autumn 1943), 508–21.

Baxter, Annette K., "Independence vs. Isolation: Hawthorne and James on the Problem of the Artist," *Nineteenth-Century Fiction, 10* (December 1955), 225–31.

Beach, Joseph Warren, *The Method of Henry James* (1918), rev. ed. Philadelphia, Albert Saifer, 1954.

———, *The Twentieth Century Novel, Studies in Technique* (New York, Appleton-Century, 1942), pp. 177–228.

Beerbohm, Max, "Jacobean and Shavian," in his *Around Theatres* (New York, Knopf, 1930), pp. 260–65, 323–26.

———, "The Mote in the Middle Distance," in his *A Christmas Garland* (New York, Oxford University Press, 1936), pp. 3–10.

Bell, Millicent, "A James 'Gift' to Edith Wharton," *MLN, 72* (March 1957), 182–85.

———, *Edith Wharton and Henry James, The Story of a Friendship,* New York, George Braziller, 1965.

Bethurum, Dorothy, "Morality and Henry James," *Sewanee Review, 31* (July 1923), 324–30.

Bewley, Marius, "Hawthorne and Henry James," in his *The Complex Fate, Hawthorne, Henry James, and Some Other*

American Writers (London, Chatto and Windus, 1952), pp. 1–149.

Blackmur, Richard P., *The Lion and the Honeycomb, Essays in Solicitude and Critique* (New York, Harcourt, Brace, 1955), pp. 61–78, 240–88.

Booth, Bradford A., "Henry James and the Economic Motif," *Nineteenth-Century Fiction, 8* (September 1953), 141–50.

Booth, Wayne C., *The Rhetoric of Fiction* (Chicago, University of Chicago Press, 1961), pp. 42–50, 339–74, and passim.

Bosanquet, Theodora, *Henry James at Work*, London, Hogarth Press, 1924.

Bowden, Edwin T., *The Themes of Henry James*, New Haven, Yale University Press, 1956.

Brooks, Van Wyck, *The Pilgrimage of Henry James*, New York, Dutton, 1925.

Brown, E. K., "James and Conrad," *Yale Review, 35* (1946), 265–85.

———, "Two Formulas for Fiction: Henry James and H. G. Wells," *College English, 8* (October 1946), 7–17.

Burgess, C. F., "The Seeds of Art: Henry James's Donnée," *Literature and Psychology, 13* (Summer 1963), 67–73.

Burke, Kenneth, *A Rhetoric of Motives* (New York, Prentice-Hall, 1950), pp. 116–17, 294–98.

Cargill, Oscar, "The First Internationl Novel," *PMLA, 73* (September 1958), 418–25.

———, *The Novels of Henry James*, New York, Macmillan, 1961.

Clair, John A., *The Ironic Dimension in the Fiction of Henry James*, Pittsburgh, Duquesne University Press, 1965.

Conrad, Joseph, "Henry James: An Appreciation," in his *Notes on Life and Letters* (New York, 1921), pp. 11–19.

Cox, C. B., "Henry James and the Art of Personal Relationships," in his *The Free Spirit: A Study of Liberal Humanism in the Novels of George Eliot, Henry James, E. M. Forster, Virginia Woolf, Angus Wilson* (New York, Oxford University Press, 1963), pp. 38–73.

———, "Henry James and Stoicism," *Essays and Studies* (English Association), *8* (1955), 76–88.

Crews, Frederick C., *The Tragedy of Manners, Moral Drama in the Later Novels of Henry James,* New Haven, Yale University Press, 1957.

Daiches, David, "Sensibility and Technique: Preface to a Critique," *Kenyon Review, 5* (Autumn 1943), 569–79.

Dupee, F. W., *Henry James, His Life and Writings,* Garden City, N.Y., Doubleday Anchor, 1956.

———, ed., *The Question of Henry James, A Collection of Critical Essays,* New York, Holt, 1945.

Edel, Leon, "The Architecture of James's 'New York Edition,' " *New England Quarterly, 24* (June 1951), 169–78.

———, *The Diary of Alice James,* New York, Dodd, Mead, 1964.

———, *Henry James,* University of Minnesota Pamphlets on American Writers, Minneapolis, University of Minnesota Press, 1960.

———, *Henry James, A Collection of Critical Essays,* Twentieth Century Views, Englewood Cliffs, N.J., Prentice-Hall, 1963.

———, *Henry James, The Conquest of London, 1870–1881,* Philadelphia, Lippincott, 1962.

———, *Henry James, The Middle Years, 1882–1895,* Philadelphia, Lippincott, 1962.

———, *Henry James, The Untried Years, 1843–1870,* Philadelphia, Lippincott, 1953.

———, Introduction to *Henry James, French Poets and Novelists* (New York, Grosset and Dunlap, 1964), pp. vii–xi.

———, "The Literary Convictions of Henry James," *Modern Fiction Studies, 3* (Spring 1957), 3–10.

———, *The Psychological Novel, 1900–1950* (Philadelphia, Lippincott, 1955), pp. 53–75 and passim.

———, "To the Poet of Prose," *Modern Fiction Studies, 12* (Spring 1966), 3–6.

Edgar, Pelham, *Henry James, Man and Author,* Boston, Houghton Mifflin, 1927.

Edwards, Herbert, "Henry James and Ibsen," *American Literature, 24* (May 1952), 208–23.

Emerson, Donald, "Henry James and the Limitations of Realism," *College English, 22* (December 1960), 161–66.

Fadiman, Clifton, Introduction and headnotes to *The Short Stories of Henry James,* New York, Modern Library, 1948.

Fergusson, Francis, "James's Idea of Dramatic Form," *Kenyon Review, 5* (Autumn 1943), 495–507.

Fiedler, Leslie, *Love and Death in the American Novel* (New York, Criterion Books, 1960), pp. 288–95, 298–300.

Firebaugh, Joseph, "The Relativism of Henry James," *Journal of Aesthetics and Art Criticism, 12* (December 1953), 237–42.

Ford, Ford Madox, *Henry James, A Critical Study,* New York, Dodd, Mead, 1916.

Fussell, Edwin, "Hawthorne, James, and 'The Common Doom,'" *American Quarterly, 10* (Winter 1958), 438–53.

Gale, Robert L., *The Caught Image, Figurative Language in the Fiction of Henry James,* Chapel Hill, University of North Carolina Press, 1964.

———, "Imagery in Henry James's Prefaces," *Revue des Langues Vivantes, 30* (1964), 431–45.

———, "Henry James and Italy," *Nineteenth-Century Fiction, 14* (September 1959), 157–90.

———, *Plots and Characters in the Fiction of Henry James,* Hamden, Conn., Archon Books, 1965.

Gibson, Priscilla, "The Uses of James's Imagery: Drama through Metaphor," *PMLA, 69* (December 1954), 1076–84.

Grattan, C. Hartley, *The Three Jameses, A Family of Minds: Henry James, Sr., William James, Henry James,* New York, Longmans, Green, 1932.

Hoare, Dorothy M., *Some Studies in the Modern Novel* (London, Chatto and Windus, 1940), pp. 3–35.

Hoffman, Charles G., *The Short Novels of Henry James,* New York, Bookman Assoc., 1957.

Holder, Alan, "The Lesson of the Master: Ezra Pound and

Henry James," *American Literature, 35* (March 1963), 71–79.

————, "On the Structure of Henry James's Metaphors," *English Studies, 41* (October 1960), 289–97.

————, "T. S. Eliot on Henry James," *PMLA, 79* (September 1964), 490–97.

Holder-Barell, Alexander, *The Development of Imagery and Its Functional Significance in Henry James's Novels,* Cooper Monographs, No. 3, Bern, Francke Verlag, 1959.

Honig, Edwin, "The Merciful Fraud in Three Stories of Henry James," *The Tiger's Eye, 9* (October 1949), 83–96.

Hopkins, Viola, "Visual Art Devices and Parallels in the Fiction of Henry James," *PMLA, 76* (December 1961), 561–74.

James, William, *The Letters of William James,* ed., Henry James II, 2 vols. Boston, Atlantic Monthly Press, 1920.

Jefferson, D. W., *Henry James,* Writers and Critics Series, Edinburgh, Oliver and Boyd, 1960.

————, *Henry James and the Modern Reader,* Edinburgh, Oliver and Boyd, 1964.

Kaye, Julian B., *"The Awkward Age, The Sacred Fount,* and *The Ambassadors:* Another Figure in the Carpet," *Nineteenth-Century Fiction, 17* (March 1963), 339–53.

Kelley, Cornelia Pulsifer, *The Early Development of Henry James* (1930), Urbana, University of Illinois Press, 1965.

Knights, L. C., "Henry James and the Trapped Spectator," in his *Explorations, Essays in Criticism* (London, 1946), pp. 155–69.

Knox, George, "James's Rhetoric of 'Quotes,'" *College English, 17* (February 1956), 293–97.

Krook, Dorothea, *The Ordeal of Consciousness in Henry James,* Cambridge, Eng., The University Press, 1962.

Leavis, F. R., *The Great Tradition: George Eliot, Henry James, Joseph Conrad* (London, Penguin Books, 1962), pp. 141–91, 275–95.

————, "Henry James and the Function of Criticism," in his *The Common Pursuit* (London, Penguin Books, 1962), pp. 223–32.

Leavis, Q. D., "The Institution of Henry James," *Scrutiny, 15* (December 1947), 67–74.

———, "Henry James: The Stories," *Scrutiny, 14* (Spring 1947), 223–29.

Lebowitz, Naomi, *The Imagination of Loving, Henry James's Legacy to the Novel,* Detroit, Wayne State University Press, 1965.

———, ed., *Discussions of Henry James,* Boston, Heath, 1962.

LeClair, Robert Charles, *Young Henry James, 1843–1870,* New York, Bookman Assoc., 1955.

Lerner, Daniel, "The Influence of Turgenev on Henry James," *Slavonic Review, 20* (December 1941), 28–54.

——— and Oscar Cargill, "Henry James at the Grecian Urn," *PMLA, 66* (June 1951), 316–31.

Levy, Leo B., *Versions of Melodrama, A Study of the Fiction and Drama of Henry James, 1865–1897,* Berkeley, University of California Press, 1957.

Liddell, Robert, *A Treatise on the Novel,* London, Jonathan Cape, 1947.

Lind, Ilse Dusoir, "The Inadequate Vulgarity of Henry James," *PMLA, 66* (December 1951), 886–910.

Lubbock, Percy, *The Craft of Fiction,* New York, Scribner's, 1921.

McFarlane, I. D., "A Literary Friendship: Henry James and Paul Bourget," *Cambridge Journal, 4* (December 1950), 144–61.

McIntyre, Clara, "The Later Manner of Henry James," *PMLA, 27* (1912), 354–71.

Mariani, Umberto, "The Italian Experience of Henry James," *Nineteenth-Century Fiction, 19* (December 1964), 237–54.

Marks, Robert, *James's Later Novels, An Interpretation,* New York, William-Frederick Press, 1960.

Martin, Terence, "Adam Blair and Arthur Dimmesdale: A Lesson from the Master," *American Literature, 34* (May 1962), 274–79.

Matthiessen, F. O., *American Renaissance, Art and Expression in the Age of Emerson and Whitman* (New York, Oxford University Press, 1941), pp. 292–305 and passim.

———, *Henry James, The Major Phase,* London, Oxford University Press, 1946.

———, "James and the Plastic Arts," *Kenyon Review, 5* (Autumn 1943), 533–50.

———, *The James Family,* New York, Knopf, 1947.

Melchiori, Giorgio, "Two Mannerists: James and Hopkins," in *The Tightrope Walkers, Studies of Mannerism in Modern English Literature* (London, Routledge and Kegan Paul, 1956), pp. 13–33.

Miner, Earl R., "Henry James's Metaphysical Romances," *Nineteenth-Century Fiction, 9* (June 1954), 1–21.

Mix, Katherine Lyon, *A Study in Yellow, The Yellow Book and Its Contributors,* Lawrence, University of Kansas Press, 1960.

Morrison, Sister Kristin, "James's and Lubbock's Differing Points of View," *Nineteenth-Century Fiction, 16* (December 1961), 245–55.

Murray, Donald M., "Henry James and the English Reviewers, 1882–1890," *American Literature, 24* (March 1952), 1–20.

Nowell-Smith, Simon, ed., *The Legend of the Master, Henry James,* New York, Scribner's, 1948.

Nuhn, Ferner, "The Enchanted Kingdom of Henry James," in his *The Wind Blew from the East, A Study in the Orientation of American Culture* (New York, Harper, 1942), pp. 87–163.

Paterson, John, "The Language of 'Adventure' in Henry James," *American Literature, 32* (November 1960), 291–301.

Perry, Ralph Barton, *The Thought and Character of William James,* 2 vols. Boston, Little, Brown, 1935.

Poirier, Richard, *The Comic Sense of Henry James, A Study of the Early Novels,* New York, Oxford University Press, 1960

Rahv, Philip, *Image and Idea, Fourteen Essays on Literary Themes* (Norfork, Conn., New Directions, 1949), pp. 42–70.

———, Introduction and headnotes to *The Great Short Novels of Henry James,* New York, Dial Press, 1944.

Raleigh, John Henry, "Henry James: the Poetics of Empiricism," *PMLA, 66* (March 1951), 107–23.

Roberts, Morris, "Henry James and the Art of Foreshortening," *Review of English Studies, 22* (July 1946), 207–14.

———, *Henry James's Criticism,* Cambridge, Mass., Harvard University Press, 1929.

———, "Henry James's Final Period," *Yale Review, 37* (Autumn 1947), 60–67.

Rosenzweig, Saul, "The Ghost of Henry James: A Study in Thematic Apperception," *Partisan Review, 11* (Fall 1944), 435–55.

Rourke, Constance, *American Humor, A Study of the National Character* (New York, Harcourt, 1931), pp. 235–65.

Rouse, H. Blair, "Charles Dickens and Henry James: Two Approaches to the Art of Fiction," *Nineteenth-Century Fiction, 5* (September 1950), 151–57.

Sharp, Sister M. Corona, *The Confidante in Henry James, Evolution and Moral Value of a Fictive Character,* Notre Dame, Ind., University of Notre Dame Press, 1963.

Short, R. W., "Henry James's World of Images," *PMLA, 68* (December 1953), 943–60.

———, "The Sentence Structure of Henry James," *American Literature, 18* (May 1946), 71–88.

———, "Some Critical Terms of Henry James," *PMLA, 65* (September 1950), 667–80.

Shroeder, John W., "The Mothers of Henry James," *American Literature, 22* (January 1951), 424–31.

Simon, Irene, "Jane Austen and 'The Art of the Novel,' " *English Studies, 43* (June 1962), 225–39.

Snell, Edwin Marion, *The Modern Fables of Henry James,* Cambridge, Mass., Harvard University Press, 1935.

Spender, Stephen, *The Destructive Element* (London, Jonathan Cape, 1935), pp. 23–110, 189–200.

Stafford, William T., "Emerson and the James Family," *American Literature, 24* (January 1953), 433–61.

———, "Henry James the American: Some Views of His Contemporaries," *Twentieth-Century Literature, 1* (July 1955), 69–76.

———, "William James as Critic of His Brother Henry," *Personalist, 40* (Autumn 1959), 341–53.

Stevenson, Elizabeth, *The Crooked Corridor, A Study of Henry James,* New York, Macmillan, 1949.

Swan, Michael, *Henry James,* London, Arthur Barker, 1952.

Terrie, Henry L., Jr., "Henry James and the 'Explosive Principle,' " *Nineteenth-Century Fiction, 15* (March 1961), 283–99.

Tillotson, Geoffrey, "Henry James and His Limitations," in his *Criticism and the Nineteenth Century* (New York, Barnes and Noble, 1952), pp. 244–69.

Tintner, Adeline, "The Spoils of Henry James," *PMLA, 61* (March 1946), 239–51.

Vaid, Krishna Baldev, *Technique in the Tales of Henry James,* Cambridge, Mass., Harvard University Press, 1964.

Vivas, Eliseo, "Henry and William (Two Notes)," *Kenyon Review, 5* (Autumn 1943), 580–94.

Volpe, Edmond L., "The Childhood of James's American Innocents," *MLN, 71* (May 1956), 345–47.

———, "James's Theory of Sex in Fiction," *Nineteenth-Century Fiction, 13* (Spring 1958), 36–47.

Ward, J. A., *The Imagination of Disaster, Evil in the Fiction of Henry James,* Lincoln, University of Nebraska Press, 1961.

———, "James's Idea of Structure," *PMLA, 80* (September 1965), 419–26.

Warren, Austin, "Henry James, Symbolic Imagery in the Later Novels," in his *Rage for Order, Essays in Criticism* (Chicago, University of Chicago Press, 1948), pp. 142–61.

Wasiolek, Edward, "Tolstoy's The Death of Ivan Ilyich and Jamesian Fictional Imperatives," *Modern Fiction Studies, 6* (Winter 1960–61), 314–24.

Watanabe, Hisayoshi, "Past Perfect Retrospection in the Style of Henry James," *American Literature, 34* (May 1962), 165–81.

Wegelin, Christof, *The Image of Europe in Henry James,* James, Southern Methodist University Press, 1958.

———, "The Rise of the International Novel," *PMLA, 77* (June 1962), 305–10.

Wellek, René, "Henry James," in his *A History of Modern Criticism, 1750–1950, 4* (New Haven, Yale University Press, 1965), 213–37.

West, Rebecca, *Henry James,* London, Nisbet, 1916.

Westbrook, Perry D., "The Supersubtle Fry," *Nineteenth-Century Fiction, 8* (September 1953), 134–40.

Wharton, Edith, *The Writing of Fiction* (New York, Scribner's, 1925), pp. 37, 45, 91, 107.

Wiesenfarth, Joseph, *Henry James and the Dramatic Analogy,* New York, Fordham University Press, 1963.

Winters, Yvor, *In Defense of Reason* (Denver, University of Denver Press, 1947), pp. 300–43.

Woolf, Virginia, "Henry James" in her *Death of the Moth, and Other Essays* (New York, 1942), pp. 129–55.

———, "Henry James's Ghost Stories," in her *Granite and Rainbow* (New York, Harcourt, 1958), pp. 65–72.

Zabel, Morton D., "Henry James, The Act of Life," in his *Craft and Character in Modern Fiction* (New York, Viking, 1957), pp. 114–43.

STUDIES OF INDIVIDUAL WORKS OF FICTION

The Ambassadors

Brown, E. K., *Rhythm in the Novel* (Toronto, University of Toronto Press, 1950), pp. 24–27.

Durr, Robert A., "The Night Journey in *The Ambassadors*," *Philological Quarterly, 35* (January 1956), 24–38.

Knoepflmacher, U. C., " 'O Rare for Strether!': *Antony and Cleopatra* and *The Ambassadors*," *Nineteenth-Century Fiction, 19* (March 1965), 333–44.

Michael, Mary Kyle, "Henry James's Use of the Word 'wonderful' in *The Ambassadors*," *MLN*, 75 (February 1960), 114–17.

O'Grady, Walter, "On Plot in Modern Fiction: Hardy, James, and Conrad," *Modern Fiction Studies*, *11* (Summer 1965), 107–15.

————— "Time and the Unnamed Article in *The Ambassadors*," *MLN*, 72 (January 1957), 27–32.

Stallman, R. W., " 'The Sacred Rage': The Time-Theme in *The Ambassadors*," *Modern Fiction Studies*, *3* (Spring 1957) 41–56.

—————, "Time and Mrs. Newsome's 'Blue Message': A Reply to Leon Edel," *MLN*, 76 (January 1961), 20–23.

—————, "Time and the Unnamed Article in *The Ambassadors*," *MLN*, 72 (January 1957), 27–32.

Stein, William Bysshe, "*The Ambassadors*: The Crucifixion of Sensibility," *College English*, *17* (February 1956), 289–92.

Tilford, John E., Jr., "James the Old Intruder," *Modern Fiction Studies*, *4* (Summer 1958), 157–64.

Watt, Ian, "The First Paragraph of *The Ambassadors*: An Explication," *Essays in Criticism*, *10* (July 1960), 250–74.

The American

Gettmann, Royal A., "Henry James's Revision of *The American*," *American Literature*, *16* (January 1945), 279–95.

Trascher, Isadore, "Henry James and the Art of Revision," *Philological Quarterly*, *35* (January 1956), 39–47.

The Aspern Papers

Stein, William Bysshe, "*The Aspern Papers*: A Comedy of Masks," *Nineteenth-Century Fiction*, *14* (September 1959), 172–78.

The Beast in the Jungle

Smith, F. E., " 'The Beast in the Jungle': The Limits of Method," *Perspective*, *1* (Autumn 1947), 33–40.

The Golden Bowl

Fergusson, Francis, "The Drama in *The Golden Bowl*," *Hound and Horn*, 7 (April–June 1934) 407–13.

Girling, H. K., "The Function of Slang in the Dramatic Poetry of *The Golden Bowl*," *Nineteenth-Century Fiction*, *11* (September 1956), 130–47.

Owen, Elizabeth, "The 'Given Appearance' of Charlotte Verver," *Essays in Criticism*, *13* (October 1963), 364–74.

Spencer, James L., "Symbolism in *The Golden Bowl*," *Modern Fiction Studies*, *3* (Winter 1957–58), 333–44.

Wright, Walter, "Maggie Verver: Neither Saint nor Witch," *Nineteenth-Century Fiction*, *12* (June 1957), 59–71.

The Liar

Kane, R. J., "Hawthorne's *The Prophetic Pictures* and James's *The Liar*," *MLN*, *65* (April 1950), 257–58.

Rosenberry, Edward, "James's Use of Hawthorne in *The Liar*," *MLN*, *76* (March 1961), 234–38.

West, Ray B., Jr., and R. W. Stallman, *The Art of Modern Fiction* (New York, Rinehart, 1949), pp. 209–16.

Madame de Mauves

Gleckner, Robert F., "James's *Madame de Mauves* and Hawthorne's *The Scarlet Letter*," *MLN*, *73* (December 1958), 580–86.

Ward, J. A., "Structural Irony in *Madame de Mauves*," *Studies in Short Fiction*, *2* (Winter 1965), 170–82.

A Passionate Pilgrim

Gegenheimer, Albert Frank, "Early and Late Revisions in Henry James's *A Passionate Pilgrim*," *American Literature*, *23* (May 1951), 233–42.

The Portrait of a Lady

Friend, Joseph H., "The Structure of *The Portrait of a Lady*," *Nineteenth-Century Fiction*, *20* (June 1965), 85–95.

Krause, Sydney J., "James's Revisions of the Style of *The*

Portrait of a Lady," American Literature, 30 (March 1958), 67–88.

Leavis, F. R., *"The Portrait of a Lady* Reprinted," *Scrutiny, 15* (Summer 1948), 235–41.

Leavis, Q. D., "A Note on Literary Indebtedness: Dickens, George Eliot, Henry James," *Hudson Review, 8* (Autumn 1955), 423–28.

Levine, George, "Isabel, Gwendolen, and Dorothea," *English Literary History, 30* (September 1963), 244–57.

Mackenzie, Manfred, "Ironic Melodrama in *The Portrait of a Lady," Modern Fiction Studies, 12* (Spring 1966), 7–23.

Powers, Lyall H., *"The Portrait of a Lady:* 'The Eternal Mystery of Things,' " *Nineteenth-Century Fiction, 14* (September 1959), 143–55.

Reid, Stephen, "The Source of Moral Passion in *The Portrait of a Lady* and *The Spoils of Poynton," Modern Fiction Studies, 12* (Spring 1966), 24–43.

Rodenbeck, John, "The Bolted Door in James's *The Portrait of a Lady," Modern Fiction Studies, 10* (Winter 1964–65), 330–40.

Sandeen, Ernest, *"The Wings of the Dove* and *The Portrait of a Lady:* A Study of Henry James's Later Phase," *PMLA, 69* (December 1954), 1060–75.

Van Ghent, Dorothy, *The English Novel, Form and Content* (New York, Rinehart, 1953), pp. 211–28, 428–39.

Williams, Paul O., "Henry James's *The Portrait of a Lady," Explicator, 22* (March 1964), item 50.

The Princess Casamassima

Dove, John Roland, "The Alienated Hero in *Le Rouge et le Noir* and *The Princess Casamassima," Studies in Comparative Literature, 7* (1962), pp. 130–54.

Dubler, Walter, *"The Princess Casamassima:* Its Place in the James Canon," *Modern Fiction Studies, 12* (Spring 1966), 44–60.

Firebaugh, Joseph J., "A Schopenhauerian Novel: James's

The Princess Casamassima," Nineteenth-Century Fiction, *13* (December 1958), 177–97.

The Pupil

Lainoff, Seymour, "A Note on Henry James's *The Pupil," Nineteenth-Century Fiction, 14* (June 1959), 75–77.

Martin, Terence, "James's *The Pupil:* The Art of Seeing Through," *Modern Fiction Studies, 4* (Winter 1958–59), 335–45).

The Sacred Fount

Andreach, Robert J., "Henry James's *The Sacred Fount:* The Existential Predicament," *Nineteenth-Century Fiction, 17* (December 1962), 197–216.

Blackall, Jean Frantz, *Jamesian Ambiguity and "The Sacred Fount,"* Ithaca, Cornell University Press, 1965.

Blackmur, R. P., *"The Sacred Fount," Kenyon Review, 4* (Autumn 1942), 328–52.

Follett, Wilson, "The Simplicity of Henry James," *American Review, 1* (May–June 1923), 315–25.

Gale, Robert L., *"The Marble Faun* and *The Sacred Fount:* A Resemblance," *Studi Americani, 8* (1962), 21–33.

Hoffmann, Charles G., "The Art of Reflection in James's *The Sacred Fount," MLN, 69* (November 1954), 507–08.

Perlongo, Robert A., *"The Sacred Fount:* Labyrinth or Parable?" *Kenyon Review, 22* (Autumn 1960), 635–47.

Raeth, Claire J., "Henry James's Rejection of *The Sacred Fount," English Literary History, 16* (December 1949), 308–24.

Ranald, Ralph A., *"The Sacred Fount:* James's Portrait of the Artist *Manqué," Nineteenth-Century Fiction, 15* (December 1960), 239–48.

The Spoils of Poynton

Gargano, James W., *"The Spoils of Poynton," Sewanee Review, 30* (Fall 1961), 650–60.

McLean, Robert C., "The Subjective Adventure of Fleda Vetch," *American Literature, 36* (March 1964), 12–30.

Quinn, Patrick F., "Morals and Motives in *The Spoils of Poynton*," *Sewanee Review, 62* (Autumn 1954), 563–77.

Roper, Alan H., "The Moral and Metaphorical Meaning of *The Spoils of Poynton*," *American Literature, 32* (May 1960), 182–96.

The Turn of the Screw

Evans, Oliver, "James's Air of Evil: *The Turn of the Screw*," *Partisan Review, 16* (February 1949), 175–87.

Heilman, Robert, B., "The Lure of the Demonic: James and Durrenmatt," *Comparative Literature, 13* (Fall 1961), 246–57.

Ives, C. B., "James's Ghosts in *The Turn of the Screw*," *Nineteenth-Century Fiction, 18* (September 1963), 183–89.

Levy, Leo B., "*The Turn of the Screw* as Retaliation," *College English, 17* (February 1956), 286–88.

Mackenzie, Manfred, "*The Turn of the Screw:* Jamesian Gothic," *Essays in Criticism, 12* (January 1962), 34–38.

Silver, John, "A Note on the Freudian Reading of *The Turn of the Screw*," *American Literature, 29* (May 1957), 207–11. Reprinted in G. Willen (next entry), pp. 239–43.

Willen, Gerald, ed., *A Casebook on Henry James's "The Turn of the Screw,"* New York, Crowell, 1960.

Watch and Ward

McElderry, B. R., Jr., "Henry James's Revision of *Watch and Ward*," *MLN, 67* (November 1952), 457–60.

What Maisie Knew

Brebner, Adele, "How to Know Maisie," *College English, 17* (February 1956), 283–85.

Gargano, James W., "*What Maisie Knew:* The Evolution of a 'Moral Sense,'" *Nineteenth-Century Fiction, 16* (June 1961), 33–46.

McCloskey, John C., "What Maisie Knows: A Study of Childhood and Adolescence," *American Literature, 36* (January 1965), 485–513.

Wasiolek, Edward, "Maisie: Pure or Corrupt?" *College English, 22* (December 1960), 167–72.

Wilson, Harris W., "What *Did* Maisie Know?" *College English, 17* (February 1956), 279–82.

Worden, Ward S., "A Cut Version of *What Maisie Knew,*" *American Literature, 24* (January 1953), 493–504.

———, "Henry James's *What Maisie Knew:* A Comparison with *The Notebook,*" *PMLA, 68* (June 1953), 371–83.

The Wings of the Dove

Allott, Miriam, "The Bronzino Portrait in *The Wings of the Dove,*" *MLN, 68* (January 1953), 23–25.

Bersani, Leo, "The Narrator as Center in *The Wings of the Dove,*" *Modern Fiction Studies, 6* (Summer 1960), 131–44.

Crow, Charles R., "The Style of Henry James: *The Wings of the Dove,*" in Harold C. Martin, ed., *Style in Prose Fiction: English Institute Essays 1958* (New York, Columbia University Press, 1959), pp. 172–89.

Kimball, Jean, "The Abyss and *The Wings of the Dove:* The Image as a Revelation," *Nineteenth-Century Fiction, 10* (March 1956), 281–300.

Koch, Stephen, "Transcendence in *The Wings of the Dove,*" *Modern Fiction Studies, 12* (Spring 1966), 93–102.

Muecke, D. C., "The Dove's Flight," *Nineteenth-Century Fiction, 9* (June 1954), 76–78.

Rypins, Harold, L., "Henry James in Harley Street," *American Literature, 24* (January 1953), 481–92.

(A full bibliography of the works on Henry James may be found in *Modern Fiction Studies, 12* [Spring 1966], 117–77.)

GENERAL INDEX

Agape, 190

Alazon, 86, 88

Ambiguity, 47, 73, 101, 138, 139, 140, 151, 152, 154, 177, 199, 206, 234. *See also* Observer

Analysis, 145, 234

Analytic: chapters, 198; passages, 63, 66; role, 71, 218

Analytical: activity, 65, 159, 209, 237; commentary, 234; conversation, 200; discussions, 223; exchanges, 209; task, 223. *See also* Choric commentator; Consciousness, center of; Epistemological; Interpreter; Narrator; Observer

Arnold, Matthew, 115

Austen, Jane, 5, 12

Authorial: activities, 144, 233; addresses, vii, 18; commentaries, 55, 93; functions, vii, ix; guide, 144; interpolations, 29 n., 191; omniscience, 233; point of view, 66; reservations, 28; reticence, 4; withdrawal, 55

Authorial narrator, 4, 17, 19, 25, 27, 28, 29, 34, 38, 39, 54, 59, 64, 70, 72, 73, 93, 95, 140, 233. *See also* Omniscient author convention

Balzac, Honoré de, 12 n., 108, 198

Blackall, J. F., 94

Booth, W. C., 33 n., 71 n., 72 n., 76, 86 n., 94 n., 111 n.; *Rhetoric of Fiction, The,* 71 n.

Boswell, James, 5

Burney, Fanny, 5

Byron, George Gordon, Lord, 75, 77, 80, 82; *Don Juan,* 80

Cargill, Oscar, 37 n., 52 n., 188, 192 n.

Cervantes, 12 n.; *Don Quixote,* 12

Chekhov, Anton, 214

Choric: commentator, ix, x, 65, 73, 149, 174, 193, 197, 200, 209, 210; fallible choric commentator, 204; interpreter, 43, 49, 53; observer, 62, 64; prophecies, 62, 198. *See also* Analysis; Consciousness, center of; Epistemological; Interpreter; Narrator; Observer; *Raisonneur*

Christ, 190; Christian, 21; imagery, 190 n.

Comedy, social, 64, 211

Comic, 69, 70, 93, 138; action, 86; comic-ironic values, 13, 16; exemplification, 64; foil, 20, 41; interest, 64; values, 66

Confidante, ix, xii, 7, 68, 71, 86, 207 n., 208 n., 213, 238

Confidential relationship, 218

Consciousness, center of, ix, 34, 49, 59, 149, 192; dramatized, ix, 28, 75, 76, 93, 140, 192, 193, 217, 233, 234; vessels of, x, 37, 46, 214, 231. *See also* Analysis; Epistemological; Interpreter; Observer

Dickens, Charles, 5, 12 n., 74, 108, 233; *David Copperfield,* 7

Double focus, 218

Dramatic agent, 23, 124

Duppee, F. W., 148 n., 174, 191 n.

Edel, Leon, xii, 78, 147 n.
Eliot, George, viii, 12 n., 37 n., 38, 74, 108, 233
    Daniel Deronda: Gwendolen, 41 n.
    Middlemarch: Dorothea, 41 n.
    Mill on the Floss, The: Philip Wakem, 37 n.
Ending: inconclusive, 143; open, 90
Epistemological: dilemma, 167; perspective, 144; predicament, 82; theme, 82, 169; uncertainties, 151. *See also* Analysis; Choric commentator; Consciousness, center of; Interpreter; Narrator; Observer; *Raisonneur*
Epistolary convention, 18 n.

Fadiman, Clifton, 212
Ficelle, 85, 117
Flaubert, Gustave, 22, 23, 29, 40, 108
Follett, Wilson, 148 n., 160
French naturalists, viii, 40, 235. *See also Impassibilité*
Freud, Sigmund, 219

Gainsborough, Thomas, 116, 117, 120
Goncourts brothers, 168

Hawthorne, Nathaniel, 12, 101 n., 102 n., 107, 108, 154, 188, 212; *Artist and the Beautiful, The*, 108; *Ethan Brand*, 212; *House of the Seven Gables, The*, 101 n.; *Marble Faun, The*, 188; *Prophetic Pictures, The*, 102 n.; *Young Goodman Brown*, 212
Hoffman, Charles, xi, 76
Howells, William Dean, 166

Imagery, 158, 183, 184, 185, 186, 190

Impassibilité, 40. *See also* French naturalists
International: conflict, 16, 64; drama, 15, 191, 203, 211; emphasis on plot, 171; impartiality, 172, 191; law, 65; marriage, 16, 18, 31, 62, 196; tales, 233; theme, 1, 2, 35, 39, 66, 69, 70, 73, 121, 170, 186, 188, 191, 194, 200
Interpretation, 233, 234
Interpretative activity, 112, 148, 209, 235
Interpreter, 32, 71, 126; commentary, 144; function, 233; role, 74, 75, 122, 149
Irony, x, 3, 14, 19, 27, 28, 29 n., 38, 39, 46, 51 n., 69, 72, 73, 86, 93, 95, 99, 103, 107, 110, 112 n., 124, 133, 135, 137, 138, 142, 155 n., 173, 188, 189, 195, 211, 213, 221; distance, 9, 13, 73; exposure, 27; interpretation, 14, 70; ironic contrasts, 31; juxtaposition, 119; parallelism, 181, 183; postscript, 17; twist of, 27, 28

Matthiessen, F. O., 8, 32, 35, 54 n., 101, 155 n., 163; *Henry James, The Major Phase*, 8 n., 180 n., 189 n.
Maupassant, Guy de, viii n., 27, 108, 192 n.; *Forte comme la morte*, 192 n.; *The Necklace*, 28; *Pierre et Jean*, introduction to, viii, 192 n.
Metaphor, 50 n., 86, 157, 158, 183, 214 n., 215 n. *See also* Style

Narration, 4, 83, 91, 233, 238
Narrative, 4, 5, 10, 17, 21, 37, 49, 76, 78, 80, 81, 156, 167, 235; devices, 83; distance, 75, 119, 183; framework, 25, 148; reliability, xi
Narrative techniques, 29 n., 73,

160; free indirect speech, 29 n., 76; report, 73; résumé, 124

Narrator, 5, 6, 7, 8, 9, 10, 11, 12, 14, 74, 75, 77, 78, 80, 81, 82, 84, 85, 87, 88, 89, 90, 91, 92, 99, 120, 123, 146, 149, 150, 151, 152, 153 n., 154, 155, 156, 157, 158, 159, 160, 161, 162, 163, 164, 165, 166, 168, 178, 179, 200, 210, 234; agent narrator, 74; experiencing self, 75, 88, 92, 119; first person narrator, ix, 74, 75, 76, 83, 140; 234; narrating self, 75, 88, 92, 119; reminiscing narrator, 124; witness narrator, 4, 5, 17, 23, 74, 149. *See also* Analysis; Epistemological; Interpreter; Observer; *Raconteur*

Nouvelle, xi, 34 n., 74 n., 113, 168, 211, 217, 218 n.

Nowell, Simon, 141; *Legend of the Master, The,* 141

Observer, vii, ix, x, xi, xii, 1, 4, 5, 9, 13, 17, 18 n., 25, 27, 30, 32, 34, 37, 40, 49, 54, 59, 64, 68, 71, 73, 81, 83, 93, 104, 109, 110, 112, 113, 119, 120, 122, 123, 129, 140, 144, 145, 147, 148, 149, 151, 167, 192, 193, 194, 196, 209, 217, 223, 233, 234, 235, 236, 237, 238, 239; as author's deputy, ix, 18, 25, 65, 235; fictional character of, x, 5, 17, 23, 28, 29, 30, 35, 66, 122, 123, 161, 233, 235, 238; functional role of, x, 28, 30, 145, 238; as guiding intelligence, 34, 73, 83, 144, 148, 149, 179, 197; interpretative role of, 30, 40, 148, 236; as lucid reflector, 37, 126, 127, 234; observer-protagonist relationship, 218, 237; as perfect mirror, 1, 5, 29, 234, 235

Omniscient author convention, vii, viii, 4, 73, 142, 144, 233, 234. *See also* Authorial narrator

Parable: open, 212 n.; closed, 212 n.

Poe, Edgar Allen, 12 n., 154

Proust, Marcel, 168, 212

Proustian analysis of character, 171

Puritanism, puritan, 16, 20, 22, 111; conscience, 25; virtue, 17, 27

Raconteur, ix. *See also* Narrator

Raisonneur, ix, 34 n., 111. *See also* Epistemological; Interpreter; Observer

Realism, viii, 12 n., 108

Revisions, xii, 14, 30, 32, 54 n. *See also* Style

Reynolds, Sir Joshua, 116, 117

Romanticism, 4, 10, 11, 13, 15, 27, 82, 167

Rossetti, Dante Gabriel, 117

Sartre, Jean Paul, 231

Satire, x, 67, 107

Shakespeare, 64

Sharp, Sister Corona, xii, 207 n.

Shaw, George Bernard, 108

Shelley, Percy Bysshe, 75

Smollett, Tobias, 5

Sterne, Laurence, vii; *Tristram Shandy,* 111 n.

Style, 32, 160, 183, 200; poetic element, 211, 224; symbol, 183. *See also* Metaphor; Revisions

Symbol, 183

Tennyson, Alfred Lord, 5, 12

Thackeray, William Makepeace, viii, 12 n., 67, 233; *Vanity Fair: Becky Sharp,* viii

Tolstoy, Leo, 168

Trollope, Anthony, vii, 4, 12 n., 233

Turgenev, Ivan, 33, 40, 108

Ullman, S., 29 n.

Vaid, Baldev Krishna, xi
Vampire, 155, 157; vampirism, 146, 150, 154. *See also* Index of James' Works, *The Sacred Fount*
Victorian literature, ix

Warren, Austin, 62, 63 n., 135 n.
Wharton, Edith, 207, 208
Wilson, Edmund, 76, 209
Woolf, Virginia, 212
Wordworth, William, 23
Wright, Walter, 189

Zola, Emile, 168

INDEX OF JAMES' WORKS

Abasement of the Northmores, The, 112 n., 168

Altar of the Dead, The, 191, 211; Preface to, 228 n.

Ambassadors, The xi, xii, 2, 8, 20, 29, 34, 38 n., 45, 57, 65, 132, 150, 155, 166, 168, 197, 211, 216, 223, 226
    Preface to, 7 n.
    Maria Gostrey, xi, xii, 45, 197, 216, 223
    Strether, 2, 45, 150
    Waymarsh, 29, 57

American, The, 3, 4; Preface to, 82 n.

Art of Fiction, The, vii
    Lesson of Balzac, The, viii n., 141
    Future of the Novel, The, vii n.

Aspern Papers, The, 74, 75, 79, 82, 83, 85, 86, 91, 93, 96, 99, 101, 142, 153, 161, 234, 238
    Preface to, 77 n., 79 n.
    Jeffrey Aspern, 77, 78, 79, 81, 85, 89

Author of "Beltraffio," The, 51, 101, 107, 109, 113, 114, 115, 118, 119, 122, 124, 127, 130, 133, 147; Mark Ambient, 108, 109, 114, 116, 118, 121, 122, 123, 236

Awkward Age, The, xi, 25, 34 n., 166, 208, 223; Longdon, 25

Beast in the Jungle, The, x, 2, 211, 212, 215, 217, 218, 219, 223, 226 n., 232, 237, 238
    May Bartram, 213, 216, 217, 218, 219, 220, 221, 223, 224, 225, 226, 227, 228, 229, 230, 231, 232
    John Marcher, 212, 213, 214, 215, 217, 218, 219, 220, 221, 223, 224, 225, 226, 227, 228, 229, 230, 231, 232

Beldonald Holbein, The, 226

Bench of Desolation, The, 211, 226

Bostonians, The, xi, 28, 74, 76, 155; Olive Chancellor, 28

Broken Wings, 112 n., 168

Bundle of Letters, A, 16, 18 n., 58

Coxon Fund, The, 107

Crapy Cornelia, 222

Daisy Miller, 51

Death of the Lion, The 76, 107, 111 n.

De Grey-Romance, 147, 155

Diary of a Man of Fifty, The, 119 n., 222 n., 223 n.

Eugene Pickering, 7

Figure in the Carpet, The, 74, 91, 96, 99, 107, 109, 111, 137 n., 142, 147, 151, 153, 164, 212, 238; Hugh Vereker, 74

Flickerbridge, 101, 226

Fordham Castle, 112 n.

Four Meetings, 2, 233

Friends of the Friends, The, 167, 236

Gabrielle de Bergerac, 12 n.

Golden Bowl, The, x, 34, 59, 63, 65, 110, 121 n., 132, 168, 169, 170, 172, 177, 178, 179, 186, 189, 190 n.,

191, 192, 193, 195, 197, 198, 207, 208, 210, 211, 212, 234, 236

Preface to, 19 n., 59 n., 110 n., 191

The Assinghams, x, 59, 65, 66, 171, 174, 187, 193, 194, 195, 196, 197, 200, 201, 203, 204, 205, 206, 207, 210

Maggie, 170, 171, 172, 173, 174, 176, 177, 179, 180, 181, 182, 183, 184, 185, 186, 188, 189, 190, 191, 192, 195, 196, 197, 198, 199, 203

Prince Amerigo, 170, 171, 172, 173, 174, 175, 176, 177, 179, 181, 182, 183, 184, 185, 186, 187, 188, 189, 191, 192, 194, 195, 196, 197, 198, 199, 200, 201, 203, 205, 206, 208 n.

Great Good Place, The, 107
Greville Fane, 107
Guest's Confession, 7

International Episode, An, 3, 16, 56, 192
Ivory Tower, The, xi

Jolly Corner, The, 2, 214 n., 215 n.
Julia Bride, 168

Lady Barbarina, 3, 16, 20, 35, 38, 56, 65, 67, 71, 72, 73, 142, 191, 193, 200, 236

Preface to, 56 n., 65, 69

Freers, 35, 38, 59, 60, 61, 62, 63, 64, 65, 66, 67, 68, 71, 72, 73, 193, 194, 198

Lady Barbarina, 56, 57, 58, 59, 61, 62, 63, 64, 65, 66, 68, 69, 70, 71, 72, 115 n.

Jackson Lemon, 56, 57, 58, 59, 62, 63, 66, 67, 70, 71, 72, 73

Landscape Painting, A, 112
Last of the Valerii, The, 185
Lesson of the Master, The, 107,

109, 113, 114, 121, 124, 125, 134, 139, 140, 141, 142, 151, 164, 237

Preface to, 109, 113

Henry St. George, 108, 126, 127, 128, 130, 131, 132, 133, 135, 136, 138, 140, 237

Paul Overt, 127, 128, 130, 131, 132, 133, 134, 135, 136, 139, 140

Liar, The, 93, 94, 96, 102, 105, 112, 123, 150, 151, 218, 236, 237, 238

Lyon Oliver, 93, 95, 96, 97, 98, 99, 100, 101, 103, 104, 105, 106, 123, 149, 218, 236

Longstaff's Marriage, 147, 155
Louisa Pallant, 236

Madame de Mauves, xii, 15, 16, 19, 24, 25, 26, 28, 30 n., 38, 94, 113, 149, 188, 236

Longmore, 17, 18, 19, 20, 21, 22, 23, 24, 25, 26, 27, 28, 29, 30, 31, 38, 149

Madame de Mauves, 18, 19, 20, 22, 24, 25, 26, 27, 28, 30

Madonna of the Future The, 14, 112, 236

Maud Evelyn, 167
Middle Years, The, 107
Most Extraordinary Case, A, 222 n.
Mrs. Temperly, 112, 119 n.

Prefaces to, ix, 3

New York edition, x, xii, 14

Next Time, The, 107, 110
Notebooks, xii, 49 n., 53 n., 70, 70 n., 72, 74, 75 n., 85, 88 n., 94, 95 n., 105, 109 n., 110, 124, 125, 126, 137, 140, 154, 155 n., 159, 160, 167, 168, 173, 179 n., 184, 187, 218, 232, 237, 239
Notes of a Son and Brother, 76 n.

Osborne's Revenge, 222 n.

Painter's Eye, The, 116 n.

Partial Portraits, 107

Passionate Pilgrim, A, x, xii, 1, 2, 4, 7, 13, 14, 16 n., 29, 53 n.; Clement Searle, i, 2, 5, 6, 7, 8, 9, 11

Path of Duty, The, 178, 179

Point of View, The, 16, 18 n., 58

Portrait of a Lady, The, 10, 16, 20, 33, 34, 35, 37 n., 38 n., 46, 49, 50 n., 52 n., 54, 55, 59, 94, 113, 142, 193, 216, 236
  Preface to, 33, 34 n.
  Isabel Archer, 20, 24, 34, 35, 37, 39, 40, 41, 42, 43, 44, 45, 46, 47, 48, 50, 51, 52, 53, 54, 68, 142
  Ralph Touchett, 34, 35, 36, 37, 38, 39, 41, 42, 43, 44, 45, 46, 47, 48, 49, 50, 51, 52, 53, 54, 149, 216, 236

Princess Casamassima, The, 34, 38 n., 74
  Preface to, 46 n., 144 n., 235 n.
  Hyacinth Robinson, 38 n., 46 n.

Private Life, The, 153, 167

Professor Fargo, 124

Pupil, The, 51, 238

Reverberator, The, Preface to, 4 n., 15 n.

Roderick Hudson, 25, 33, 111
  Preface to, 4, 33 n., 142, 143 n.
  Roderick Hudson, 25
  Rolland Mallet, 25, 33 n., 34 n., 111

Round of Visits, A, 218

Sacred Fount, The, 76, 81, 83, 91, 96, 98, 106, 142, 145, 146, 147, 148, 149, 150, 152, 154, 159, 160, 162, 166, 167, 168, 169, 195, 200, 209, 210, 217, 234, 238, 239. *See also* General Index, Vampire

Sense of the Past, The, xi, 79

Sir Edmund Orme, 167

Small Boy and Others, A, 76 n.

Spoils of Poynton, The, xi, 167; Preface to, 148 n., 165 n.

Story of a Masterpiece, The, 101 n., 112, 222 n.

Sweetheart of M. Briseux, The, 7, 112

Third Person, The, 167

Tragic Muse, The, xi, 34, 74, 111, 112, 116, 134, 139, 142; Preface to, 112, 145 n.

Tree of Knowledge, The, 104 n., 168

Turn of the Screw, The, xi, 25, 51, 74, 99, 104, 115, 236, 238; Governess, xi, 25, 238

Two Faces, The, 236

Watch and Ward, 12 n.

What Maisie Knew, xi, 34, 112 n., 119 n., 167, 168

Wheel of Time, The, 276

Wings of the Dove, The, xi, 34, 36, 37 n., 38 n., 51, 52, 65, 132, 138, 169, 191, 192 n.